# Substituting a Value-Added Tax for the Corporate Income Tax

# NATIONAL BUREAU OF ECONOMIC RESEARCH
## FISCAL STUDIES

# Substituting a Value-Added Tax for the Corporate Income Tax

## First-Round Analysis

Stephen P. Dresch
*Institute for Demographic and Economic Studies
and National Bureau of Economic Research*

An-loh Lin
*Federal Reserve Bank of New York*

David K. Stout
*National Economic Development Office (London)*

*with contributions by* Milton L. Godfrey, *Cybermatics, Inc.*

Published for the National Bureau of Economic Research, Inc.
by Ballinger Publishing Company
*A Subsidiary of J.B. Lippincott Company*
Cambridge, Massachusetts
1977

Copyright © 1977 by The National Bureau of Economic Research, Inc. All rights reserved. No part of this publication may be reproduced, stored in a retrieval system, or transmitted in any form or by any means, electronic mechanical photocopy, recording or otherwise, without the prior written consent of the publisher.

International Standard Book Number: 0-88410-474-5

Library of Congress Catalog Card Number: 77-5778

Printed in the United States of America

**Library of Congress Cataloging in Publication Data**

Dresch, Stephen P
    Substituting a value-added tax for the corporate income tax.

    Bibliography: p. 199
    Includes index.
    1. Value-added tax. 2. Corporations—Taxation. 3. Prices. 4. Income distribution. I. Lin, An-loh, joint author. II. Stout, David, joint author. III. Title.

HJ5711.D67                      336.2'71                      77-5778

ISBN 0-88410-474-5

*Relation of the Directors to the Work and Publications of the*
*National Bureau of Economic Research*

1. The object of the National Bureau of Economic Research is to ascertain and to present to the public important economic facts and their interpretation in a scientific and impartial manner. The Board of Directors is charged with the responsibility of ensuring that the work of the National Bureau is carried on in strict conformity with this object.

2. The President of the National Bureau shall submit to the Board of Directors, or to its Executive Committee, for their formal adoption all specific proposals for research to be instituted.

3. No research report shall be published by the National Bureau until the President has sent each member of the Board a notice that a manuscript is recommended for publication and that in the President's opinion it is suitable for publication in accordance with the principles of the National Bureau. Such notification will include an abstract or summary of the manuscript's content and a response form for use by those Directors who desire a copy of the manuscript for review. Each manuscript shall contain a summary drawing attention to the nature and treatment of the problem studied, the character of the data and their utilization in the report, and the main conclusions reached.

4. For each manuscript so submitted, a special committee of the Directors (including Directors Emeriti) shall be appointed by majority agreement of the President and Vice Presidents (or by the Executive Committee in case of inability to decide on the part of the President and Vice Presidents), consisting of three Directors selected as nearly as may be one from each general division of the Board. The names of the special manuscript committee shall be stated to each Director when notice of the proposed publication is submitted to him. It shall be the duty of each member of the special manuscript committee to read the manuscript. If each member of the manuscript committee signifies his approval within thirty days of the transmittal of the manuscript, the report may be published. If at the end of that period any member of the manuscript committee withholds his approval, the President shall then notify each member of the Board, requesting approval or disapproval of publication, and thirty days additional shall be granted for this purpose. The manuscript shall then not be published unless at least a majority of the entire Board who shall have voted on the proposal within the time fixed for the receipt of votes shall have approved.

5. No manuscript may be published, though approved be each member of the special manuscript committee, until forty-five days have elapsed from the transmittal of the report in manuscript form. The interval is allowed for the receipt of any memorandum of dissent or reservation, together with a brief statement of his reasons, that any member may wish to express; and such memorandum of dissent or reservation shall be published with the manuscript if he so desires. Publication does not, however, imply that each member of the Board has read the manuscript or that either members of the Board in general or the special committee have passed on its validity in every detail.

6. Publications of the National Bureau issued for informational purposes concerning the work of the Bureau and its staff, or issued to inform the public of activities of Bureau staff, and volumes issued as a result of various conferences involving the National Bureau shall contain a specific disclaimer noting that such publication has not passed through the normal review procedures required in this resolution. The Executive Committee of the Board is charged with review of all such publications from time to time to ensure that they do not take on the character of formal research reports of the National Bureau, requiring formal Board approval.

7. Unless otherwise determined by the Board or exempted by the terms of paragraph 6, a copy of this resolution shall be printed in each National Bureau publication.

*(Resolution adopted October 25, 1926, as revised*
*through September 30, 1974)*

# Table of Contents

# List of Figures

# List of Tables

# Preface

This book is divided into two basic parts: identification of probable first-round price changes resulting from the tax substitution and discussion of the potential implications of these changes for such substantive issues as income distribution, international trade, etc. Chapter 2 gives a detailed analysis of the theoretical issues which must be resolved if changes in tax structure are to be translated into changes in the structure of prices. These include (a) criteria for defining a compensating tax substitution, i.e., for determining tax rates, (b) alternative variants of a value-added tax, (c) the meaning of tax shifting and the treatment of depreciation, (d) fiscal implications of a tax substitution, and (e) the input-output model as a means of analytical synthesis. On the basis of the model developed in Chapter 2, compensating VAT-CIT substitutions and price changes by component of final demand and by industry are examined in Chapter 3, under alternative stipulations concerning the degree of CIT reduction and shifting.

Chapters 4 through 7 analyze the potential consequences of the probable price changes in various substantive dimensions. In Chapter 4, the initial consequences for the size distribution of income are considered. The effects of the tax substitution for the level and composition of desired investment are examined in Chapter 5. The focus of Chapter 6 is on the broad subject of the potential consequences of the tax substitution for international trade. Finally, Chapter 7 contains a miscellany of additional topics, including intergovernmental fiscal effects, interindustry changes in tax liabilities, implications of potential short-run wage adjustments (across industries), regional consequences, and allocative effects.

At the outset we should briefly summarize the purposes which we do *not* intend this book to serve. First, our analysis does not project the consequences which would occur if this change in tax structure was used in a prevailing economic environment; that is, the study does not represent a conditionally predictive or projective exercise. Second, the study does not provide comparative static estimates, either quantitative or qualitative, of the long-run equilibrium consequences of this type of change in tax structure; this is explicitly indicated by the reference in the title to "first-round" effects. Clearly, we could have undertaken a more aggregate analysis of the long-run differential or absolute consequences of such a change in tax structure, focusing on implications for, e.g., macroeconomic balance, capital-labor ratios in the corporate and noncorporate sectors, and relative factor shares. However, because such analyses are well represented in the literature, with results that are quite well-known and accepted, we felt that a somewhat different study would be of potentially great value.

In general terms, we had two interrelated objectives in undertaking the writing of this book: first, to identify the mechanisms by which the effects of the tax substitution would be transmitted through the economy, and second, to indicate the relative magnitudes of the various short-term disequilibria which would result, responses to which would ultimately constitute the long-term effects of the change in tax structure. In general, the available aggregate analyses obscure the very uneven short-run impacts of a tax change at more disaggregate levels, even within the "corporate" and "noncorporate" sectors. However, at this more micro level we do not have well-articulated general equilibrium models capable of supporting comparative static analyses of long-run equilibrium states. The focus on the micro dimension thus has implied an analysis of the short-run, or "first-round," effects of the change in tax structure and of their transmission through the economy, especially through interindustry transactions, since these are particularly important in the case of a tax on value added at each stage of production.

Given this initially restricted focus, however, it was important for us to identify the relative magnitudes of the various disequilibria which would emerge in the intermediate run as the result of such a large-scale change in fiscal structure. This has led to our examination, in the second half of the study, of the initial impacts of the tax change (and of resultant first-round changes in prices, profits, and terms of trade) on income distribution, investment demand, import and export demand, and the balance of payments. While we have limited ourselves to a first-round analysis which does not trace the later-round effects of the indicated initial changes in, e.g., invest-ment, import and export demands, the indicated short-run demand shifts suggest the longer-run general equilibrium adjustments which will be induced. Thus, we have attempted to indicate (1) immedi-ate consequences, behavior in response to which long run adjustment will be brought about, and (2) the differences at the micro (e.g., industry) level in the degree of initial disequilibrium and disruption which can be expected to accompany the change in tax structure.

In light of our objectives, the use of an input-output framework has not been greatly restrictive. In the long run, certainly, as capital-labor ratios, the composition of demand, etc., are altered in direct or indirect response to the change in tax structure, an input-output formulation would effectively dissolve many of the most interesting questions. But, in the short run, the restrictive relationships imposed by the input-output system can in fact be viewed as fixed. Since we have attempted to identify initial impacts on, e.g., investment, on the basis of a theoretical formulation not confined by input-output rigidities, utilization of the input-output framework has not been seriously confining. On the contrary, it has provided the only basis available for meaningfully examining the transmission of initial re-sponses between industries and identifying the concomitant initial impacts on the structure of final demand.

Because we have been interested in the differential, not absolute, effects of this change in tax structure, it has been necessary to com-pensate for the macroeconomic impacts of the change. Clearly, as has been discussed, in the long run the level and composition of aggregate demand can be anticipated to change, and such changes would require further compensatory action if differential effects were to be identified. This is not to say that we are uninterested in later-round adjustments, as indicated by our concern with shifts in investment and international trade demands. However, we have not attempted, because we are unable, to trace through the ultimate differential consequences of the change in tax structure. Nonethe-less, we have emphasized (and indicated the short-run disequilibrium origins of) the various macroeconomic effects which will constitute the most important consequences of this change in tax structure.

We particularly acknowledge the attention and advice given throughout the course of the study by Carl S. Shoup, without whose intellectual contributions and encouragement the inquiry would never have taken place. We are also especially grateful to John R. Meyer for his continuing interest and constructive criticisms. Edward K. Smith, with whose support this program of research in public finance was developed, has been a constant source of advice and support. The form, structure, and substance of the manuscript have benefited greatly from the incisive criticism provided by a review committee consisting of Shoup, Richard A. Musgrave, Wassily Leontief, and Dan Throop Smith. Our research has also been strengthened by the responses of the Harvard and Stanford public finance seminars to earlier versions. Finally, the study has benefited, in substance and in exposition, from critiques by Emilio G. Collado and by the NBER's Board Reading Committee consisting of Frank Boddy, Roy Moor, and William Vickrey. The intensive examination by Vickrey has been most helpful in emphasizing the restrictions and limitations of the analysis. Of course, the authors alone bear final responsibility for any shortcomings of the study.

This study was greatly assisted by the contribution of services and data by Cybermatics, Inc.; Milton L. Godfrey of Cybermatics prepared the basic input-output data, implemented the tax substitution simulations, provided the appendixes to this volume, and served generally as a source of expert advice and technical information. We also acknowledge grant support of the National Bureau's program of Research on Federal Tax, Expenditure and Transfer Substitutions from the Office of Economic Research of the Economic Development Administration, Department of Commerce [Grant Number OER 396-G-71-17 (99-7-13227)]. This broader program of research has also been assisted financially by the United Nations Department of Economic and Social Affairs and by the International Division (European and International Affairs) of the Ford Foundation, under whose auspices a parallel study of large-scale changes in government expenditure (disarmament) was undertaken.

We are thankful to Frances Selhorst for her capable research assistance during the basic stages of our effort. Elisabeth Parshley, Sydney Shulman, Wendy Graves, and Nellie Zorc deserve our appreciation for their participation in the preparation of the manuscript. Finally, we must also acknowledge the ability and insight of our editor, Ester Moskowitz. The charts were drawn by the late H. Irving Forman with his customary skill.

During the preparation of this study the authors were affiliated with the NBER, Dresch and Lin as research associates and Stout as visiting fellow.

# Substituting a Value-Added Tax for the Corporate Income Tax

 *Chapter 1*

# The VAT-CIT Substitution

## 1.1 ORIGINS AND OBJECTIVES

In this book an initial attempt is made to assess the possible first-round consequences of a major change in fiscal structure: partial or complete replacement of the United States corporate income tax by an indirect tax on value added. The study has two primary dimensions and is intended to fulfill two rather different functions. First, the value-added tax (VAT) has been a recurrent focus of interest among those concerned with tax policy, and discussion of the VAT has often been linked with the possibility of a reduction in the corporate income tax (CIT). Thus, the particular aspects of fiscal change we examine warrant serious analysis in their own right. However, the second and ultimately more important objective is the development and adaptation of techniques of analysis which are applicable to the evaluation of the impacts of large-scale changes in fiscal structure on specific segments of the economy. It has long been recognized that this type of analysis cannot be undertaken within the confines of the easy ceteris paribus assumptions of partial equilibrium economics. "All else" does not remain constant when major changes in tax structure are undertaken. The identification and meaningful evaluation of the full consequences of such changes would require the use of a general equilibrium analysis, one which would permit the explicit recognition of responses in various sectors of the economy to changes in fiscal variables. While the need for a general equilibrium approach to fiscal changes that are pervasive in their impacts is recognized in contemporary public finance theory, little progress has been made in applying this type of analysis to concrete policy situations. The present study is a partial step in this direction, limited in its scope and policy implications, in that the possible macro-economic consequences flowing from the stimulus to real investment involved in the reduction of the CIT are not taken into account, the basis of comparison being in each case alternatives that involve the maintenance of a constant budgetary deficit or surplus, rather than attempting to work in terms of a constant aggregate real demand.

The development of a general equilibrium framework for the evaluation of major changes in fiscal structure was first set forth as a focus for future NBER research by John Bossons and Carl S. Shoup. In a 1969 report, they specifically proposed the VAT-CIT substitution as a subject of priority concern [Bossons and Shoup]. A number of factors contributed to the then-current interest in the value-added tax as an alternative to direct corporate taxes. This proposed change in tax structure had its origins in a general dissatisfaction with the existing system of taxation and in several specific policy concerns which came to the fore in the early 1960s. First, and probably most important, was the concern with economic growth which had emerged as a major issue in the late 1950s. One explanation offered for lagging rates of growth was the alleged depressive effect of high marginal rates of income taxation on the rate of investment. The corporate income tax became a particular target. It was thought that elimination of the CIT would stimulate investment either through increased after-tax rates of return to capital or through enhanced corporate liquidity (net-of-tax cash flow) or some combination thereof. The VAT, on the other hand, at least in its popular form as a consumption tax, would not involve any offsetting, depressive effects on growth.

A related variant of the growth argument was concerned with the adverse consequences of the corporate income tax for the composition, rather than the level, of investment. As a partial income tax, not applying to noncorporate business income, the CIT insofar as it was not allowed for in any way in the personal income tax provisions regarding dividends and capital gains, created incentives to redirect investment from the taxed corporate sector to the untaxed noncorporate sector. This allocative inefficiency was criticized by economists: an equalization of net-of-tax rates of return in the corporate and noncorporate sectors could be achieved only by higher gross returns in the corporate sector and excessive investment in the noncorporate sector. Elimination of the CIT would raise net-of-tax returns in both sectors through a flow of capital from the unincorporated to the incorporated sector. However, the possibly more serious charge was that the CIT, in discriminating against the corporate sector, in fact discriminated against those industries which were most dynamic. If the corporate sector, for reasons of technology and organization, is the engine of productivity growth and economic progress, then the adverse consequences of discriminatory tax treatment are both static and dynamic. Within the corporate sector, moreover, the CIT discriminates also against those investments in new and specialized plant and equipment that cannot readily be made the basis for mortgage or debt finance (e.g., investment in railroad rolling stock could often be more easily financed with debt than investment in yard automation). The rate of growth, as well as the level of income and output, would be increased by a movement toward greater fiscal neutrality.

The second major impetus for advocacy of the VAT was provided by the recurrent balance-of-payments crises which have plagued the United States from the mid-1960s through the early 1970s. The deterioration in the United States trade position revived concern for the effects of tax policy on the international competitive position of the economy. In this context the apparent contrast between extensive reliance of the United States on origin-based direct taxes, which are nonrebatable under the General Agreement on Tariffs and Trade (GATT), and dominance abroad, particularly in Europe, of indirect, destination-based taxes suggested the possibility of a tax substitution, e.g., the VAT for the CIT, as an alternative to devaluation as a means of correcting trade imbalances. Somewhat more generally, the discussion of the evolving United States relationship with Western Europe embraced the VAT because of its role in the tax harmonization efforts of the European common Market.[1] The concern with international trade and economic integration leads back to the issue of growth because of the benefits to the balance of payments of sustained increases in productivity. It is primarily with reference to these issues of growth, trade, and economic integration that the Committee for Economic Development has advocated (a) an initial partial substitution of a VAT for the CIT and (b) the confinement of any future tax reductions to the remaining CIT rather than to any newly adopted VAT [Committee for Economic Development, p. 28].

---

1. The role of the VAT for the Common Market countries was primarily one of tax rationalization. In general, it was introduced as a replacement for other, less desirable forms of indirect taxation, e.g., wholesale and retail sales taxes and manufacturers' and turnover taxes. As will be discussed later, these prior taxes were also generally applied on a destination basis, i.e., were rebated on exports and applied as border taxes on imports, consistent with GATT regulations. Thus, their replacement by the VAT should not have implied in itself a systematic change in the terms of trade between the European Economic Community (EEC) and other countries.

In the early 1970s, discussion of the VAT was stimulated by speculation that the Nixon administration would tie the value-added tax to a proposal for federal assumption of major responsibility for the financing of primary and secondary education and by the proposed imposition of a United States VAT in the context of post-August 1971 international monetary adjustments.

In addition to these topical sources of interest, the VAT has attracted attention partially because of its seeming novelty. Only recently enacted on a comprehensive basis by any developed, industrial nations, the VAT differs sufficiently in administration from other closely related forms of indirect taxation, e.g., the retail sales tax, as to appear to be a new, potentially far-reaching fiscal instrument.[2] Thus, government officials and legislators, particularly at the federal level, view it as a major untapped source of stable revenues.

Economists have been attracted to the VAT because of its allocative efficiency. Unlike direct taxes, which affect incentives, e.g., changes in work effort, in willingness to bear risk, or in investment and savings, and also unlike selective ad valorem taxes, which lead to distortions in factor and commodity prices, the consumption-type VAT can be shown to be relatively neutral in its allocative effects. In principle, the VAT rate is the same for all activities. Therefore, it would not create artificial incentives to use particular productive inputs, production processes, or commodities.[3]

Finally, the concern, particularly in business circles, with the alleged depressive effects of high, nominally progressive rates of income taxation on investment, risk-taking, and growth has led to a continuing interest in alternative revenue sources. In this regard, the probable regressivity of the VAT, as a replacement for some part of the personal or corporate income tax, may be viewed as a positive attribute.

---

2. The history of the VAT is relatively brief. A variant was employed by France between 1948 and 1953. The Shoup Tax Mission to Japan proposed the VAT as a revenue source for prefectures in 1950, but this recommendation was never adopted. Brazil, Greece, and Turkey have, at various times, employed the VAT as a manufacturers' sales tax. The VAT was formally adopted as a replacement for other forms of indirect taxation by the European Economic Community (Common Market) in 1963, and has recently been enacted by the final remaining EEC members [Shoup, 1970, p. 250].

3. The only area in which the consumption-type VAT is not allocatively neutral is in the allocation of time between work (and the consumption of purchased, hence taxed, commodities) and leisure (an untaxed consumption commodity).

## 1.2 DIFFERENTIAL INCIDENCE ANALYSIS

The theoretical origins of this study are embedded in the development in public finance theory of differential incidence analysis. The most important single insight of modern incidence theory is that the effects of government policies can be assessed only with reference to some base, i.e., the configuration of the economy (e.g., price and output structure, factor and size distributions of income) under some alternative public policy. In brief, it makes no sense to talk of the "absolute" effects of any policy; it is only possible to identify the differential effects of one policy as an alternative to another. Thus, with the substitution of one tax for another, the economic configuration under the replaced tax provides a basis or benchmark for the analysis of the effects of the newly introduced tax.

Because the term "differential incidence" has become somewhat ambiguous, having been applied to almost any examination of the effects of alternative taxes, its meaning in the present context must be explored and clarified. Most succinctly, its use here is synonomous with *compensated tax* (policy) *substitution*. In effect, a reduction in the rate of one tax is compensated for by the imposition of another. Obviously, the meaning of "compensates" is not immediately clear: a wide range of useful and valid interpretations is possible, depending on the objective of the particular analysis.

In its most simple sense compensation might be interpreted to require only equal monetary (nominal revenue) yield of two alternative taxes. In its most elaborate sense compensation implies holding all relevant economic magnitudes constant except one, and measuring the effect of the tax change in the remaining dimension.

The issue of criteria for a compensating tax substitution is related, but not identical, to the issue of the range of effects of the tax substitution which are to be explicitly considered in the analysis. Again, at the most simple extreme it could be assumed that everything other than the nominal yields of the taxes being altered will remain constant, i.e., that the tax changes will have only direct effects and that the system will not further respond to the changes in tax variables. At a more complex level a comparative statics analysis of the system in equilibrium under each tax configuration provides one alternative, and a dynamic analysis of the response of the system to the tax change provides another. Thus, parallel to the definition of a compensating tax change is the identification of the effects which must be compensated. A more sophisticated definition of compensation requires a more elaborate representation of economic processes in relation to the fiscal environment. It is in this sense that meaningful differential incidence analysis requires a general equilibrium framework.

Our study represents only a first step in the process of applying the insights of public finance theory to an analysis of concrete policy choices. Formally, the analysis is of the input-output or flow of funds variety, i.e., it does not attempt to take account of elasticities of supply, demand, or substitution through which the economy adjusts to fiscal change. Because of a number of restrictive assumptions which have been imposed by the complexity of relevant economic processes, the analysis is limited to an assessment of "first-round," or analytically short-run responses to the indicated tax change.[4] Since the range of responses analyzed is restricted, e.g., wages, production coefficients, and final demands are assumed fixed, a number of factors pertinent to a complete general equilibrium assessment of a large-scale change in fiscal structure are not examined. Nevertheless, the range of responses is broad enough to require a more complex compensation criterion than equal monetary yield.

A distinguishing feature of the analysis is its emphasis on the highly disaggregated consequences of the policy actions examined. A number of very different policies composed in part of the elements studied here may be capable of producing basically similar aggregate effects, although their consequences at more disaggregated levels may be quite diverse. The analytic richness of alternative policies resides precisely in this micro-level diversity, and differential microconsequences ultimately must constitute the basis for policy choice.

It should be clearly understood at the outset that this study consists of an analysis of the underlying implications of this or that potential change in the tax system, and *not* of a prediction of the actual consequences were the particular policy to be enacted. This analysis-prediction dichotomy is particularly important to the comprehension and evaluation of the study. Many large-scale econometric models predict relatively accurately. However, policy changes in general operate (exert their effects) at the margin and only slowly over time. Even a highly accurate econometric model may not be able to identify the marginal effects of a specific policy change, particularly when these effects become fully apparent only

---

4. By "short-run" we do not mean to imply temporally short-term responses, but rather a limitation on the extent of adaptive response by different elements of the economy to the change in tax structure which can be examined. Thus, "short-run" here is used in its analytical, microeconomic sense.

over longer periods of time. The nonpredictive, analytic purpose of a policy evaluation model, it is argued, justifies at least provisionally many of the oversimplifications incorporated in its empirical implementation. Thus, the objective of the analysis is *not* to predict quantitative shifts or precise time-profiles of response (lag structures, etc.) but to identify qualitative changes in "first-round" impacts, e.g., in income distribution, relative growth of various industries, or international trade. It should be clearly understood that these represent only intermediate-state tendencies, due to limitations on our capacity to assess empirically the full range of ultimate responses to a particular change in fiscal structure.

In the remainder of this introduction the emphasis is on the substance of the VAT-CIT substitution, while in later sections the two levels of analysis are intermingled.

## 1.3 CHARACTERISTICS OF THE VAT

As indicated above, it has been commonly argued that a partial or complete substitution of the VAT for the CIT would have favorable effects for the level of investment, for the interindustry and corporate-noncorporate distribution of investment, for allocative efficiency, and for the balance of payments. Nevertheless, its regressive effects on income distribution are admitted, and they provide the focus for opposition to a simple substitution of the VAT for the CIT [National Economic Development Office; Smith]. However, both the magnitude and timing of these effects will necessarily depend upon the specific nature of the legislated tax changes and upon the constellation of price changes in goods and factor markets resulting from the tax substitution. Thus, discussions of the VAT must proceed in terms of anticipated consequences on prices and factor returns of a specific VAT-CIT substitution.

The variants of the value-added tax we examine are all of the consumption type,[5] the one universally adopted by countries that have enacted a VAT. The choice is further dictated by the administrative convenience of this form, which is reflected in its adoption abroad, and by desirable economic characteristics, particularly as contrasted with the gross-product variant, which has received extensive attention elsewhere [Aaron].

---

5. Ignoring governments, the tax base of a consumption-type VAT consists only of private domestic consumption expenditure, in contrast to a base of consumption plus net investment (national income or net national product) for the income type, and consumption plus gross investment (gross national product) for the gross-product type.

The obvious, although not unique, technique for administering a consumption-type VAT is the *invoice method*: each potential tax-paying entity computes a gross tax liability on all sales, as invoiced to purchasers, and then receives a credit for all VAT invoiced on its own intermediate or investment purchases. Net tax due is then the excess of the gross liability on sales over total credits for taxes paid on purchases.[6]

Since the VAT is a destination tax, it would not be invoiced on export sales, but a full credit for previously invoiced (earlier stage) VAT would be provided, resulting in a zero net rate of tax on exports. On the other hand, imports would be fully subject to VAT as a border tax. Investment purchases themselves would be wholly free of tax, since the entire VAT on investment purchases would be creditable against the gross VAT liability in computing actual tax due. A tax liability would arise only as capital services were embodied in taxable consumption output. As will be discussed later, this procedure is equivalent to *instantaneous depreciation* under an income tax.

Clearly, to exempt export or investment purchases completely, any excess of credits over liabilities must result in a rebate to the taxpayer. However, the value of the net credit would be reduced, and nominally exempted purchases would be partially taxed, if the credit were simply carried over to be applied against future VAT liabilities.[7]

The treatment of government purchases under a VAT is in the aggregate (national accounts) sense moot, since any VAT liability invoiced on government purchases is simultaneously government revenue and expenditures. However, under a multilevel government system, with the VAT imposed at the national level, the introduction of the VAT and the specific treatment of government purchases may differentially affect the fiscal status of various government units. Particularly in the context of substituting a federal VAT for both federal and state CITs, achievement of intergovernmental neutrality will not be possible.

The equivalence of a value-added tax and its corresponding single-stage tax (which in the case of the consumption-type VAT would be the retail sales tax, RST), has been a subject of continuing debate

---

6. For a more detailed discussion of administration, with a consideration also of VATs of the income and gross-product types, see Shoup [1970, pp. 257–261].

7. If provision were made only for a carryover to the future of net credits, the effective tax would be the difference between the nominal credit and its present value. This point is worth noting because it has commonly been ignored, e.g., under the French carryover treatment of net credits arising from high rates of investment undertaken by new or rapidly growing firms.

[Lindholm, 1970 and 1971; National Economic Development Office, 1971, Chapter 5, Annex 1; Shoup, 1972; Due, 1972]. Formally, the two are clearly equivalent. A consumption-type VAT and an RST in principle apply to an identical base, private domestic consumption expenditure. Under the usual competitive assumptions this would imply corresponding economic effects, i.e., the degree of tax shifting would be the same under both, with no effect on relative prices. It has been argued, however, that since the VAT is a multiple stage tax, there would be greater "slippage"[8] in forward shifting of the tax, although the logic which would lead to an expectation of systematic differences between the RST and consumption-type VAT in tax shifting does not seem particularly compelling. With a credit for earlier against later stage VAT liabilities, for example, differential shifting would imply that net-of-tax prices of *exempted* commodities (investment, export, and government purchases) would decline if a VAT replaced an equivalent RST. On the other hand it can be argued that since the VAT is in part paid considerably sooner than the RST on the final output, the added financing charge would cause forward shifting of somewhat more than the VAT, to an extent not entirely offset by the gain to the government through earlier receipts, given the higher cost of capital to private firms as compared to interest rates paid by government. This tendency would be enhanced to the extent that conventional markups might be applied to costs inclusive of VAT.

Apart from this dispute over the economic equivalence of appropriately designed value-added and retail sales taxes, the choice between them reduces to the relative ease and effectiveness of administration. For the retail sales tax it has been argued that collection is less costly since only the final-stage seller must be included in the tax administration network. Offsetting this is the greater likelihood that some taxable sales will escape tax entirely. Thus, if for administrative ease, small retail establishments are exempted from the tax, their sales entirely escape an RST, while only the markup of the retailer escapes under the VAT if the exemption takes the form of filing no tax return. Similarly, tax evasion is more difficult with a VAT. More generally, the consumption-type VAT, under the invoice method, is argued to be self-enforcing. To obtain a credit for VAT paid, a seller must report his VAT liability on sales, and the invoiced credit claimed by a purchaser can be compared with the VAT liability reported by the seller. Thus, with dual reporting a

___
8. I.e., lower price increases than would be observed if the change in tax liability were fully translated into a change in price.

minimal rate of random checks would be expected to be quite effective in identifying tax evasion.

A major advantage claimed for the VAT is its ability to distinguish between business and nonbusiness purchasers. A significant complaint against the RST and related single-stage, seller-administered taxes is the difficulty of crediting purchasers. In extreme cases this even extends to exports, when, e.g., wholesaler taxes are unable to distinguish between domestic and foreign purchasers. The virtue of the VAT is that both buyer and seller are taxpaying units; thus, the tax charged at one stage can be rebated at another if a sale is nontaxable. Under any sales-type tax only one stage is directly involved in tax collection, and credits and rebates become difficult if not impossible.

A common argument for the RST relates to the ease with which "multiple rate" systems can be accommodated. Thus, the retail sales taxes of many states exempt, or tax at lower rates, purchases of such "necessities" as food, clothing, utilities, medical care and drugs, etc., and it has been alleged that such practices would be more difficult under a VAT. While it will be argued below that multiple rates are undesirable in principle and are quite ineffective in terms of their stated objectives, most commonly the mitigation of regressivity, the provision of a VAT credit to the seller of an untaxed commodity could as easily, and completely, exempt these selected transactions from taxation as would exemption under an RST.

Apart from the merits of the VAT versus the RST, it can be safely suggested that at worst a VAT would be more easily administered than an equally universal profits tax, if only because it requires no inventory accounting and no estimate of depreciation.

## 1.4 CHARACTERISTICS OF THE VAT-CIT SUBSTITUTION

Our focus is on the first-round cost and price consequences of varying degrees of replacement of the CIT by a consumption-type VAT with the characteristics just described. The analysis is based upon an input-output model representing the U.S. economy in 1969.[9] It is assumed that factor incomes *other than corporate profits*, interindustry input-output coefficients, and final demands are initially unaffected by the tax substitution. It is in this sense that the analysis is restricted to "first-round" consequences of the

---

9. The model is described more completely in Chapter 2.

change in tax structure. Adjustments of these variables will imply further-round consequences of the tax substitution.

The first phase of the study is concerned with the effects of the tax substitution on prices, by industry and by component of final demand. Thus, the input-output model serves the function of translating changes in tax liabilities into changes in prices. Given the restrictive assumptions imposed, first-round price effects, strictly speaking, represent "tax allocation" effects reached under common assumptions for all industries, concerning the reflection of various tax changes in pricing decisions.

It is assumed throughout that the VAT is fully shifted forward and that VAT-exclusive prices are identical for all classes of purchasers (consumption, investment, export, and government). The assumption of an appropriately flexible, monetary policy is required to support the assumed patterns of VAT shifting. More generally, under the assumption of profit-maximizing behavior on the part of producers and traders, monetary and fiscal policies are assumed to be compatible with maintaining the original (pre-VAT) level of real income along with proportionate changes in all prices and unchanged net-of-VAT demands for all commodities, with effectively complete forward shifting. This is the classical price theory argument for full shifting of a general ad valorem tax.

Correspondingly, the classical assumption regarding the CIT is that *in the short run* the returns to capital (profits, corporate income) are quasi-rents (the capital stock is fixed and the supply of capital services is inelastic with respect to the rate of return or price, as long as output price is greater than variable cost), and therefore forward shifting should not occur. That is, the elimination of the CIT should not affect output prices in the short run if the latter are determined subject to the classical condition that marginal cost equals marginal revenue.

However, in this case professional opinion is much more divided, with empirically based assertions ranging from zero shifting [Gordon] to shifting in excess of unity [Krzyzaniak and Musgrave]. In light of this dispute a range of alternative shifting assumptions is employed in the analysis, and the sensitivity of the consequences of the tax substitution to the degree of forward CIT shifting is given particular attention. For purposes of translating tax changes into price changes, CIT shifting is simply defined as the change in gross-of-tax profit relative to the change in tax liability.

To justify short-run forward shifting of the CIT it is necessary to introduce "nonclassical" theories of price determination: oligopolistic theories, in which interdependence is recognized between producers who are subject to external constraints on collusive joint maximizing decisions or who engage in entry-restricting pricing; long-run "normal cost" and administered-pricing theories; etc. However, whatever the underlying price-formation process, forward shifting of the CIT implies that net profits, capital earnings, and rates of return enter into price determination. If market pressures on net earnings are not perfectly competitive, then CIT increases or the benefits of CIT reductions will be shifted to consumers.

This relationship of price to net capital earnings in the case of forward CIT shifting has two primary implications for the analysis of the VAT-CIT substitution. First, it determines our treatment of depreciation, which is included at replacement cost. If the returns to capital are quasi-rents, as classical price theory indicates, then changes in capital goods prices do not alter commodity prices in the short run. However, if prices are influenced by *net* profits, then changes in capital goods prices must be incorporated in commodity pricing. This is achieved by including depreciation in intermediate interindustry transactions rather than in the residual component of industry value added.

Secondly, the relationship between net capital earnings and price implied by forward CIT shifting provides a heuristic justification for the assumption of full forward shifting of the VAT, even if non-classical price formation is assumed. Thus, a failure to shift the VAT completely would reflect imperfectly competitive market pressures similar to those required for generating short-run CIT shifting. However, the "net rate of return" constraints will already have been incorporated through CIT shifting. It therefore appears redundant to impose them a second time through an incomplete shifting of the VAT, since the tax changes are assumed to be simultaneous.

Initial presubstitution rates of CIT were determined from aggregate data by input-output sector, and are thus industry-specific. The reduction in CIT rates is assumed to be proportionate to these rates industry by industry. Because it was impossible at this level of disaggregation to distinguish among state and federal CIT liabilities, it was assumed that the proportionate reduction in effective CIT rates applies to all corporate income taxes.

The reduction or elimination of the CIT has several consequences for government. First, assuming that prices (and gross profits) are unchanged, i.e., assuming that the benefits of the CIT reduction are not shifted forward as lowered prices (exclusive of the newly imposed VAT), the government experiences only a *primary CIT revenue loss*, equal to the change in tax rates multiplied by the pretax-substitution levels of corporate income. But, *if* instead, the CIT reduction is shifted forward, lowering prices, and *if* the CIT is not completely eliminated, then with gross-of-tax profits reduced, the CIT at the new, lower rates will be reduced even further than the primary loss would indicate. This *secondary revenue loss* obviously occurs only if the CIT is retained, since the maximum revenue loss, primary and secondary combined, cannot exceed the revenue yield prior to the tax substitution. Finally, the level of nominal government expenditures will be reduced if, as a result of CIT reduction and shifting, the (VAT-exclusive) *prices of government purchases decline.*

An ultimately major effect of the tax substitution is *not* taken into consideration in the present analysis: Unless the CIT is considered to be entirely shifted forward, or the effect of CIT reduction is offset by monetary stringency and increased interest rates, investment demand will increase. Thus, if real disposable income, and with it the level of consumption demand, are initially maintained at a constant level by maintaining an unchanged government budgetary deficit or surplus, an increase in aggregate demand will occur, resulting in an increase in real income or in the rate of inflation. A change in the interest rate, if used to offset the effect of the CIT reduction on the aggregate volume of investment, would in itself involve a severe redistribution of incomes and differential effects on prices. In effect, in what follows, the analysis reflects only extreme short-run impacts which occur before investment has had time to respond to the changed circumstances.

The VAT rate is determined at that level which will just compensate for the three initial governmental impacts described above: the primary CIT revenue loss, the secondary CIT revenue loss, and the reduction in the cost of government purchases. Compensation is thus defined in terms of an unchanged government surplus or deficit, rather than in terms of an unchanged level of aggregate demand. This VAT-yield criterion, which equates the net change in tax revenue to the net change in government expenditure under the assumption of a constant bill of final demand, incorporates price changes for government resulting from CIT reduction and shifting. It can be argued that this yield criterion is a politically and legislatively relevant condition, given the way such legislation is usually thought of by those responsible for its formulation. It is consistent with short-run budgetary neutraility in accordance with the restriction of the present analysis to "first round" effects. It makes no attempt, however, to avoid a net stimulative or sedative effect on the economy as a whole in the medium or longer run; indeed the levels of VAT revenue specified in this analysis as the equivalent of various levels of CIT reduction can be expected under most circumstances to lead within a fairly short period after the change to a substantial stimulus to the economy or to increased inflationary pressure.

Just as the required VAT revenue varies with the degree of CIT reduction and shifting, so the VAT base also varies. The greater the degree of the CIT shifting, the greater will be the decline in (VAT-exclusive) prices of consumption goods, necessitating a higher VAT rate.

Thus, the relationship between the VAT rate and the degree of CIT reduction and shifting is somewhat complex. At one extreme, if the CIT is not shifted, then (a) the prices of government-purchased commodities are unchanged, (b) gross profits are not reduced and no secondary CIT revenue loss is experienced, and (c) net-of-VAT consumption expenditure is unaltered. Thus, the VAT rate is simply determined by the primary CIT revenue loss relative to the pre-substitution level of consumption expenditure. At another extreme, if the CIT is completely eliminated, then the secondary CIT revenue loss, which is due to the reduction in gross profits induced by shifting the CIT, is necessarily zero. In between these extremes, as the degree of shifting increases, required VAT revenue declines as the result of reduced government prices, while the VAT base declines as a result of reductions in VAT-exclusive consumer prices. Whether the VAT rate will rise or fall with an increase in the degree of shifting of the CIT depends on whether required revenue declines more or less rapidly than the VAT base. For intermediate degrees of CIT reduction and shifting, the required VAT rate will vary systematically with primary and secondary CIT revenue loss and with changes in government and consumer expenditures induced by CIT shifting.

Once the first-round price effects of the tax substitution have been determined, it is possible to assess the probable later round consequences for income distribution, investment, international trade and the balance of payments, etc.

## 1.5 CONSEQUENCES OF THE VAT-CIT SUBSTITUTION

This section contains a brief summary of the substantive consequences of the tax substitution for varying assumed degrees of CIT reduction and shifting. Because, as indicated above, the degree of forward CIT shifting determines the CIT revenue loss and the change in government and consumer prices resulting from CIT reduction, the CIT-compensating VAT rate depends crucially upon the assumed degree of CIT shifting. Using the model described in Chapter 2, the estimated relationship between CIT reduction and shifting, on the one hand, and the CIT-compensating VAT rate, on the other, are outlined in Table 1-1. For relatively small reductions in CIT rates the VAT rate *rises* with increases in shifting, simply because (1) the secondary CIT revenue loss is greater than the savings in government expenditures resulting from the decline in prices, i.e., as shifting rises, the amount of VAT revenue needed to compensate also rises, while (2) the VAT base necessarily declines. Thus, on the basis of our model, if CIT rates are reduced across the board by 25 percent, the VAT rate which will just hold the government surplus (deficit) constant rises from 1.9 percent if CIT savings are not shifted to 2.9 percent if these savings are shifted forward completely in the form of lower prices. However, if the relative reduction in the CIT is large, then the secondary revenue loss due to the decline in gross profits will be small, since the remaining CIT rate, applying to the now lower pretax profits, will be relatively low, while government expenditure savings resulting from price reductions may be quite large relative to the net change in CIT revenue. If the government expenditure reduction net of the secondary CIT revenue loss, relative to the primary CIT revenue loss, is greater than the shifting-induced decline in consumer expenditures, relative to their presubstitution level, then the required VAT rate will *decline* with increased CIT shifting. In fact, in the extreme case of complete CIT removal, for which there is no secondary revenue loss (the new CIT rate is zero), government expenditure reductions result in a decline in the VAT rate from 7.7 percent in the absence of CIT shifting to 7.2 percent if the benefits of CIT removal are fully translated into lower prices.

Since an increase in CIT shifting calls for an increase in the required VAT rate when the CIT reduction is small, and a decrease when it is large, there must be, for some intermediate degree of CIT reduction, a stationary point, at which a small increase or decrease in CIT shifting calls for neither an increase or decrease in

**Table 1-1. VAT Rate for Varying Degrees of CIT Reduction and Shifting**

| *Degree of CIT Shifting*[a] | *Degree of CIT Reduction*[b] | | |
|---|---|---|---|
| | *25%* | *75%* | *100%* |
| 0.0 | 1.92% | 5.76% | 7.68% |
| 0.4 | 2.19 | 5.91 | 7.50 |
| 1.0 | 2.91 | 6.19 | 7.22 |

Source: Table 3-1.

[a]The *proportion* of any reduction in CIT liabilities which accrues to purchasers in the form of lower prices.

[b]Percentage reduction in all corporate income tax rates.

the required VAT rate. At this level of CIT reduction, the relative change in VAT revenue required to offset the reduction must equal the relative change in the VAT base resulting from increased shifting, implying a VAT rate invariant to the degree of shifting. In our model, this equality is found at a relative CIT reduction of between 85 and 90 percent, for which the VAT rate is constant at about 6.8 percent, regardless of CIT shifting.

Invariance of the VAT rate is significant because the actual degree of CIT shifting is unknown and subject to dispute. More generally, the degree of forward shifting may not be fixed for all time, but may rather be a symptom of underlying conditions of demand, supply, and competition prevailing at the time of the tax change. In this context of uncertainty, if great weight is placed upon avoidance of unanticipated government surpluses or deficits, then on the basis of our model the risk-adverting policy would be to undertake a major reduction in the CIT, since the budgetary surplus would then be virtually unaffected by the degree of CIT shifting. Of course, the range of conceivable variability in the degree of shifting may itself be a function of the degree of CIT reduction. In that case, a VAT rate unaffected by CIT shifting may be purchased at the price of greater unpredictability concerning the degree of shifting [NEDO, pp. 43–44].

The sensitivity of the tax-substitution-induced price changes to the assumed degree of CIT shifting determines the relationship between the degree of CIT shifting and the compensatory VAT rate. Again, zero shifting of the CIT provides an extreme; in this case, prices exclusive of VAT are unaltered by the tax substitution, while VAT-inclusive prices rise by the VAT rate. With any degree of positive forward shifting of the CIT, however, VAT-exclusive prices (investment, exports, and government) decline, and the net rate of increase in VAT-inclusive consumption prices is less than the VAT rate. Thus, in our model, if the CIT is not shifted, repeal of the CIT requires a compensatory VAT rate of 7.68 percent, and consumption prices rise just by this percentage. But with full forward CIT shifting, the required VAT rate is 7.22 percent, while consumption prices increase by only 1.68 percent. In the first case (no shifting), VAT-exempt prices are unaffected. In the second case (full shifting), these prices decline, in the extreme by 5.45 percent (private fixed investment). The size of consumption price increases and VAT-exempt price decreases are of course smaller if the CIT is only partially removed, but increases in the degree of shifting invariably increase the magnitude of VAT-exclusive price declines and reduce the magnitude of VAT-inclusive price increases, as indicated in Table 1-2.

At the first-round stage all of the consequences of the VAT-CIT substitution flow from alterations in tax liabilities and, corrspondingly, in prices. The most important dimensions in which these consequences are explored are income distribution, investment, and international trade.

### 1.5.1 Consequences for Income Distribution

In unrelieved form the change from the CIT to the VAT is invariably regressive. Consider specifically the case of complete repeal of the CIT. With zero CIT shifting consumption prices rise by the VAT rate while after-tax corporate profits increase by the full amount of the former CIT revenue (equal to the revenue yield of the newly imposed VAT). If the increases in consumption expenditures are allocated to households on the basis of the level and composition of these expenditures and the increases in profits are allocated on the basis of wealth, then changes in *tax liability relative to income* decline with income class: from a net increase in liability of 6 percent at incomes between $5,000 and $7,500 to a net decrease of 7 percent at incomes above $15,000.

Table 1-2. Price Indices for Consumption and Nonresidential Fixed Investment for Varying Degrees of CIT Reduction and Shifting

| Degree of CIT Shifting | Price Indices | |
|---|---|---|
| | Consumption[a] | Investment[b] |
| | *CIT Reduction of 25 Percent* | |
| 0.0 | 101.92 | 100.00 |
| 0.4 | 101.57 | 99.36 |
| 1.0 | 100.69 | 97.76 |
| | *CIT Reduction of 75 Percent* | |
| 0.0 | 105.76 | 100.00 |
| 0.4 | 104.18 | 98.28 |
| 1.0 | 101.45 | 95.31 |
| | *CIT Reduction of 100 Percent* | |
| 0.0 | 107.68 | 100.00 |
| 0.4 | 105.28 | 97.82 |
| 1.0 | 101.68 | 94.55 |

Source: Table 3-5.

[a] VAT-inclusive prices.

[b] VAT-exclusive (exempt) prices.

If the CIT reduction is fully shifted forward in the form of lower prices, the rest of the world reaps a net benefit of $2.5 billion as a result of export price reductions. Similarly, the prices of capital goods decline, due to the shifted reduction in the CIT. Only VAT-inclusive consumption prices rise, although to a lower degree than in the case of zero CIT shifting. After-tax profits under the full-shifting assumption are unaffected by the tax substitution. If the reduction in prices of investment goods is distributed to households on the basis of wealth holdings, and if consumption price increases are distributed as indicated in the preceding paragraph, it is again possible using our model to estimate the impact of the change in tax structure on the distribution of income. The domestic burden of the price increases, although positive in the aggregate, declines by income class from about 2 percent at incomes between $5000 and $7500 to minus 0.2 percent at incomes above $15,000.

Perhaps the most interesting finding concerning income distribution is that multiple-rate and VAT-exemption schemes do not mitigate the underlying regressivity of the VAT. To maximize the progressivity of a multiple-rate VAT in our model, all consumption commodities exhibiting income elasticities less than unity were assumed to be completely exempt from the VAT.[10] We thus carried to an extreme the common practice of exempting "necessities" from state retail sales taxes, in order to reduce the regressivity of that particular ad valorem levy.

This exemption scheme failed in significantly reducing the regressivity of the VAT-CIT substitution. For example, if the CIT is eliminated, the exemption of commodities in inelastic demand in our model reduces the Gini coefficient (*index of inequality*) only from 0.397 to 0.394 if the CIT is not shifted, and from 0.380 to 0.377 if the CIT reduction is fully shifted, the initial figure in each of these comparisons being to the postsubstitution value of the Gini coefficient in the absence of an exemption. These increases in equality compare to a pre-tax-substitution Gini coefficient of 0.374, indicating that the exemption partially reduces the regressive effect of the VAT-CIT substitution, especially if the CIT is fully shifted.

Moreover, this marginal mitigation of regressivity is purchased at the price of a significant increase in the basic VAT rate, from about 7 percent to over 15 percent for those commodities still subject to VAT. This extreme rate differential, zero for some classes of

---

10. Administratively, sellers would *not* invoice VAT on final sales of these commodities, but would receive full credit for VAT on intermediate purchases, even if this resulted in a net credit.

commodities versus 15 percent for others, could be expected to produce significant allocative distortions as households change their consumption patterns, by substituting exempt for taxable commodities, in an attempt to minimize tax liabilities.

In a more realistic context, in which fewer commodities were subject to exemption, this rate differential could be significantly reduced but only at the price of an even less effective amelioration of regressivity. In addition, the allocative distortions that occur in response to differential rates of taxation would remain; thus, the allocative neutrality of the VAT, its most significant positive attribute, would be lost. Finally, the European experience indicates quite clearly that the private and governmental costs of tax administration are greatly increased by the incorporation of dual and multiple VAT rates [NEDO, p. 5].

Thus, dual rates can be objected to on a number of counts, and use of such schemes has little mitigating effect on the basis regressivity of the tax substitution. However, this finding does not provide a substantial argument against the VAT-CIT substitution on distributional grounds. First, the position could be taken that the U.S. tax structure would be improved by the regressivity implied by a VAT-CIT substitution. The overall progressivity-regressivity of the tax system as a whole would be only marginally influenced in any event. Secondly, other means could be found to compensate for the regressivity of the VAT-CIT substitution while retaining the basic allocative neutrality of the VAT. For example, systems of rebatable credits against personal income tax liabilities have often been proposed in the context of otherwise regressive ad valorem taxes. Thus, the VAT could be levied at a higher rate than estimated to be required here to compensate for the CIT, with a credit against the income tax permitted for VAT imputed on a basic level of per capita consumption. The additional revenue requirements resulting from income tax losses could be reduced if the credit were of the "vanishing" variety, i.e., were itself included as a component of taxable income and subjected to tax. Alternatively, but somewhat more radically, the VAT itself could be replaced by a direct *progressive expenditures tax* of the type proposed by Kaldor. This tax would preserve the allocative neutrality and many of the other desirable characteristics of the VAT that relate to investment and trade. In a system already employing an income tax, administration of a progressive expenditures tax would only require in addition that taxpayers consistently adjust the realized income as now reported by the flows into and out of investment, and by gifts and bequests made or received.

### 1.5.2 Investment Consequences

We assessed the investment effects of the VAT-CIT substitution on the basis of the liquidity theory of investment elaborated by Kuh, Meyer, and Glauber. Following Brittain, Lintner, and Dobrovolsky, we assumed that dividends are determined by nominal profits. Investment is then a function of *real* cash flow net of dividends and corporate profits taxes. If it is assumed that the CIT is not shifted, its repeal will not alter the prices of capital goods. Profits (net of tax) would then increase in our model by $42.68 billion, equal to total CIT liabilities, which would imply an increase of $18.43 billion in dividends. The remainder, a $24.25 billion increase in real net cash flow, would result in a *cumulative* increase in gross investment of $32.05 billion.[11] In the short run the Meyer-Glauber elasticities indicate that gross investment in plant and equipment would increase by 5.3 percent, or $5.3 billion. In this case, since capital goods prices are unaffected by the tax change the investment stimulus operates only in the incorporated sector.

With elimination and full forward shifting of the CIT, nominal net cash flows are unaffected by the tax substitution. However, the shifted CIT reduction has the effect of reducing capital goods prices by more than 5 percent. Thus, *real* net cash flows are necessarily increased, by $4.24 billion. The cumulative increase in gross investment stimulated by this price reduction is projected to be $8.98 billion, with a short-run increase of 1.5 percent or $1.5 billion. In this case the stimulus operates on the investment activity of both the incorporated and the unincorporated sectors since the price reductions benefit all investment activity. Of the $8.98 billion increase in cumulative gross investment, the unincorporated sector would account for $3.37 billion and the incorporated sector for $5.61 billion.

Thus, under either CIT shifting assumption the replacement of the CIT by the VAT might significantly stimulate aggregate investment demand. In addition, the composition of investment demand would be significantly altered in favor of the corporate sector if the CIT were not shifted. It must be pointed out, however, that in the input-output model itself, the assumption has been adhered to that no change occurs in the level or composition of real final demand. The above estimates of increases in investment resulting from the substitution are "second round" effects not included in the model. Since increases in effective (VAT-inclusive) consumption prices might

---

11. This amount represents the undiscounted sum of all future increases in investment resulting from an increased real cash flow in the current period.

reduce real consumer demand, it could be expected that the investment stimulus would operate in more than one way. Investment could be shifted toward sectors supplying disproportionately large components of final demand that are exempt from the VAT and for which prices may have declined. Alternatively, the process of "capital deepening" (greater capital intensity of production), rather than "capital widening" (growth in productive capacity) could accelerate in response to a reduction in the cost of capital relative to wages.

### 1.5.3 International Trade Effects

Our contention is that the international trade consequences of the VAT-CIT substitution have often been misunderstood and confused. On the realistic assumption that the VAT is fully shifted forward, any balance-of-trade effects of the change in tax structure must result from the reduction or elimination of the CIT, not from the imposition of the VAT itself. In general, the VAT has no effect on the terms of trade. As a destination-based tax the VAT will have trade effects only if it is substituted for an origin-based tax, the reduction of which is shifted forward in lower prices of exports and of import-competing goods. Thus, if the CIT is *not* shifted the terms of trade are unaltered. Prices of imports and of import-competing commodities (if subject to the VAT) rise by equivalent proportions (the VAT rate), while VAT-exclusive export prices are unaltered. Thus, zero shifting of the CIT would imply an unchanged balance of trade.

If the CIT reduction is shifted in the form of lower VAT-exclusive prices, then its replacement by a VAT will serve (at least in the short run) to stimulate exports and reduce imports. If the CIT is completely eliminated, the improvement in the balance of trade is estimated in our model to be between $2.7 billion and $4.7 billion, depending on the export and import elasticities employed. To place these estimates in perspective, the complete removal of a forward-shifted CIT is demonstrated to be equivalent to an effective devaluation of about 5 percent. Since such a devaluation is a perfectly conceivable alternative to the VAT-CIT substitution, and has in fact been effected between 1971 and 1973, balance-of-trade consequences provide no substantial argument in favor of the tax substitution. This is particularly true since one quite conceivable outcome of the tax substitution is an unchanged balance of trade (if the CIT is not shifted).

However, while the effect of VAT-CIT substitution on the balance of trade under the most favorable assumptions would be equivalent to a 5 percent devaluation, the effect on international capital flows might be quite different. Depending on the degree to which elimination of an unshifted CIT increased after-tax corporate profits and rates of return, significant capital inflows might be predicted, which might well reduce the deficit in the balance of payments. In brief, a devaluation would operate primarily on the trade account, while the tax substitution might operate either on the trade account (if the CIT is shifted), on the capital account (if the CIT is not shifted), or on both trade and capital accounts (intermediate degrees of CIT shifting). Unfortunately, it has not been possible within the confines of this study to assess quantitatively the potential implications of the tax substitution for international capital flows.

As a final note on trade consequences, it should be pointed out that the elimination of a shifted CIT and a 5 percent devaluation are equivalent only in terms of the *net* change in the balance of trade. In general, the devaluation apparently operates more strongly through increases in exports than through the substitution of import-competing goods for imports, while the reverse would be true under the tax substitution with CIT shifting.[12] However, changes in *real* export and import flows would be quite similar under either of these policies.

### 1.5.4 Regional Effects

In Chapter 7, particular attention is devoted to the *differential regional consequences* of the tax substitution, especially its implications for the relatively low-income South. It is shown that, depending on the degree of CIT shifting (complete versus zero), repeal of the CIT would increase net southern tax liabilities by between 0.7 and 2.1 percent of disposable personal income in that region. In contrast, the rest of the country, with per capita incomes one-third greater than in the South, would experience a 0.7 percent reduction in tax liabilities relative to income if the CIT were not shifted, and only a 0.3 percent increase if the CIT were fully shifted.

On a regional basis, the tax-substitution-induced investment expansion is found to be significantly nonneutral. To project the probable regional investment increases the ad hoc assumption was employed that a region's share of any industry's investment expansion would be equal to its share of base (actual 1969) investment in that industry. Applying the model to a selected group of manufacturing industries for which regional investment statistics were

---

12. This statement will be true if the relative price elasticity of exports (U.S. export prices to world prices) is greater than the relative price elasticity of imports (domestic prices of import-competing goods to world prices).

available and assuming complete CIT repeal, it was found that zero CIT shifting would generate a 10 percent increase in investment nationally; by region, the investment expansion would range between 7.5 percent in the West South Central to 12.5 percent in New England. The South as a whole would experience an increase of 9.3 percent, versus 10.3 percent for the rest of the nation. In the case of full CIT shifting the national expansion of 1.9 percent would decompose into a regional range of from 1.5 percent (West South Central) to 2.2 percent (New England), with an aggregate Southern expansion of 1.7 percent in contrast to an expansion of 2.0 for the rest of the nation. Thus, the South would experience a marginally lower investment stimulus than the rest of the United States, primarily because of differences in the South's industrial composition.

In terms of changes in international trade flows, the South would benefit most from the potential stimulus to import-competing industries of a shifted CIT reduction, but would be only marginally affected by any export expansion. Thus, if the CIT is shifted, the stimulus to income and output in the South flowing from the VAT-CIT substitution might be quite great.

### 1.5.5 Other Substitution Effects

Virtually no attention has been given to *intergovernmental fiscal effects* of a VAT-CIT substitution. In the discussion of these effects it is usually pointed out that, notwithstanding the large direct labor component in expenditures by state and local governments, these jurisdictions would benefit significantly from complete elimination of the federal CIT, if this were shifted forward in the form of lower prices of government-purchased goods and services. However, if federal repeal caused states simultaneously to repeal their own corporate income taxes, as might be expected, then state-local governments, as a group, would suffer a significant net decline in budget surpluses regardless of the degree of CIT shifting.[13] This adverse change in budgetary status would be aggravated if these governments were not effectively exempted from the VAT (via either a

---

13. In section 1.4, we pointed out that since we could not separate federal and state CIT liabilities at the individual industry level, we were forced to assume that all CITs would be proportionately reduced. However, as discussed later, the net burden of a state CIT is significantly reduced by the existence of a federal CIT, since state CIT liabilities can be deducted in computing the base for the federal CIT. This advantage would be lost if the federal CIT were greatly reduced or repealed. Thus, it is not unlikely that states would in fact follow the federal suit in CIT reduction. Also, elimination of the federal CIT could significantly increase the administrative costs of the state CIT.

credit or exemption from invoicing). Thus, if a federal VAT were substituted for the state-federal CIT, explicit provision for sharing of federal revenues with affected state-local governments would be necessary if the tax substitution were not adversely to affect the fiscal condition of individual jurisdictions. Whether such compensatory federal action would in fact be desirable and, if so, how such a distribution of federal revenues should be designed remain open questions.

An assumption of the analysis is that nominal factor incomes other than corporate profits are unaffected by the tax substitution. However, consumer prices (inclusive of VAT) are found to increase under all CIT shifting and reduction assumptions, implying declines in real wages. To assess the differential short-run pressures for further-round price and output adjustments in different industries, *wage adjustments* required to restore pre-tax-substitution levels of real wages are compared by industry with the decline in CIT liabilities, under the assumption of repeal and zero shifting of the CIT. Not surprisingly, it is found that the CIT savings greatly exceed potential short-run labor cost increases in relatively capital-intensive, highly incorporated industries. Conversely, labor-intensive, unincorporated industries could experience aggregate increases in wage bills greatly in excess of CIT savings.

Much popular concern has focused on the potential *interindustry redistribution of tax burdens* implicit in a VAT-CIT substitution. To provide some evidence on this score the principal assumption of the study, that the VAT is fully shifted forward in higher prices, is dropped. It is demonstrated that, in the short run, if neither the CIT nor the VAT were shifted, and if VAT-exclusive prices to all purchasers were equalized,[14] then highly incorporated and rapid growth (high-investment) industries would experience significant increases in net profits, while after-tax profits would decline for relatively unincorporated, low-growth industries.[15]

The strongest argument for the VAT-CIT substitution is the positive effect it would have on the overall allocative efficiency of the United States economy. This increase in efficiency would follow from improvements in production (in particular from a reallocation

---

14. Retaining the assumption of equal VAT-exclusive prices for all purchasers implies that introduction of an unshifted VAT will reduce effective prices on investment, export, and government sales. Thus, the change in after-tax profits need not equal the net change in government tax receipts.

15. By "highly incorporated industries," we mean those industries in which a large share of value added is accounted for by incorporated enterprises, and conversely for "relatively unincorporated industries."

of capital from the noncorporate to the corporate sector), from reallocation of consumption, and from probable increases in the rate of capital accumulation.

As has been indicated throughout, the consequences of the VAT-CIT substitution discussed here represent estimates only of the results of first-round, short-run responses to this change in tax structure, projected under a highly restrictive and confining set of assumptions. However, ultimate consequences of the substitution will only flow from the more pervasive responses of households and producers, not to mention fiscal and monetary authorities, to these initial effects. This in itself is sufficient justification for the analysis; it at least provides a basis for qualitative estimates of the probable ultimate effects on important economic magnitudes and of further policy adjustments which would be necessary or desirable.

In conclusion, it would appear that the only unique argument in favor of the VAT-CIT substitution is the probable improvement in allocative efficiency which such a movement toward a more neutral system of taxation would induce. Redistributive effects certainly do not provide a basis for advocating this substitution, and putative investment and international trade effects could be more confidently achieved by other means.

*Chapter 2*

# The Theoretical Structure
# of the Analysis

## 2.1 BASIC THEORETICAL ISSUES

The major difficulty encountered in the assessment of the differential effects of a substitution of one tax (VAT) for another (CIT)[1] is the isolation of the effects of the change in tax structure from the effects of other simultaneous changes. Thus, John Bossons has stated that "one of the most frequent sources of spurious issues [in evaluating tax substitutions] is the confusion of macroeconomic control problems with problems of tax structure" [Bossons, p. 255]. More generally, Carl Shoup has argued that, in a context of multiple goals, the effects of a tax substitution on the achievement of one goal can only be assessed by making simultaneous changes in other fiscal instruments sufficient to maintain presubstitution levels of other goal variables [Shoup, 1970, pp. 12-15].

Of course, the difficulty is that such a multidimensional differential incidence analysis requires both a completely specified general equilibrium approach and a knowledge of the "goals" of the tax substitution, neither of which is available to the analyst concerned with the evaluation of a VAT-CIT substitution. Even the achievement of aggregative neutrality is beyond the confines of the input-output model used in this study. Rather than requiring as a *condition*

---

1. Throughout this study, the reduction or repeal of the CIT refers to the total CIT in the United States economy, that is, the federal CIT and the CIT of those states that impose this tax. "Government" refers, therefore, to the combined federal-state government. But the VAT is assumed to be imposed only by the federal government (see Chapter 7, section 1).

of the tax substitution that the level of real income and output be unchanged, the input-output model imposes this as an *assumption*, i.e., the final demand vector is assumed to be exogenously given and unaffected by the tax substitution. It should be emphasized that this constraint seriously limits the practical usefulness of the results, especially to the extent that division of the final demand vector between investment and consumption goods is likely to be substantially altered by the tax changes examined.

As a result of these conceptual and empirical limitations, the analysis is confined to the first-round consequences of the tax substitution. However, even though the model is restricted to a rather simple representation of interdependent economic processes, a number of difficult theoretical and conceptual issues arise. In this chapter, we discuss the most important of these issues, their specific representation in an input-output model, and the restrictive assumptions incorporated in the model.

**Criteria for a Compensating Tax Substitution.** Between the extremes of simple equal monetary yield of the two tax instruments and simultaneous adjustments in a sufficiently large set of instruments to offset any unintentional consequences of the tax substitution, a number of compensatory criteria can be developed. The issue reduces to the identification of a criterion which limits the response as much as possible to the change in tax structure (as opposed, e.g., to implicit changes in stabilization policy) but does not exceed our analytical capabilities.

**Alternative Variants of the Value-Added Tax.** The VAT can take on a number of different forms, each of which has significantly different economic consequences. Although the empirical analysis is limited to examination of a VAT of the consumption type, it is important to point out the substantive differences between alternative variants.

**Price Determination and Tax Shifting.** The consequences of the tax substitution ultimately follow from the change in tax rates, the effect of these changes on prices, and the responses of producers and consumers to these tax-rate and price adjustments. Furthermore, unless the responses of prices to tax changes can be identified, criteria for a compensatory tax substitution cannot be concretely specified and realized.

**Fiscal Implications of the Tax Substitution.** On the basis of the discussion of price determination and tax shifting, it is possible to specify concretely the elements entering the compensation criterion, thus determining a VAT rate which just compensates, in terms of the government budget balance, for the reduction or repeal of the CIT.

To place this discussion in context the tax substitution used in this analysis must be briefly outlined: a uniform (proportionate) reduction from the initial average CIT rate in each industry is assumed.[2] The VAT then imposed is to be invoiced on all sales, on the basis of the VAT-exclusive value. The VAT is assumed to be applied on a destination basis, with exports exempted and the VAT applied to imports as a border tax. As the VAT is of the consumption type, a refund is permitted for VAT invoiced on business purchases, including gross investment. The VAT is set at a *rate* that allows the government to purchase the original (presubstitution) bill of goods and services at the new (postsubstitution) prices without incurring a change in its nominal (i.e., money) budget surplus or deficit.

## 2.2 CRITERIA FOR A COMPENSATING VAT-CIT SUBSTITUTION

A number of considerations entered into our selection of a compensation criterion, as we tried to bridge gaps between what is theoretically desirable and actually feasible:

The goals of the VAT-CIT substitution actualy are not clear. Advocates have stressed a range of real or imagined benefits which would flow from this change in tax structure. However, a fundamental uncertainty exists concerning the actual implications of this fiscal change. One purpose of an analysis of this change is to identify these implications; the compensation criterion should then be designed to bring out, rather than disguise, obscure, or define away, the differential impacts of these two taxes.

The compensation criterion should clearly avoid the merging of changes in macroeconomic stabilization policy with changes in tax structure. Expansion or contraction of government budgets could

---

2. The CIT rate reduction utilized in the analysis is somewhat artificial. First, since state and federal corporate income tax liabilities could not be empirically separated at the level of input-output sectors, it has been necessary to assume that the reduction applies to the total corporate tax liability. More seriously, the reduction is expressed in terms of *effective* rates (actual average tax liabilities, i.e., ratios of CIT to profit), which bear no simple or consistent relationship to statutory corporate tax rates. This will not introduce a bias into the analysis if the simple fact of a reduction in nominal tax rates does not alter the relationship between these and effective rates of tax. In any event, the distortions resulting from this assumption should be of minor importance.

certainly be achieved without reliance on a substitution of a VAT for the CIT. Since our fundamental concern is with the differential consequences of the tax substitution itself, it is necessary to focus the analysis on a specific substitution which does not intermingle these consequences with the consequences of overall changes in government stabilization policy.

The compensation criterion must be consistent with analytical capabilities. On the one hand, to be meaningful compensation must be defined in terms of economic variables whose movements can be captured by the underlying model. For example, a reasonable definition of aggregative neutrality would be unchanged total employment.[3] However, to translate tax changes into changes in employment would require a well-developed representation of the labor market, relating employment changes to tax-substitution-induced changes in wages, capital-labor ratios, and output prices. Unfortunately, we do not now have the analytical capabilities to trace out these relationships.

On the other hand, the compensation criterion should include relevant responses which can in fact be projected. Thus, to require only that the monetary yield of the two taxes be equal, under the assumption that, e.g., prices or corporate profits will be unchanged, represents a waste of available information if it is in fact possible to project price and corporate profit changes resulting from the tax substitution, and if these changes will alter tax revenue yields.

Finally, it could be argued that the compensation criterion should be politically and legislatively relevant, since the purpose of studies such as this one is the identification of an open-ended range of uncompensated differential consequences of a potential change in the tax structure.

Of the foregoing, the most important substantive objective in the choice of a compensation criterion is the achievement of aggregative neutrality. However, as noted above this cannot be required as a condition of the tax substitution since it is imposed as an assumption of the input-output model, given the stipulation of a fixed bill of final demands. Thus, the analysis is forced to rely on a more rudimentary criterion which would be *consistent with* (rather than a *reflection of*) a stable macroeconomic control policy.

Specifically, price changes that result from application of the criterion chosen for determining a CIT-compensating VAT rate must be a consequence only of the tax substitution and not of an overall ex-

---

3. This criterion has been employed in a study of alternatively-compensated reductions in military expenditure [Dresch, 1972b; Dresch and Goldberg].

pansion or contraction of the government budget. Since real government demands for goods and services are assumed to be given, this reduces to a search for a definition of unchanged effective revenue yield. Four possible equal-budgetary-yield criteria can be proposed:

a. *Equal Monetary Yield.* Let $C$ be the CIT revenue loss (either from partial or full repeal of the CIT) and $V$ be the VAT revenue gain, including amounts attributed to purchases by the government.[4] Equal monetary yield simply requires that $C = V$, a condition that necessitates analysis of "money differential incidence" [Shoup, 1970, p. 13]. Obviously, this condition will entail an unequal real yield of the tax substitution (not to mention of the tax system as a whole, as indicated in b, below) if the prices of government-purchased goods and services rise as a result of the tax substitution. Thus, even if the CIT were the only tax employed initially, a constant bill of goods and services could be maintained only if the government's deficit (surplus) increased (decreased). In the analysis of money differential incidence, then, the effects of two government budget changes are necessarily merged: the tax substitution and an increase or decrease in deficit. In the present case, if $P_g$ is the government price index (in VAT-inclusive terms, compared to a pre-VAT base of unity), it is unlikely that $C = V/P_g$ would also be achieved when the yield criterion is $C = V$.

b. *Equal Real Yield of the Tax Changes.* Here it is required that $C = V/P_g$, i.e., that the VAT revenue be adequate to command the same real resources after the tax substitution as were previously commanded by the CIT revenue forgone through CIT reduction or repeal. But government-purchased goods and services are also financed by tax sources other than the CIT. Consequently, if $P_g$ changes and if the original bill of goods and services is to be purchased by the government, *either* the original net government budget position will change (increase or decrease in deficit or surplus) *or* rates of other taxes must be simultaneously increased or decreased. Thus, this criterion is consistent with differential incidence analysis only under some further stipulation regarding the nature of concomitant, compensating changes in all other tax rates. One possible condition for simultaneous change in other taxes could be referred

---

4. Actual or imputed VAT on government purchases is included for logical consistency: since the corporate profits resulting from sales to government are subject to the CIT, parallel treatment suggests that VAT attributable to government also be included.

to as "revenue source neutrality": all other tax rates should be changed enough so that the *proportion* of total governmental revenue derived from each revenue source is the same as before the tax substitution.

It should be clearly understood that the analysis then concerns the differential incidence of the VAT-CIT substitution *and* the simultaneous changes in other taxes; relative price changes and their effects cannot be viewed as consequences of the tax substitution alone. Nevertheless, equal real VAT-CIT yield and revenue source neutrality appears to be a more interesting combination of budgetary changes than equal monetary yield supplemented by changes in the deficit (criterion a, above).[5]

c. *Equal Real Budget Surplus or Deficit.* Let $R$ and $G$ refer to government revenue and expenditure; $b$, before the tax substitution; $a$, after the substitution. With the relevant postsubstitution price index $P$, this condition stipulates that $(R_b - G_b) = (R_a - G_a)/P$, meaning that the preexisting real fiscal imbalance is maintained after the tax substitution.[6]

Under one conceivable interpretation, this condition is consistent with differential incidence analysis (as described in condition b, above) on the assumption that the surplus (deficit) will be used to increase (reduce) governmental (private) expenditure in the future, i.e., that the government is *saving* in order to increase, in later years, government expenditure, or, via future lower taxes, private expenditure, or is *dissaving* at the expense of future government or (via future higher taxes) private expenditure. The relevant price index for the evaluation of the real surplus or deficit then depends upon the future use of the surplus or deficit, public or private, and must reflect the impact of the tax substitution on these future prices.

More likely, the government surplus or deficit does not reflect savings or dissavings but instead is the result of overall government

---

5. Aaron clearly intends to employ the second criterion, although it is not clear what assumptions he makes regarding changes in the real yields of other taxes (rate changes versus increase in deficit). He is also ambiguous about the price index used to evaluate real yields. In referring to government purchasing power of the changed taxes he seems to imply a government price index, but elsewhere he refers to four available alternatives: GNP deflator, government expenditure deflator, wholesale price index, and retail (consumer) price index [Aaron, pp. 165–166.].

6. $P$, rather than $P_g$, is used to denote the "price index" because, as will become clear, the appropriate index need not relate to changes in the prices of government-purchased goods and services.

stabilization (macroeconomic control) policy. Under this interpretation, the criterion of equal real surplus implies some concept of aggregative neutrality, i.e., an avoidance of expansion or contraction in the economy. In this case the appropriate "price" index must really be an index of the change in the surplus (deficit) required to maintain the existing level of real aggregate demand. In fact, as has been discussed, our model does not attempt to identify that specific substitution which would be fiscally neutral. In view of the probable effects of the substitution on investment (as discussed in Chapter 5), it would indeed appear that a fiscally neutral substitution would require substantially higher VAT rates than the ones estimated by this model.

d. *Change in Revenue Equal to Change in Expenditure*, or *Equal Monetary Surplus or Deficit.* Under this criterion $V = C + (P_g G - G) = C + (P_g - 1)G$, where $(P_g - 1)G$ is the change in government expenditure due to the tax-substitution-induced price changes. Equivalently, this criterion implies a constant monetary surplus or deficit, i.e., $(R_b - G_b) = (R_a - G_a)$. This condition could simply be referred to as (narrow) budgetary neutrality, with the VAT compensating for both the nominal CIT revenue loss and the change in government expenditures due to induced price changes. In the present application of this criterion, it is assumed for reasons of tractability that the nominal revenue yield of other tax sources is unaffected by the tax substitution. In principle, the *rates* of other taxes should be held constant, and the VAT rate should be set sufficiently high to compensate for the tax-substitution-induced changes in the nominal yields of these taxes as well as for the CIT revenue loss and the price-change-induced increase in government expenditure.

Of these four criteria the second (equal real yield) and fourth (equal changes in revenue and expenditure) will be identical if original government expenditure on goods and services equals the amount of CIT revenue which is lost by the reduction in the CIT rate (or by CIT repeal, if the rate is reduced to zero).[7] The third and fourth (equal real versus equal monetary surplus) will be identical if the original government budget is in balance, but they will be quite different if the government surplus or deficit is large and prices change significantly. Only under the fourth criterion is the VAT

---

7. This can be easily shown: Criterion d requires that $G(P_g - 1) + C = V$. Criterion b requires that $C = V/P_g$. For criteria d and b to be equivalent, therefore, it is necessary that $G(P_g - 1) + C = CP_g$, i.e., that $G = C$.

treatment of government purchases a matter of indifference: since the VAT on these purchases is simultaneously government revenue and expenditure; whether government purchases are considered subject to or exempt from the VAT will not alter the government surplus or deficit. In all four cases, it is assumed that the tax substitution would have no significant consequences for the nominal yields of other taxes, e.g., ad valorem sales taxes.

For our purposes criterion d seems perferable: It provides a more interesting context than the "money differential incidence" of the simultaneous tax and deficit change implied by the first criterion; it appears to be more in line with legislative realities than the second, which would in principle require simultaneous changes in all tax rates,[8] and it contrasts with the third, which would require unavailable knowledge regarding fiscal neutrality or the future use of government (dis)savings. Our dominant consideration has simply been to achieve a differential incidence analysis of changes in the tax *structure* consistent with legislative-political realism. For these reasons, we used the fourth criterion, a constant nominal surplus or deficit (or alternatively stated, a net change in revenue equal to the substitution-induced change in expenditure).

## 2.3 THE CONSUMPTION-TYPE VAT AND ALTERNATIVES

The consequences of a complete or partial replacement of the CIT by a VAT will depend crucially on the precise characteristics of the tax substitution. Identification of the specific CIT change is relatively straightforward: it is assumed that the existing characteristics of the CIT as reflected in observed differentials between nominal and actual (or effective) rates, are unaltered by the tax substitution. Thus, the analysis concerns the complete or partial replacement of the *existing* U.S. CIT (federal and state), rather than an *idealized* CIT, by the VAT.

The same procedure cannot be employed for the VAT, since it is

---

8. As indicated, it is assumed, for simplicity, that nominal yields of other taxes are unaffected by the tax substitution; a more appropriate assumption would be that other tax *rates* are unaffected. In the initial incidence analysis presented here, the distortion is limited to (a) ad valorem taxes, the yields of which will be sensitive to price changes induced by the VAT–CIT substitution and (b) personal income taxes, the bases of which are altered by changes in after-tax corporate profits. Aaron also assumes constant nominal yields of other ad valorem taxes, an assumption which is particularly inconsistent with the suggested "revenue source neutrality" interpretation of his yield criterion (see note 6). In both our own and Aaron's analyses, however, the effects of these inconsistencies should be of only secondary importance.

not in effect in the United States. Thus, it is necessary to choose the characteristics of the VAT, and we will therefore be substituting an idealized VAT for an actual CIT.

Given this freedom in defining the VAT, we were guided by the following considerations in selecting a specific variant: First, as in the case of the selection of a yield criterion, we sought political and legislative realism. Secondly, and related to the first, we took into account and were guided by the practices of other industrialized nations that impose a VAT. Finally, desirable economic characteristics, relating both to allocative efficiency and to the range of specific objectives advanced by advocates of the VAT, have provided a basic set of criteria for VAT specification.

On the basis of these considerations the *consumption-type VAT* was ultimately selected for analysis. This variant of the VAT has a number of important characteristics which differentiate it from others, particularly in terms of economic effects. In the following discussion, we explain these differences in detail.

The main variants of the VAT are the *consumption, income,* and *gross product* types. Under a VAT of the consumption type the tax is invoiced on all sales other than exports. The seller is then credited for VAT invoiced on all business purchases in determining his net VAT liability. Thus, the apparent net base of the VAT consists of final sales to households and government. Since the VAT invoiced on government purchases represents both revenue and expenditure of the government, the ultimate *net* VAT base consists only of final sales to consumers, i.e., private domestic consumption expenditure.

Although the VAT is invoiced on capital goods sales, that tax payment is concurrently recouped by way of an "input tax" credit against the gross VAT liability of the business purchaser of the capital good. A VAT liability arises only at some future date when the capital is transmuted into consumption output. As a result of this immediate tax rebate, the tax funds of users of capital goods are not tied up, as would otherwise occur if the VAT could only be recouped gradually through depreciation of the capital good; in this sense the exemption of investment is equivalent to instantaneous (accelerated) depreciation under a profits tax (full write-off at the time of purchase) [Musgrave, pp. 343-344].[9]

---

9. Depending on the sophistication of depreciation policy a VAT of the income type may also discriminate against investments of different duration. However, under equivalent depreciation rules an income tax and the income-type VAT would be equally discriminatory [Musgrave, pp. 338-343]. In any event, the degree of discrimination under a VAT of the income type would be small relative to that inherent in the gross-product variant.

It is this instant-rebate feature which differentiates the consumption-type VAT from its alternatives, the income and gross-product types.[10] Under a VAT of the *income type* the tax is "recouped" only through depreciation of the capital good: investment purchases are subject to tax but a credit is allowed only for depreciation. Thus, the net base of the income-type VAT consists of net investment plus consumption. A *gross-product* VAT goes further: it is levied on capital purchases but no credit is permitted for depreciation; the resulting net VAT base consists, therefore, of gross investment plus consumption. Effectively, a VAT on gross investment implies double taxation of capital goods: first at the time when the capital good is purchased, and again when the capital good is transmuted into consumption output and the latter is sold.

In addition, the base of a gross-product VAT is highly sensitive to the definition of the accounting period (differentiating intermediate from capital purchases) while that of the income and consumption types is not. Thus, the gross-product type strongly discriminates against lengthy investments.[11] On the other hand, the relation of the consumption type to the life of a capital investment is completely neutral, but only at the expense of a total exemption of capital goods from the tax (Shoup, pp. 251–252; Musgrave, pp. 336–346). Similarly, it is neutral to the degree of capital-intensiveness of production techniques.

As in the case of instantaneous depreciation under an income or profits tax, the exemption of investment under a consumption-type VAT logically requires that the investor receive an immediate refund if he enjoys a *net* credit (excess of credits on intermediate and capital goods purchases over liability on sales). Simply providing for a carryover of net credits to future periods is not adequate, since the value of a credit of a given dollar amount is reduced the longer the refund is delayed. This consideration could be quite significant in the case of newly formed or rapidly expanding firms, for which the value of the credit would be greatly eroded if the credit were not realized until years later. It is now the practice in all European countries to refund net VAT credits without delay.

---

10. In addition to the gross-product, income and consumption types of VAT, Shoup [1970, pp. 352–354] identifies the wages, or investment-income-exclusion, variant, the base of which will be equal to consumption in any period only if net investment is equal to profits (more generally, to nonwage income).

11. The invoice method of administering the collection of the VAT, described in the text, breaks down if either an income or gross-product, rather than consumption VAT, is applied. For a discussion of alternative methods of administration, see Shoup [1970, pp. 257–261].

For goods in international trade, it is assumed that the VAT is imposed on the destination principle, i.e., export sales are exempt from the VAT while it is imposed as a border tax on imports.[12] Value added at all stages in the course of production for export is ultimately VAT-free since a full tax credit is enjoyed at the final stage on all export-embodied inputs while export sales are exempted from tax. Thus, the relation of the VAT itself to the terms of trade is neutral: the imposition of the tax should leave export prices unchanged and alter import and import-competing prices equivalently.

Finally, in contrast to (broadly based or partial) income taxes or to an income or gross product VAT the consumption VAT is neutral in its relation to consumption versus savings. In brief, the present value of all future consumption is unaffected by the timing of consumption, since the consumption-type VAT does not create a gap between the gross- and net-of-tax rate of return to capital. Because of this characteristic, a consumption-type VAT, by diverting resources from consumption to investment, would stimulate growth if it were substituted for a CIT or other income tax. This would be in addition to any stimulus due to strengthened demand which might result from the substitution of the VAT for the CIT on the basis of a balanced budget criterion.

Primarily as a result of these allocatively neutral efficiency characteristics the consumption-type VAT has commanded wider attention that its alternatives, and has been advanced as an alternative to other types of taxes, particularly the CIT. For these reasons, our analysis is restricted to the consumption type.

A final issue concerns the treatment of other taxes in determining the base of the VAT, and vice versa. In our analysis the VAT is excluded from the bases of other taxes, e.g., the CIT, while all components of value added, including other taxes, are included in the VAT base. The reason for this treatment can be indicated using indirect business taxes (IBT) as an example. Under our assumptions the VAT is invoiced at a uniform rate on VAT-exclusive but IBT-inclusive value. Employing the invoice method, with each firm invoicing VAT on sales (other than exports) and receiving a credit for VAT invoiced on purchases, the ultimate ratio of aggregate net VAT liabilities (excluding VAT on government purchases) to aggregate consumption expenditures will equal the VAT rate. This equal-

---

12. A destination-based VAT is somewhat difficult to contemplate in the case of the United States. Invoicing the tax on export sales might raise questions of an unconstitutional tax on exports. Exemption of imports would require that some kind of credit for a hypothetical tax on imports be allowed, since imports as intermediate goods cannot be distinguished in final transactions.

ity would break down if the VAT were imposed on IBT-exclusive value *unless* all elements of IBT imposed at all previous stages (e.g., real property, excise, sales, motor vehicle and fuel taxes) could be separately identified and excluded, at the stage in question, from all purchases by the firm, which is obviously impossible.[13] The invoice method would result in an indeterminate relationship between VAT liabilities and consumption expenditures if each firm simply excluded from sales its own IBT in determining its net VAT liability, because IBT imposed at earlier stages of production would still bear the VAT at later stages. Thus, the ratio of total VAT yield to aggregate consumption (exclusive of IBT) would diverge from the VAT rate uniformly invoiced on IBT-exclusive sales, since the IBT would have been only partially excluded.[14] In fact, the effective VAT rate would necessarily be greater than the invoiced rate since a portion of the IBT (from earlier stages of production) could not be identified and excluded from the invoice sales basis. This inconsistency between the nominal and effective VAT rate disappears if the IBT is uniformly *included* in the VAT invoiced sales base.

## 2.4 TAX SHIFTING AND TAX-SUBSTITUTION-INDUCED PRICE ADJUSTMENTS

### 2.4.1 The Translation of Tax Changes into Price Changes

As noted previously, the crucial first-round response to a change in tax structure is the effect of the tax change on commodity and factor markets. In the analysis of the price effects of the tax substitution, macroeconomic effects have simply been ignored. Thus, at this stage, we are interested only in those extremely short-run impacts which will occur before any significant macroeconomic reactions have manifested themselves. For even an intermediate-term policy it will be necessary to take thse reactions into account,

---

13. Indirect business taxes in the national income accounts include federal excise taxes, customs duties, and "nontaxes" (user charges and fees), state and local sales taxes, motor vehicle licenses, property taxes, and nontaxes. In 1969, indirect business tax revenue amounted to about $85 billion. Excise taxes and sales tax accounted for 48.12 percent and property taxes for 36.25 percent of this total.

14. This can easily be shown by a simple numerical example. Assume that the economy consists of two firms, *A* and *B*, and a consumer, *C*. Before any taxes are imposed, *A* has a sale of $100 to *B*, and *B* resells to *C* at $200. Suppose that a 5 percent sales tax is imposed. *A* sells to *B* for $105. *B* adds value, as above, of $100, and so he pays 5 percent tax on $205, or $10.25, and sells to *C* for $205 + $10.25 = $215.25. Total IBT is $5 + $10.25 = $15.25. A 2 percent VAT is now imposed. Sales inclusive of taxes now are: *A* to *B*, $107,

and as discussed in the latter chapters of this book, these effects are likely to be so substantial as to overwhelm the first-round consequences. This will be true whether macroeconomic balance is restored through a higher VAT rate than presented here, together with a budget surplus or diminished deficit, or whether the balance is restored through monetary stringency and higher interest and net profit rates.

In principle, even the microeconomic consequences of the substitution should be traced through by means of a fully articulated general equilibrium representation of interrelated commodity and factor markets. Since this is beyond current capabilities, our analysis is focused on the narrower issue of the probable *initial* effects of the tax substitution on commodity prices, rather than moving directly to economic effects, e.g., changes in the allocation of resources. A completely fixed (price-inelastic) bill of final demands is assumed as well as unchanged factor earnings (other than corporate profits). The "price effects" we project actually represent "tax allocation effects." Instead of observing the translation of tax changes into price changes, a range of assumptions is employed concerning the characteristics of this tax change-price adjustment relationship. In this context, the term "tax shifting" is simply a shorthand reference to these assumed tax allocation relationships. Thus, our concern with the shifting of a particular tax in fact reflects our inability to identify the ultimate effects of the tax change on relevant economic magnitudes.

The alternative "tax shifting" assumptions employed in the analysis should, then, be viewed simply as alternative characterizations of the initial effects of a change in tax instruments on prices.[15]

## 2.4.2 CIT Shifting

With reference to first-round price adjustments, the issue of CIT shifting is concerned with the degree to which a reduction (increase) in the CIT is translated into reductions (increases) in prices. This

---

*B* to *C*, $215.25 plus VAT imposed on a basis exclusive of VAT plus *B*'s *indirect tax only* (i.e., on $215.25 - $10.25 = $205). This VAT, at 2 percent, is $4.10. *B* therefore sells to *C* for $215.25 + $4.10 = $219.35. Consumption expenditures exclusive of all taxes are $200. Dividing this into total VAT revenue ($4.10), we get 2.05 percent, which is greater than the nominal VAT rate of 2 percent. This is so because elements of the sales tax in the earlier stages of production cannot be excluded from sales in the later stages on which the VAT is invoiced.

15. Discussions with Wassily Leontief have served to clarify both our understanding and exposition of this issue.

differs somewhat from previous discussions which have questioned
the effect of such a tax change on gross- or net-of-tax profits or rates
of return [Krzyzaniak and Musgrave]. However, under the assumption of unchanged factor (except capital) earnings and final demands,
the effects of a change in the CIT on profits (gross or net) and on
prices will be directly related. Thus, in the following discussion
profit can be conceived of either as an aggregate or per unit of
output. Similarly, tax revenues may be interpreted interchangeably
as either aggregate or per unit. The objective is to devise a flexible
and internally consistent relationship between changes in CIT rates
and changes in per unit CIT liabilities (and hence, under current
assumptions, prices).

Consider a corporation with after-tax net profits of $\pi_N$ (total or
per unit), resulting from gross profits of $\pi$ taxed at a rate $t$, i.e.,

$$\pi_N = (1 - t)\pi.$$

A tax change is then introduced which reduces the corporate tax
rate from $t$ to $\gamma t$, i.e., tax rates are reduced by a percentage
$S = 100(1 - \gamma)$, where $0 \leqslant \gamma < 1$. If it is assumed that the benefit
of the corporate tax reduction is entirely shifted to consumers, then
with unchanged unit sales *net* profits will not change as a result of
the rate reduction, i.e.,

$$\pi_N = (1 - \gamma t)\pi',$$

where $\pi'$ denotes gross profits after the tax reduction. Then,

$$(1 - \gamma t)\pi' = (1 - t)\pi,$$

and

$$\pi' = \frac{(1 - t)}{(1 - \gamma t)}\pi.$$

Corporate income tax revenue before the rate reduction was simply
$t\pi$. If gross profits had not changed as a result of the tax change,
revenue would have been reduced to $\gamma t\pi$, implying a revenue loss of
$(1 - \gamma)t\pi$. However, because of the shifting of the tax benefit,
corporate tax revenues are reduced by a larger amount, i.e., by

$$\Delta T = t\pi - \gamma t\pi'$$

$$= t\pi - \gamma t \frac{(1 - t)}{(1 - \gamma t)}\pi$$

$$= \frac{(1 - \gamma)}{(1 - \gamma t)} t\pi > (1 - \gamma)t\pi$$

since $(1 - \gamma t)$ is less than unity. If, for example, pretax profits were $100 and the original tax rate were 50 percent, the presubstitution revenue would be $50. The tax rate is then reduced to 25 percent ($\gamma = 0.5$). With no shifting, revenue would be reduced to $25 and net profits would rise to $75. However, if the full benefit of the tax reduction is shifted forward, pretax profits fall to $66.67, tax revenue falls to $16.67, and net-of-tax profits remain constant at $50. Thus, forward shifting of the corporate tax savings (*un*shifting in Aaron's terminology) results in greater corporate tax revenue losses and price reductions than might be superficially anticipated [Shoup, 1959, pp. 323–324].

Most generally, the true shifting parameter for the CIT, $\alpha$, can be defined as the ratio of the change in gross profits to the change in tax liabilities, itself a consequence of a change in CIT rates, i.e.,

$$\alpha = \frac{\pi - \pi'}{t\pi - t'\pi'}, \qquad (2\text{-}4\text{-}1)$$

where $t' = \gamma t$. If gross profits are expressed per unit of output, then the numerator of this expression is simply the price-reduction benefit to purchasers of a tax reduction of the *amount* specified in the denominator, assuming that other components of price are unaffected by the tax change.[16]

---

16. The CIT shifting parameter as defined here differs from that employed by Aaron [p. 164], whose specification is correct only under the assumption that the CIT is completely removed. That is, Aaron mistakenly assumes that the reduction in CIT liability (per unit output) is predetermined, independently of the value of the shifting parameter. In effect, he makes the reduction in CIT liability a function only of the original level of gross profit (or CIT liability) and of the change in the tax rate. The change in CIT liability under Aaron's formulation is simply

$$\Delta T^A = (t - t')\pi,$$

the change in the tax rate multiplied by the original level of gross profit. The purchaser price reduction is then $a\Delta T^A = a(t - t')\pi$, where $a$ is the Aaron shifting parameter. In fact, of course, that price reduction implies a further reduction in profits and tax liabilities, a reduction which again must be assumed to be shifted, ad infinitum (an infinite series that converges toward a limit). Most importantly, these further reductions depend upon the value of the shifting parameter. In consequence, it is necessary to express $\Delta T$ as a *function* of the true shifting parameter, $\alpha$. Thus, $\Delta T = t\pi - t'\pi'$; and from the definition of $\alpha$ (above),

$$\pi' = \frac{(1 - \alpha t)}{(1 - \alpha t')}\pi$$

From equation (2-4-1) the absolute change in (per unit) gross profit (price) can be determined as a function of the degree of CIT reduction, the shifting parameter, and the level of gross profit prior to the CIT reduction:

$$\pi - \pi' = \frac{\alpha(t - t')}{(1 - \alpha t')}\pi$$

$$= \frac{(1 - \gamma)}{(1 - \alpha\gamma t)}\alpha t\pi \tag{2-4-2}$$

since $t' = \gamma t$. (For $\pi$; see the preceding footnote.)

This change in gross profit or price takes into account the fact that if the benefits of the CIT reduction are shifted forward, a corresponding initial price and gross profit reduction implies a further reduction in tax liability, a reduction which in turn must be shifted through further reduction in price and gross profit, ad infinitum.

In summary, the effect on price of a given reduction in effective corporate income tax rates will necessarily depend on the degree of CIT shifting. If any part of the CIT savings are shifted forward, gross-of-tax corporate profits will decline, implying an equivalent reduc-

---

so that

$$\Delta T = t\pi - t'\frac{(1 - \alpha t)}{(1 - \alpha t')}\pi$$

$$= \frac{(t - t')}{(1 - \alpha t')}\pi$$

and the resultant price reduction is

$$\pi - \pi' = \alpha\Delta T = \frac{\alpha}{(1 - \alpha t')}(t - t')\pi = \frac{\alpha}{(1 - \alpha t')}\Delta T^A$$

Thus, if the true shifting parameter is $\alpha$, Aaron's parameter "$a$" is given by

$$a = \frac{\alpha}{(1 - \alpha t')},$$

and only when $t' = 0$ does $a = \alpha$, i.e., only when the CIT is fully removed is Aaron's parameter "$a$" equal to the true shifting parameter $\alpha$. The most serious consequence of this misspecification is that in cases of partial CIT reduction the true shifting parameter will be a function of the effective tax rate. Since the present analysis examines partial replacement of the CIT by the VAT, it is necessary to employ the correct, although mathematically more complex, shifting parameter $\alpha$.

tion in price. Only if the tax savings are completely retained by producers, i.e., if gross profits remain constant and net profits increase by the amount of the tax savings, will the CIT reduction have no effect on prices.

Thus, it is necessary to specify CIT shifting parameters for all industries. Unfortunately, there exists no consensus concerning the degree to which the corporate income tax has been shifted in the short run; empirical estimates range from no shifting to shifting in excess of the increase in tax liabilities [Gordon; Krzyzaniak and Musgrage]. Classical price theory suggests no short-run shifting. However, the diversity of empirical shifting estimates and the plausibility of market structure hypotheses which would give rise to some degree of shifting dictate that alternative CIT shifting assumptions be examined. In the empirical analysis, CIT shifting parameters ranging between the logical extremes of zero (no shifting) and one (full shifting) are employed. As has been discussed, these shifting parameters are defined as the ratios of the change in gross profit to the change in tax liability, where the latter reflects the full effects of both (a) the initial change in tax rates, and (b) the change in tax liability due to the change in gross (taxable) profit resulting from shifting. Under full forward shifting of the CIT reduction *net*-of-tax profit is unchanged, while under zero shifting *gross* profit remains constant.

In principle, it is necessary to specify a CIT shifting parameter for each industry. While there is no basis for assuming that shifting parameters will be equal for all industries, except under the classical assumption of zero short-run shifting, the lack of any reasonable basis for determining differential CIT shifting parameters dictates the provisional assumption that all industries shift equal proportions of their reduced CIT liabilities. CIT shifting parameters that vary by industry are not employed.

In summary, if any part of a given CIT reduction is shifted, the result is a price reduction to the consumer. The reduction in price is then a function of the degree of CIT reduction, of the value of the shifting parameter (assumed equal for all industries), and of the initial CIT liability per original dollar of sales (*not* equal for all industries). The higher the initial CIT liability, the greater the resultant reduction in price. Thus, a very capital-intensive industry or an industry with a very high profit rate or one which is highly incorporated will experience above-average reductions in price due to the shifted CIT reduction: the *initial* tax rate per dollar of sales will be higher, and the consequent reduction in gross profit will be greater [Shoup, 1959], implying greater reductions in price on both counts.

### 2.4.3 Effects of the VAT on Prices

Shifting of the VAT, i.e., the relationship between the VAT rate and prices (inclusive or exclusive of VAT itself) is also more complex than might at first appear. Let $P$ denote price prior to the introduction of the VAT; $P'$, the VAT-exclusive price after VAT imposition; $P*$, the VAT-inclusive price; and $Z$, the VAT rate. Then the VAT-inclusive price will simply be $(1 + Z)P'$. As in the case of the CIT, the VAT shifting parameter, $\beta$, can be defined as the ratio of the change in price to the change in tax liability, the comparison in each case being to the situation prior to VAT introduction:

$$\beta = \frac{(1 + Z)P' - P}{ZP'} \qquad (2\text{-}4\text{-}3)$$

In the analysis of the VAT-CIT substitution the pre-VAT (but post-CIT reduction) price is adjusted by the effect of the VAT, i.e., $P'$ is expressed as a function of $\beta$, $Z$, and $P$:

$$P' = \left(\frac{1}{1 + Z - \beta Z}\right)P \qquad (2\text{-}4\text{-}4)$$

Thus, in terms of VAT-inclusive prices

$$P* = (1 + Z)P' = \left(\frac{1 + Z}{1 + Z - \beta Z}\right)P$$

$$= \left[1 + Z\left(\frac{\beta}{1 + Z - \beta Z}\right)\right]P. \qquad (2\text{-}4\text{-}5)$$

In this formulation, the effect of any failure fully to shift the VAT (i.e., $P > P'$) will be to reduce the VAT-exclusive value added, which will in turn reduce the VAT liability, again ad infinitum.[17] As a result, the ultimate VAT-exclusive price will lie between the pre-VAT

---

17. The formulation here again contrasts with Aaron's [p. 164], which is simply

$$(1 + Z)P' = P[1 + Zb]$$

where $b$ is Aaron's misspecification of the VAT shifting parameter. By inspection, it can be seen that Aaron's $b$ is given by

$$b = \frac{\beta}{(1 + Z - \beta Z)}$$

which is independent of the VAT rate, $Z$, only if $\beta = 0$ or $\beta = 1$, i.e., if the VAT is fully absorbed by profits or is fully shifted forward. Thus, the effective degree of VAT shifting assumed by Aaron differs from that nominally indicated.

price $P$ (unitary shifting) and $[1/(1 + Z)]P$ (zero shifting), depending on the degree of VAT shifting ($\beta$).

It should be noted that under a VAT of the consumption-type only consumption purchases are ultimately subject to the tax. Since credit is granted the buyer for VAT invoiced on business purchases, investment and exports are effectively exempt from tax, while the VAT on government purchases is simultaneously government revenue and expenditure. However, this does not imply that effectively exempt transactions will be unaffected by the imposition of the VAT. Specifically, if producers fail to fully shift the VAT, then VAT-exclusive prices will decline. Thus, imposition of the VAT would reduce the *effective price* of VAT-exempt purchases. This result will be further examined in the later discussion of interindustry changes in tax liabilities.

In summary, the introduction of the VAT will increase VAT-inclusive prices in each industry unless the VAT liability is fully absorbed by profits or other factor earnings. Again, it is necessary to specify a tax-shifting parameter. Unlike CIT shifting, for which various alternative parameter values are examined, the VAT in our model is assumed to be fully shifted forward by all industries. The difference in treatment rests on three considerations. First, if it is assumed that the VAT is not fully shifted forward, difficult issues are raised concerning the actual incidence of the VAT and the consequent changes in the yields of other taxes, e.g., the remaining CIT (as will be discussed below). Secondly, full shifting of the VAT is at least consistent with classical price theory, given that final demand is completely price-inelastic, a condition implicit in our assumption of an unchanged final demand vector. Finally, we have argued that nonclassical assumptions concerning the shifting of the CIT necessarily relate to *net* rates of return. Similar market considerations must underlie a short-run failure to fully shift the VAT. However, the "net rate of return" constraints have already been incorporated through CIT shifting. It therefore seems redundant to impose them a second time through less than full shifting of the VAT since the two tax changes are simultaneous. As a result, full forward shifting of the VAT is assumed throughout.

Thus, it is assumed that, in response to the VAT introduction, producers mark-up their pre-VAT prices by the full amount of the VAT liability. Furthermore, it is assumed that *VAT-exclusive* prices for each industry are uniform for all purchasers. For investment goods purchases and exports, the effective price is VAT-exclusive, since a full VAT credit is allowed. Since government incurs no net VAT liability, only domestic consumers, having no tax credit, pay at VAT-inclusive prices.

### 2.4.4 Price Formation and the Rate
### of Depreciation

Because in the short run the *gross* earnings of existing capital goods are necessarily a kind of quasi-rent, short-run changes in capital goods prices and the replacement cost of depreciated capital should not influence output price under the usual profit maximization assumptions. However, the assessment of the VAT-CIT substitution under a range of assumptions concerning the degree of forward CIT shifting logically necessitates the inclusion in the base of the VAT of depreciation at post-tax-substitution prices.

Specifically, classical price theory, positing profit-maximizing behavior on the part of producers, implies that a corporate profits tax will not be shifted in the short run; any output-price configuration which maximized profits prior to the introduction (removal) of the CIT will also maximize profit after the CIT change. Short-run capital earnings are indeed purely a quasi-rent. With unchanged final demands (shifts in demand functions in which all final outputs are held constant), the reduction of the CIT and introduction of the VAT will simply increase prices by the amount of the VAT.

However, in this "classical case," whether depreciation is evaluated at replacement cost or not, is a matter of indifference *as far as the price effects of the substitution are concerned.* VAT-exclusive prices will be unchanged, and VAT-inclusive prices will be increased by the VAT rate applied to total value added originally embodied in a unit of final output. Since gross investment is effectively VAT-exempt the replacement cost of depreciated capital is unaltered by the tax substitution. Thus, the inclusion of depreciation at replacement cost is consistent with the classical treatment of *gross* capital earnings as a quasi-rent *as long as classical assumptions regarding tax shifting are also employed.*

Any other short-run shifting assumptions necessarily violate the classical model. To justify, e.g., forward shifting of a CIT, it is necessary to introduce nonclassical theories of price determination, oligopolistic theories relating to recognized interdependence between producers, "administrative" and "entry-restricting" pricing, etc. A thorough exposition of these issues is beyond the scope of the present study, but a central observation can be made: whatever the underlying price determination process, in any case involving forward shifting of a CIT or nonshifting of a VAT, the price determination must operate on the basis of net profits; i.e., net capital earnings and rates of return must underlie price formation. Thus, short-run shifting of CIT increases or of the benefits of CIT reductions must result from (imperfectly competitive) market pressures, or potential pressures, on net earnings. In consequence, when the classical assumptions are given up, i.e., when forward shifting of a CIT or less-than-full shifting of a VAT are introduced, net earnings are logically implied as the determinants of prices. And for true net earnings to determine price, changes in the replacement cost of capital must be translated into equivalent changes in output price.[18]

In an input-output model, the translation of changes in capital goods prices into changes in output prices requires that depreciation be removed from gross value added and included in interindustry transactions. Depreciation is thus treated as having been contributed by capital-goods-producing industries rather than by capital-goods-using industries. Consistent with nonclassical shifting assumptions, price will then be determined by net rather than gross value added.

It should be clearly understood that the issue of the appropriate treatment of depreciation concerns criteria for price determination and is not unique to the analysis of the consumption-type VAT. In fact, the initial price effects of the tax substitution will be unaffected by the inclusion of depreciation in value added or in interindustry transactions regardless of the type of VAT (consumption, income, or gross-product) examined, as long as the classical shifting assumptions are maintained. Under nonclassical shifting assumptions, determination of prices by *net* earnings of capital (value added net of depreciation) requires that depreciation *not* be included unchanged in value added. For the consumption and income types of VAT, prices will be determined by net capital (and other) earnings only if depreciation is included at replacement cost, i.e., in interindustry transactions.

For a gross-product VAT, the necessary treatment in nonclassical cases is even more complex, because gross investment (net investment plus depreciation) is included in the VAT base, and depreciation is taxed twice, first as a component of value added of final output and second as a component of final output itself. Unlike a consumption or income VAT, a gross-product type permits no credit against final VAT liabilities of VAT on gross investment (consumption type) or on depreciation (income type). To achieve a given level of net earnings it is necessary to alter prices to reflect both changes in replacement cost and the additional taxation of depreciation.

The treatment of depreciation under a gross-product VAT is in-

---

18. As a result, Aaron's inclusion of depreciation in value added is acceptable only under classical shifting assumptions, i.e., zero shifting of the CIT and full shifting of the VAT. When, however, the Aaron model is used to experiment with nonclassical shifting assumptions, it incorrectly includes depreciation in value added, i.e., at original rather than replacement prices, and prices are incorrectly determined by gross rather than net value added.

deed complex, regardless of the shifting assumptions employed. Even under classical shifting assumptions, interpretation of depreciation and price formation depends on whether depreciation is allocated to intermediate transactions or to value added. If to value added, the *net* earnings of capital can be domonstrated to decline by the amount of the VAT liability on depreciation, even though VAT-exclusive capital goods prices and gross value added are unchanged. This is simply because VAT on depreciation cannot be credited against final VAT liabilities. However, if depreciation is instead allocated to intermediate transactions, this will not imply, as it does in the cases of VATs of the consumption and income types, that net earnings will be unaffected: the VAT on depreciation as an intermediate good, i.e., as a component of final value added, is not the only tax on depreciation. The capital-using industry will itself be forced to pay the VAT on depreciation, and true net earnings will decline by this amount.

In consequence, it is not sufficient to include depreciation in interindustry transactions for the analysis of nonclassical cases in which prices are to be determined by net capital earnings. To achieve any given level of *net earnings* it is necessary to adjust depreciation for both changes in capital goods prices and the noncreditability of VAT on depreciation. If depreciation for some industry is $D$ at original capital goods prices, and if $P_K$ is an index of VAT-exclusive capital goods prices after the tax substitution, then the value of depreciation which must enter final prices, *if a predetermined level of net earnings is to be attained*, is $P_K D(1 + Z)^2$, where $Z$ is the VAT rate. Simply including $D$ as an intermediate transaction would result in a contribution to final output price of $P_K D(1 + Z)$, and net earnings would fall short of the predetermined level by $Z P_K D$, the net VAT liability of the capital-using industry on account of depreciation. The "true" replacement cost of capital now includes the noncreditable VAT, i.e., becomes $P_K D(1 + Z)$. To obtain a given level of net earnings this amount must be included in total value added embodied in final output. The depreciation contribution to final output price is then $[P_K D(1 + Z)](1 + Z) = P_K D(1 + Z)^2$. The VAT liability on sales attributed to depreciation is simply $P_K D(1 + Z)Z$; deducting this amount from the depreciation component of final (VAT-inclusive) sales price, we are left with the VAT-inclusive replacement cost of capital, i.e.,

$$P_K D(1 + Z)^2 - P_K D(1 + Z)Z = P_K D(1 + 2Z + Z^2 - Z - Z^2)$$

$$= P_K D(1 + Z).$$

Thus, it is necessary (a) to include depreciation at VAT-exclusive replacement capital prices, i.e., as an intermediate good, and (b) to augment this amount by the VAT liability on depreciation $(1 + Z)$, if a given level of net earnings is to be achieved under a gross-product VAT.

To reiterate, under our assumptions, price is determined by value added *net* of true economic depreciation (capital consumption evaluated at replacement cost). This is equivalent to treating capital earnings as quasi-rents *if the corresponding classical shifting assumptions are employed* (zero CIT and full VAT shifting), since in this case consumption prices would rise just by the amount of the VAT and capital goods prices would be unchanged. It is also consistent with nonclassical cases in which prices change through the influence of tax shifting on *net* earnings, and thus on value added net of true depreciation.

## 2.5 FISCAL IMPLICATIONS OF THE TAX SUBSTITUTION

### 2.5.1 Revenue and Expenditure Effects

The VAT-CIT substitution will have both direct and indirect effects for all levels of government. Directly, the tax involves a loss in CIT revenue and a more-or-less compensatory increase in revenues from the VAT. Indirectly, any changes induced in prices of governmental-purchased goods and services by the tax substitution will alter either government expenditure or real levels of government demand, while changes in consumer prices may lead to adjustments of public employees' wages. Also, changes in prices and wages in the rest of the economy will lead to secondary changes in the revenue yields of other taxes, and in each of these cases the effects may be quite different at different levels of government.

For a first-round analysis of the change in tax structure, the following effects are considered: Direct changes in VAT and CIT revenue yields due to increases or decreases in the rates of these taxes; indirect changes in VAT and CIT revenues due to changes in value added or in corporate profits resulting from the tax substitution, a consequence of the direction and degree of tax shifting; and finally, changes in the level of nominal government expenditure, due to price changes, assuming a fixed bill of real final demands of government.

It is specifically, if unrealistically, assumed that the nominal yields of taxes other than the VAT and the CIT are unaffected by the tax substitution. A more complete analysis would incorporate changes in other revenues following from effects on factor earnings and prices, requiring that the VAT be sufficient to compensate for these as well as changes in the CIT and in government prices. Adjustments of actual government demands and of public employees' wages are considered second-round responses to the change in tax structure and are ignored in the formal analysis. Differential intergovernmental fiscal consequences are briefly considered at a later stage. For present purposes government is viewed in integrated, national income accounts terms.

### 2.5.2 CIT Revenue Loss

Although the tax substitution involves a simultaneous reduction or elimination of the CIT and compensating imposition of the VAT, it is useful heuristically to view the change in tax structure as a series of individual tax changes. Thus, the revenue loss resulting from a reduction in effective CIT rates can first be considered independently of later changes in VAT rates.

The CIT revenue loss is straightforward if either (a) the CIT is completely repealed or (b) the benefits of the CIT reduction are not shifted forward in the form of lower prices (and profits). If the CIT is repealed, the nominal revenue loss is simply the prior yield of this tax. Regardless of any resultant changes in profits, the revenue loss is unchanged. If the CIT is only partially eliminated, then the revenue loss will simply equal the change in yield at the original level of profits only if the benefits of CIT reduction are not shifted forward, reducing gross-of-tax profits.

Shifting of the CIT will, however, reduce taxable profits, resulting in a revenue loss greater than would be implied by the change in rates at original profit levels. Recall that CIT shifting was defined as the ratio of the change in profits to the change in tax liabilities:

$$\alpha = \frac{\pi - \pi'}{t\pi - t'\pi'}$$

where as before $\alpha$ represents the shifting parameter, $\pi$ the level of gross profits (aggregate or per unit output), $t$ the tax rate, and primes (') indicate post-tax-substitution values.

The change in CIT revenues, $\Delta T_C$, is then simply

$$\Delta T_C = t\pi - t'\pi'$$

$$= t\pi - t'\frac{(1 - \alpha t)}{(1 - \alpha t')}\pi$$

$$= \frac{(t - t')}{(1 - \alpha t')}\pi \qquad (2\text{-}5\text{-}1)$$

Because of the shifting-induced decline in taxable profits, the ultimate CIT revenue loss is a multiple $[1/(1 - \alpha t')]$ of the loss due to the rate reduction alone $[(t - t')\pi]$.

### 2.5.3 VAT Revenue and Interdependence in Tax Yields

The revenue gained by imposition of the VAT is similarly dependent on the degree to which the VAT itself is shifted. If the VAT is fully shifted forward through higher prices, then value added (price) exclusive of the VAT is unaffected by the imposition of the tax. Thus, VAT revenue would be given by the VAT rate multiplied by taxable (consumption) expenditure (accumulated value added). However, if the VAT is not fully shifted, then value added exclusive of the VAT will decline, resulting in a concomitant decline in VAT revenue.

Thus, if the value of taxable sales, prior to imposition of the VAT but after CIT reduction, is denoted by $P'$ (previously denoting price), the VAT rate by $Z$, and the degree of VAT shifting by $\beta$, then the VAT-exclusive value of taxable sales after introduction of the VAT, $P''$, is

$$P'' = \left(\frac{1}{1 + Z - \beta Z}\right)P' \tag{2-5-2}$$

implying VAT revenue of

$$\Delta T_V = ZP'' = \frac{Z}{(1 + Z - \beta Z)}P' \tag{2-5-3}$$

However, the ultimate change in tax revenue resulting from the imposition of the VAT is still more complex, unless the VAT is fully shifted forward. First, it is necessary to identify the component of price (the factor return) that bears the unshifted part of the VAT. Provisionally, assume that the failure fully to shift the VAT is reflected by a reduction in profit (aggregate and per unit of output). Then, as a result of the shifting of part of the VAT burden to profits, profits will decline by $P' - P''$, which will result in a decline in corporate income tax revenues. With the given (post-CIT-reduction) CIT rate, $t'$, the change (positive or negative) in CIT revenue will be $t'(P'' - P')$, i.e.,

$$
\begin{aligned}
\Delta T_{CV} &= t'(P'' - P') \\
&= t'\left[\left(\frac{1}{1 + Z - \beta Z}\right)P' - P'\right] \\
&= t'P'\frac{-Z + \beta}{1 + Z - \beta Z}
\end{aligned}
\tag{2-5-4}
$$

where $\Delta T_{CV}$ is the change in CIT revenue resulting from the proportion of the VAT liability borne by profits. $\Delta T_{CV}$ will be zero only if $\beta = 1$, i.e., if the VAT is fully shifted, or if $t' = 0$, i.e., the CIT is totally repealed. The full change in revenue following the imposition of the VAT is, then,

$$\Delta T = \Delta T_V + \Delta T_{CV}$$

$$= \left(\frac{Z}{1 + Z - \beta Z}\right)P' + \left(\frac{-Z + \beta Z}{1 + Z - \beta Z}\right)t'P'$$

$$= \left[\frac{(1 - t' + \beta t')}{1 + Z - \beta Z}\right]P' \qquad (2\text{-}5\text{-}5)$$

Of course, this would not be the end of the tax revenue effects of incomplete forward shifting of the VAT, e.g., personal income tax liabilities would be altered through reductions in dividends or capital gains. Furthermore, any shifting of the CIT savings would generate additional reductions in profits and prices, and hence in VAT *and* CIT revenues. Most generally, any backward shifting of the VAT will simultaneously affect federal and state CIT, other income tax, and possibly non-income-tax revenues. Similarly, changes in prices, through either the forward shifting of the CIT reduction or backward shifting of the VAT, will reduce government revenues from existing ad valorem excises, even if final demands are unaffected by the price and disposable income changes. Thus, unless the rates of these taxes are simultaneously altered, their revenue yields will also be affected.

In brief, revenue yields of different taxes are interdependent, and this interdependence, not to mention the identification of economic effects, would require that a tax substitution be examined in a general equilibrium context. The model used here to assess the effects of a VAT-CIT substitution goes only partially in this direction. A number of artificial assumptions have had to be made to render the problem tractable; one of the most important of these is the assumption that the nominal yields of other taxes will be unaffected by the VAT-CIT changes.

### 2.5.4 Change in Government Expenditure
Since government final demands are assumed to be constant and changes in public employee wages and in transfer payments (e.g., relief to needy) induced by the VAT-CIT substitution are relegated to later-round adjustments, government expenditure will be altered

only by changes in the prices of government-purchased goods and services. Since the VAT invoiced on government purchases in the aggregate represents both revenue and expenditure, it makes no difference whether VAT is charged on government purchases and the amount entered as additional VAT revenue, or whether government purchases are exempt and government prices are VAT-exclusive.

The reduction or repeal of the CIT will benefit government to the degree to which CIT savings are translated into lower prices. Employing the yield criterion that the government surplus or deficit be unchanged by the tax substitution, CIT shifting reduces the total VAT revenue required to compensate for the CIT.

If the VAT is fully shifted, government prices after the imposition of the VAT will be determined only by the reduction or repeal and the degree of shifting of the CIT. However, if the VAT is not fully shifted, but is partially or completely absorbed by profits or other factor earnings, then government prices, *exclusive of VAT*, will decline, on the reasonable assumption that VAT-exclusive prices are identical for all purchasers. In brief, a firm cannot easily distinguish between ultimately taxable and nontaxable sales, and the failure to shift the VAT fully will result in price reductions in the case of sales entitled to a VAT credit. Even if the firm could distinguish between taxable and nontaxable transactions, the maintenance of VAT-exclusive prices on nontaxable sales, when VAT-exclusive prices of taxable sales declined, would necessitate an inherently unstable dual price system.

In fact, it is assumed throughout that the VAT is fully shifted forward. Thus, government expenditures will be affected only by the possible shifting of the CIT reduction.

## 2.6 THE INPUT-OUTPUT MODEL
## ANALYTICAL SYNTHESIS

### 2.6.1 Overview of the Model
All the foregoing elements, including (a) the criteria for a compensating tax substitution, (b) the special characteristics of the consumption-type VAT, (c) price formation, tax shifting, and the appropriate treatment of depreciation under nonclassical pricing assumptions, and (d) direct and indirect fiscal implications of the tax substitution are structurally integrated in the context of an input-output model. Essentially, the input-output model provides a framework for a static general equilibrium price determination within which the first-round economic effects of a compensated tax substitution can be identified.

In input-output analysis, price for each industry's output is defined as the total value of primary resources directly and indirectly used in the production of a unit of final output. Ultimately, this price consists of *imports* and *value added,* with value added defined to include all primary factor income, including employee compensation, profits, and all other factor payments. If output is measured in constant dollars, i.e., as the *value* of output prior to the tax substitution, then the unit price of each industry's output is initially unity by definition. Any change in this "price per dollar of final output" will then measure the change in value added (including imports) per original dollar of final output resulting from the tax substitution.

Defined in this way, output price for *any* industry is related to value added of *all* industries by a set of technical input coefficients which specify total inputs (direct and indirect) from each industry required to produce a dollar of final output of the given industry. Thus, given the total input coefficients, value added per unit of output for all industries can be transformed into output price for any particular industry. A change in any price is then necessarily the consequence of a change in the value added of some industry or industries. As a result, the input-output relationships between industries imply that a change in the value added of any industry will be passed forward automatically as a price change of other industries.

In input-output practice, depreciation, or capital consumption can be treated either as a component of gross value added or as an intermediate input. Depreciation is conventionally included in value added simply because of the empirical difficulty of allocating it over capital-goods-producing industries. However, by use of a capital flow table, supplemented by a number of assumptions concerning the relationships between investment and output, it is possible to distribute depreciation over capital-goods-producer industries. Because net value added is logically implied as the determinant of price in cases of short-run shifting of the CIT, depreciation allowances by industry have been subtracted from both gross investment and gross value added and have been added to interindustry transactions. [19]

---

19. Specifically, two basic assumptions are required to estimate capital consumption on an interindustry basis. First, depreciation of capital goods supplied by industry $i$ to industry $j$ is assumed to be proportionate to the stock of $i$th industry capital goods in industry $j$ in the previous period, i.e.,

$$D_{ij,t} = d_{ij}K_{ij,t-1}$$

where $D_{ij,t}$ is depreciation of the $i$th good in the $j$th industry in period $t$, $K_{ij,t-1}$ is the stock in the preceding period, and $d_{ij}$ is the depreciation rate as approx-

As a result of the depreciation adjustment, the price effects of the VAT-CIT substitution incorporate the tax-substitution-induced changes in the prices of capital good inputs: capital consumption per unit of output is evaluated at postsubstitution replacement cost rather than at original cost. Value added will then include only *net* earnings of capital, in addition to other factor incomes. However, because only final consumption sales constitute the base of the consumption-type VAT after allowances and credits, only value added directly or indirectly entering consumption is ultimately subject to tax.

It must be reiterated that this treatment of depreciation, entering it into prices at replacement cost, is equivalent to treating capital earnings as quasi-rents *if the corresponding classical tax shifting assumptions are employed* (zero CIT and unitary VAT shifting). In this case consumption prices rise just by the amount of the VAT, capital goods prices are unchanged, and the treatment of depreciation, whether as an interindustry transaction or as a component of gross value added, is a matter of indifference. However, only the former treatment of depreciation (as an interindustry transaction, i.e., at replacement cost) is consistent with nonclassical shifting assumptions, under which prices respond to the effects of tax changes on net earnings of capital.

---

imated by the reciprocal of the average useful life of the $i$th capital good in the $j$th industry. Secondly, the growth rates of all types of capital goods stocks in an industry are assumed to be uniform, equal to the normal (average) growth rate of real output of the industry, $g_j$, i.e.,

$$\frac{K_{ij,t} - K_{ij,\,t-1}}{K_{ij,\,t-1}} = g_j$$

Thus, the unobserved stock in the preceding period, $K_{ij,t-1}$, can be determined on the basis of gross investment, $I_{ij,t}$, given by the capital flow table, and the rates of growth and depreciation, $g_j$ and $d_{ij}$:

$$K_{ij,t-1} = \frac{I_{ij,t}}{g_j + d_{ij}}$$

Depreciation, by user and supplier industry, is then

$$D_{ij} = d_{ij}\ \frac{I_{ij}}{g_j + d_{ij}}$$

The details of the conversion of depreciation into interindustry transactions are contained in Appendix A, section 4.

In the analysis of the first-round effects of the tax substitution, it is assumed that the constant-dollar bill of final demands (by industry) and the input-output coefficients (inclusive of depreciation) are unaffected by the tax changes. Demand and input-substitution responses to the tax-induced changes in relative prices are relegated to later-round reactions. Thus, the initial (first-round) price effects of the tax substitution must be interpreted primarily as indices of potential demand and production-process responses to the tax substitution, rather than as price changes which would actually be observed.

The substance of the foregoing model can be outlined conceptually in terms of its application to the VAT-CIT substitution. The effects of the tax substitution on prices can be most conveniently broken into two independent phases: First, the reduction in the CIT, and second, the imposition of the VAT. In each phase, the effect on prices results from tax-substitution-induced changes in value added (defined inclusive of CIT and VAT liabilities).

A reduction in effective CIT rates will have no effect on prices if reduced CIT liabilities are simply converted into higher net profits. However, if the CIT savings are shifted to purchasers, then to that degree gross-of-tax profits, value added, and hence price, will decline. Note that a decline in the value added of any one industry will be reflected in the prices of all industries that use the product of that industry as an intermediate good.

Thus, the effect of the CIT reduction on prices is a function of the degree of CIT reduction, of the magnitude of the CIT shifting parameter (assumed to be equal for all industries), and of the initial *direct and indirect* CIT liability per original dollar of output.

In the second phase, introduction of the VAT will increase value added in each industry (inclusive of VAT) if the VAT is fully shifted forward in higher prices. However, if the VAT is of the consumption type and is fully absorbed by profits or other factor earnings, then under the assumption of equal VAT-exclusive prices for all purchasers aggregate value added (inclusive of net VAT) will decline, i.e., consumption prices will be unchanged by the VAT, while effective prices for nonconsumption purchasers will *decline* by the (rebated) VAT liability. At intermediate degrees of VAT shifting, value added may increase or decrease, but in any event will increase by less than the nominal VAT liability.

If the VAT is fully shifted forward, VAT-exclusive prices will be determined only by the reduction in and shifting of the CIT, i.e., prices after the CIT reduction but before the VAT introduction are equal to VAT-exclusive prices after inauguration of the VAT. Thus,

VAT-inclusive prices will be known as soon as the VAT rate is determined.

In addition, the CIT-compensating VAT rate is dependent only on the previously determined VAT-exclusive prices. The selected criterion for VAT yield is simply that net change in government revenue equal net change in government expenditure, i.e., that the net change in the government surplus be zero. The *net* change in government surplus *after the CIT reduction* but before the VAT is given by the algebraic sum of the decrease in CIT revenue (direct decrease due to rate reduction, and indirect decrease due to shifting) and the decrease in government expenditure (due to reductions in the prices of governmentally purchased goods and services, resulting from CIT shifting). In addition, government expenditure will be increased by the amount of the VAT invoiced on government purchases; however, since the VAT on government purchases is government revenue as well as expenditure, these items cancel out and can be ignored, i.e., government can be assumed to pay at VAT-exclusive prices. Thus, *with full VAT shifting* the required VAT *revenue* is known as soon as the CIT is reduced.[20] The base of the VAT, private domestic consumption at VAT-exclusive prices, is also known if the VAT is fully shifted. Therefore, the required VAT rate is simply the ratio of the pre-VAT net change in government surplus to the VAT base, both computed *after* reduction of the CIT. The resultant VAT rate will be just sufficient to produce a net change in government revenue equal to the net change in expenditure, i.e., an unchanged monetary surplus or deficit. Given the VAT *rate* and VAT-exclusive prices, VAT-inclusive consumption prices can then be determined.

In the more general case of incomplete VAT shifting, VAT-exclusive prices would not be known until the VAT rate was determined. That is, *VAT-exclusive* prices would depend on the shifted VAT rate. In this case, not examined here, the VAT rate and prices (both inclusive and exclusive of VAT) would have to be determined simultaneously.

### 2.6.2 The Analytics of the Model
The mathematical representation of the foregoing model is straightforward. Consider a depreciation-adjusted input-output system, in which estimates of depreciation (use of capital services) are added to

---

20. If the VAT were not fully shifted, then VAT-exclusive prices of government purchases would decline further with the introduction of the VAT, as noted previously.

interindustry flows and correspondingly subtracted from gross value added and from gross investment for each industry. Final demand ($y$) is disaggregated into private domestic consumption ($c$), government purchases ($g$), net private domestic investment ($i$), and exports ($e$).[21] Net value added per dollar of output ($v$) is divided into gross corporate profits ($\pi$) and other elements ($o$), including imports.[22] The input-output model is thus given by

$$x = (I - A)^{-1}y = (I - A)^{-1}(c + g + i + e) \qquad (2\text{-}6\text{-}1)$$

$$p' = v'(I - A)^{-1} = (\pi + o)'(I - A)^{-1} \qquad (2\text{-}6\text{-}2)$$

where $I$ is an $n$ by $n$ identity matrix, $A$ is an $n$ by $n$ matrix of direct requirements coefficients, $x$ is a vector of total output, $p$ is a vector of prices, and primes indicate transposes.

Equations (2-6-1) and (2-6-2) represent two veiws of an input-output system. Equation (2-6-1) relates total outputs of all industries to final demands from all industries. Equation (2-6-2) relates final output prices of all industries to primary factor costs of all industries and reveals the cost structure of producing a dollar of final output in terms of the primary resources eventually used. These two equations indicate the dual aspects of the input-output system.

Equation (2-6-2) is appropriate for answering the question: What would be the relative price consequences if all or part of the corporate income tax were replaced by a consumption-type value-added tax, assuming that the bills of real final demand, $c$, $g$, $i$, and $e$ and the input-output structure, $A$, are unchanged by the tax substitution?

Let $S/100 = s$ be the uniform proportionate reduction in initial effective CIT rates. The pre- and postsubstitution CIT rates for industry $j$ are denoted by $t_j$ and $t_j'$ [$= t_j(1 - s)$], respectively. The CIT shifting parameter for industry $j$, $\alpha_j$, is defined as the ratio of the change in gross profit to the change in tax liability, i.e.,

$$\alpha_j = \frac{\pi_j - \pi_j^*}{t_j\pi_j - t_j^*\pi_j^*}, j = 1, 2, \ldots, n, \qquad (2\text{-}6\text{-}3)$$

where asterisks (*) represent post-CIT-reduction values. As a consequence of the CIT reduction and shifting, per unit value added for industry $j$, $v_j$, is reduced by $\Delta\pi_j$,

---

21. Each of these final demands represents a vector by industry.
22. Value added and its components are again vectors by industry.

$$\Delta\pi_j = \pi_j - \pi_j^* = \frac{\alpha_j}{1 - \alpha_j (1-s)t_j}(st_j\pi_j), j = 1, 2, \ldots, n, \quad (2\text{-}6\text{-}4)$$

assuming that other value-added elements remain unchanged. Thus, the per unit value added for industry $j$ after the CIT reduction but before the VAT introduction is simply

$$v_j^* = v_j - \Delta\pi_j = v_j - a_j st_j\pi_j \qquad (2\text{-}6\text{-}5)$$

with

$$a_j = \frac{\alpha_j}{1 - \alpha_j (1 - s) t_j} \qquad (2\text{-}6\text{-}6)$$

for $j = 1, 2, \ldots, n$. For the reasons indicated in section 2.4.2, it is assumed that $\alpha$ is uniform across the industries.

Therefore, value added for all industries after CIT reduction is

$$v^{*\prime} = v' - s\pi'tb, \qquad (2\text{-}6\text{-}7)$$

where $\pi'$ is a $1 \times n$ row vector containing initial gross profits, $t$ is an $n \times n$ diagonal matrix containing initial CIT rates, and $b$ is an $n \times n$ diagonal matrix containing the elements $a_j$. From equation (2-6-2), the price vector of final output after the CIT reduction, in terms of value added, is

$$p_2' = v^{*\prime} (I - A)^{-1}, \qquad (2\text{-}6\text{-}8)$$

with the price reduction equal to $s\pi'tb(I - A)'$. Since it is assumed that the VAT is fully shifted forward, the VAT-inclusive price vector after the VAT introduction is simply the price vector $p_2$ multiplied by 1 plus the VAT rate, i.e.

$$p_3' = (1 + Z) p_2' = (1 + Z) v^{*\prime} (I - A)^{-1}, \qquad (2\text{-}6\text{-}9)$$

where $Z$ is VAT rate. With the introduction of the VAT, $p_2'$ can be interpreted as a vector of VAT-exclusive prices.

The VAT rate is still not determined. To solve for the VAT rate, individual gross changes in government revenue and expenditure resulting from the CIT-VAT substitution must be calculated. To satisfy the yield criterion, an unchanged monetary surplus (or deficit), net changes in revenue and expenditure must be equal. On the revenue side, the reductions in CIT rates cause original government revenue to decrease by an amount $s\pi'tx$ plus an additional amount $s(1 - s)\pi'tbtx$ if the tax saiving is shifted forward. CIT revenue will not be further reduced since the VAT is assumed to be fully shifted forward. Second, the introduction of VAT increases government revenue by an amount equal to $Zp'_2 (c + g)$, with $c$ and $g$ standing for private domestic consumption expenditures and government purchases at their original values. It can be assumed that, since the government is not itself a VAT-payer, it will not enjoy a credit for the VAT invoiced to it on its purchases from the tax-paying sector. It therefore pays the VAT-inclusive price on all purchases, including its purchases of capital goods, but correspondingly it is the recipient of these invoiced tax revenues.[23] The net change in the government revenue is thus

$$\Delta R = Zp'_2 (c + g) - s\pi'tx - s(1 - s)\,\pi'tbtx. \qquad (2\text{-}6\text{-}10)$$

On the expenditure side, the change in the government expenditure is simply the difference between the post-tax substitution and the original expenditure, i.e.,

$$\Delta G = (1 + Z)p'_2 g - p'g. \qquad (2\text{-}6\text{-}11)$$

Setting $\Delta G = \Delta R$ to satisfy the equal yield condition and utilizing equations (2-6-2), (2-6-7), and (2-6-8), a quadratic equation in $Z$, the VAT rate, can be derived:

$$k_1 Z^2 + (k_1 - k_2)Z - k_2 = 0, \qquad (2\text{-}6\text{-}12)$$

where $k_1$ and $k_2$ are scalars with

$$k_1 = v'(I - A)^{-1}c - s\pi'tb\,(I - A)^{-1}c,$$

and

$$k_2 = s\pi'tx + s(1 - s)\pi'tbtx - s\pi'tb(I - A)^{-1}g.$$

---

23. As has been noted repeatedly, under the constant surplus condition the VAT treatment of government purchases is, in the aggregate, a matter of indifference.

Examining the elements of these expressions:

1. $s\pi'tx$ = primary loss in CIT revenue, an increasing function of the degree of CIT reduction.

2. $s(1 - s)\pi'tbtx$ = secondary loss in CIT revenue resulting from any partial or full shifting of the CIT reduction. The loss increases and then, when the CIT reduction approximates 50 percent, decreases at a diminishing rate. Also, it increases at an increasing rate with increases in the shifting parameter.

3. $s\pi'tb(I - A)^{-1}g$ = reduction in government expenditure resulting from lower VAT-exclusive prices due to CIT shifting. It increases at a diminishing rate with increases in the degree of CIT reduction. It also increases, but at an increasing rate, as the CIT shifting parameter increases.

4. $v'(I - A)^{-1}c$ = total private domestic consumption expenditure before the tax substitution.

5. $s\pi'tb(I - A)^{-1}c$ = reduction in private domestic consumption expenditure due to CIT shifting, increasing at a diminishing rate with increases in the degree of CIT reduction and at an increasing rate with increases in the CIT shifting parameter.

Thus, $k_1$ and $k_2$ can be easily interpreted: $k_1$ is total private domestic consumption expenditure after the CIT reduction but before the VAT introduction; $k_2$ is change in the government surplus or deficit after the CIT reduction but before the VAT introduction. Since the VAT invoiced to the government on its purchases represents equal amounts of increases in government expenditure and revenue, the invoiced VAT does not appear in $k_2$, nor does government expenditure appear in $k_1$. Therefore, $k_1$ is the VAT base and $k_2$, the VAT revenue required to preserve the government budget position before the tax change. Thus the solution of equation (2-6-12) for the VAT rate, $Z$, is

$$Z = \frac{k_2}{k_1} = \frac{s\pi'tx + s(1 - s)\pi'tbtx - s\pi'tb(I - A)^{-1}g}{v'(I - A)^{-1}c - s\pi'tb(I - A)^{-1}c}.$$ (2-6-13)

That is, the required VAT rate is equal to the ratio of the required compensatory VAT revenue to the VAT base. With the VAT rate determined, the price equations (2-6-8) and (2-6-9) provide, respectively, VAT-exclusive and -inclusive prices after the tax substitution.[24]

---

24. Since prices were initially unity by definition, postsubstitution prices can be interpreted as ratios to presubstitution prices.

Aggregate price indices are obtained from these indices of individual prices. For domestic private consumption the index is computed by dividing consumption expenditures at VAT-inclusive prices by the consumption expenditures prior to the tax substitution, i.e.,

$$P_c = 100(p_3'c/p'c). \qquad (2\text{-}6\text{-}14)$$

Similarly, the VAT-exclusive price indices for government purchases, net investment, and exports are respectively:

$$P_G = 100(p_2'g/p'g) \qquad (2\text{-}6\text{-}15)$$

$$P_I = 100(p_2'i/p'i) \qquad (2\text{-}6\text{-}16)$$

$$P_E = 100(p_2'e/p'e). \qquad (2\text{-}6\text{-}17)$$

*Chapter 3*

# CIT-Compensating
# VAT Rates, Revenues,
# and Price Adjustments

## 3.1 CIT-COMPENSATING VAT RATES
## AND REVENUES

To identify VAT rates and revenues which would just compensate for the reduction or removal of the corporate income tax, the model described in the preceding chapter was applied empirically to data for the United State economy in 1969. The remainder of the study contains the results of this application. In this section we discuss VAT rates and revenues required to compensate for various degrees of CIT reduction under alternative assumptions concerning forward CIT shifting. The effects of these specified tax substitutions on prices (by industry and by component of final demand) are examined in the following section of this chapter. In the remaining chapters we then consider the implications of these tax and price changes for income distribution, investment, and international trade.

Six degrees of CIT reduction ($S$) are examined: $S$ = 25 percent, 50 percent, 75 percent, 85 percent, 90 percent, and 100 percent. As we discussed earlier, it is assumed throughout that producers fully shift the newly imposed VAT forward by raising their prices. Prices exclusive of VAT are determined by the reduction and shifting of the CIT, and are then simply marked up by the amount of the VAT in determining VAT-inclusive prices. To assess the effects of possible shifting of the CIT, six alternative degrees of CIT shifting are considered: $\alpha$ = 0, 0.2, 0.4, 0.6, 0.8, 1.0.

Superficially, the examination of such a large number of alternative cases (6 degrees of CIT removal by 6 degrees of CIT shifting = 36 separate cases) might seem unnecessary; however, since the degree of CIT shifting is an "unknown," examining the *sensitivity* of the VAT rate to the CIT shifting parameter seemed necessary. In fact, we will discover that for a specifiable degree of CIT reduction (about 90 percent) the appropriate compensating VAT rate is independent of the CIT shifting parameter. Because the interrelationships between the compensating VAT rate, CIT shifting, and the degree of CIT reduction can only be assessed numerically, it is necessary to approximate the general relationships by the empirical solution of a number of permutations.[1]

The importance of the interrelationships between the VAT rate and the degrees of CIT reduction and shifting should not be underestimated. The substitution of one broad-based tax for another (VAT for the CIT) involves a number of uncertainties and potentially serious unanticipated effects. At least one significant criterion for the actual selection of a particular tax substitution is the *minimization* of the most serious of these unexpected consequences. In the present case, while a budget-balancing approach to fiscal policy might cause concern to be felt over the possibility of unanticipated revenue surpluses or shortfalls, the more significant and fundamental problem would lie in the possibility of unanticipated enhancement or represssion of aggregate demand. In the analysis being presented

---

1. Equations (2-6-6) and (2-6-13) indicate why, e.g., the derivative of the VAT rate, $Z$, with respect to the CIT shifting parameter, $\alpha$, cannot be determined analytically:

$$a_j = \frac{\alpha}{1 - \alpha(1-s)t_j} \tag{2-6-6}$$

$$Z = \frac{s\pi'tx + s(1 - s)\pi'tbtx - s\pi'tb(I - A)^{-1}g}{v'(I - A)^{-1}c - s\pi'tb(I - A)^{-1}c} \tag{2-6-13}$$

where

$$b = \begin{bmatrix} a_1 \cdots 0 \cdots 0 \\ \vdots & \vdots & \vdots \\ 0 & a_j & 0 \\ \vdots & \vdots & \vdots \\ 0 \cdots 0 \cdots a_n \end{bmatrix}$$

By inspection it can be seen that the derivative cannot be reduced to a scalar magnitude because $\alpha$ only enters the VAT rate equation through the vector $b$, which also incorporates initial industry-specific CIT rates and the degree of CIT reduction. Furthermore the sign of the derivative is ambiguous.

here, however, both the CIT and VAT revenues as well as net impacts on aggregate demand are in general sensitive to the unknown CIT shifting parameter. Moreover, within our model the government's only way of minimizing the consequences of variations in shifting is by manipulating the size of the CIT reduction. Thus, it is important at least to investigate the degree to which unanticipated consequences can be avoided by selecting an appropriate value for this policy-controlled variable.

CIT-compensating VAT rates and revenues are presented in Table 3-1 for all 36 combinations of CIT reduction and shifting. Each column contains VAT rates and revenues required to compensate for a given CIT reduction under varying shifting assumptions. Conversely, the shifting parameter is held constant and the degree of CIT reduction is varied across each row. The final row and column provide the relative ranges of VAT rates and revenues for each of the CIT shifting and reduction assumptions.

To interpret the variations in VAT rates and revenues it is necessary to recall that the criterion for the VAT yield being used in this model is that the nominal government surplus or deficit be unaffected by the tax substitution: the VAT rate is determined such that the net change in government revenue (difference between VAT revenue gain and CIT revenue loss) equals the change in government expenditure.

Stated another way, VAT revenue must equal the CIT revenue foregone plus the (algebraic) change in government expenditure. The change in CIT revenue can be further decomposed into two components: the "primary" loss due to the rate reduction and the "secondary" loss due to CIT shifting. Adopting the convention that government prices are VAT-exclusive, the change in government expenditure is due solely to the shifting of the CIT reduction.

The VAT *rate* is simply given by the ratio of required VAT revenue to the VAT base, i.e., to private domestic consumption expenditure at VAT-exclusive prices. With zero CIT shifting, consumption prices are not changed by the CIT reduction and the VAT base is simply private domestic consumption expenditure prior to the tax change. However, with forward shifting of the CIT reduction, the consumption base declines by the amount of the shifted reduction in CIT liabilities.

Thus, the change in the VAT rate as the degree of shifting ($\alpha$) and of CIT reduction ($S$) are varied depends upon the consequent changes in the components of required VAT revenue and in the VAT base. These changes in the components are given in Table 3-2.

In the following analysis we concentrate first on the sensitivity

Table 3-1. VAT Rates and Revenues[a] for Varying Degrees of CIT Reduction and Shifting (rates in percentages; revenues in billions of dollars)

| CIT Shifting Parameter | Degree of CIT Reduction (S) | | | | | | | | | | | | Range (percent) | |
|---|---|---|---|---|---|---|---|---|---|---|---|---|---|---|
| | 25 Percent | | 50 Percent | | 75 Percent | | 85 Percent | | 90 Percent | | 100 Percent | | | |
| | Rate | Revenue | Rate | Revenue | Rate | Revenue | Rate | Revenue | Rate | Revenue | Rate | Revenue | Rate | Revenue |
| 0.0 | 1.92 | 10.67 | 3.84 | 21.34 | 5.76 | 32.01 | 6.53 | 36.28 | 6.91 | 38.41 | 7.68 | 42.68 | 300 | 300 |
| 0.2 | 2.04 | 11.33 | 3.99 | 22.02 | 5.83 | 32.14 | 6.55 | 36.04 | 6.90 | 37.95 | 7.59 | 41.72 | 271 | 268 |
| 0.4 | 2.19 | 12.11 | 4.15 | 22.79 | 5.91 | 32.28 | 6.57 | 35.79 | 6.89 | 37.48 | 7.50 | 40.77 | 242 | 237 |
| 0.6 | 2.38 | 13.07 | 4.34 | 23.66 | 6.00 | 32.43 | 6.59 | 35.53 | 6.87 | 37.00 | 7.41 | 39.81 | 212 | 205 |
| 0.8 | 2.61 | 14.27 | 4.56 | 24.65 | 6.09 | 32.59 | 6.61 | 35.26 | 6.86 | 36.52 | 7.32 | 38.86 | 175 | 172 |
| 1.0 | 2.91 | 15.83 | 4.82 | 25.80 | 6.19 | 32.76 | 6.63 | 34.99 | 6.84 | 36.02 | 7.22 | 37.91 | 148 | 139 |
| Range (percent) | 51.6 | 48.4 | 25.5 | 20.9 | 7.5 | 2.3 | 1.5 | -3.6 | -1.0 | -6.2 | -5.9 | -11.2 | | |

Source: For derivation, see accompanying text.

[a]VAT revenue = net loss in government revenue before the VAT introduction, but after reduction of the CIT.

Table 3-2. Components of Change in VAT Revenues and Base (dollars in billions)

| CIT Shifting Parameter (α) | CIT Revenue Loss | | Government Expenditure Savings (3) | Reduction in Consumption (VAT) Base (4) | Net CIT Loss as Percent of Primary Loss (5) | Col. 4 as Percent of Preshifted VAT Base (6) | Ratio: VAT Rate with Shifting to Rate Without Shifting (7) |
| | Primary (1) | Secondary (2) | | | | | |
|---|---|---|---|---|---|---|---|
| | | | *CIT Reduction of 25 Percent* | | | | |
| 0.0 | $10.67 | 0 | 0 | 0 | 0 | 0 | 1.0 |
| 0.2 | 10.67 | $0.91 | $0.25 | $1.56 | 6.16% | -0.28% | 1.065 |
| 0.4 | 10.67 | 1.99 | 0.55 | 3.40 | 13.53 | -0.61 | 1.142 |
| 0.6 | 10.67 | 3.31 | 0.90 | 5.63 | 22.53 | -1.01 | 1.238 |
| 0.8 | 10.67 | 4.95 | 1.34 | 8.40 | 33.80 | -1.51 | 1.359 |
| 1.0 | 10.67 | 7.07 | 1.90 | 11.95 | 48.48 | -2.15 | 1.517 |
| | | | *CIT Reduction of 50 Percent* | | | | |
| 0.0 | 21.34 | 0 | 0 | 0 | 0 | 0 | 1.0 |
| 0.2 | 21.34 | 1.18 | 0.49 | 3.03 | 3.23 | -0.54 | 1.038 |
| 0.4 | 21.34 | 2.49 | 1.03 | 6.41 | 6.86 | -1.15 | 1.081 |
| 0.6 | 21.34 | 3.98 | 1.64 | 10.21 | 10.97 | -1.84 | 1.131 |
| 0.8 | 21.34 | 5.67 | 2.33 | 14.52 | 15.68 | -2.61 | 1.188 |
| 1.0 | 21.34 | 7.62 | 3.11 | 19.45 | 21.14 | -3.50 | 1.255 |
| | | | *CIT Reduction of 75 Percent* | | | | |
| 0.0 | 32.01 | 0 | 0 | 0 | 0 | 0 | 1.0 |
| 0.2 | 32.01 | 0.86 | 0.71 | 4.42 | .46 | -0.80 | 1.013 |
| 0.4 | 32.01 | 1.76 | 1.46 | 9.08 | .95 | -1.63 | 1.026 |
| 0.6 | 32.01 | 2.72 | 2.25 | 14.01 | 1.47 | -2.52 | 1.041 |
| 0.8 | 32.01 | 3.74 | 3.09 | 19.22 | 2.03 | -3.46 | 1.057 |
| 1.0 | 32.01 | 4.82 | 3.97 | 24.25 | 2.64 | -4.45 | 1.074 |
| | | | *CIT Reduction of 85 Percent* | | | | |
| 0.0 | $36.28 | 0 | 0 | 0 | 0 | 0 | 1.0 |
| 0.2 | 36.28 | $0.58 | $0.80 | $4.57 | -0.61% | -0.82% | 1.002 |
| 0.4 | 36.28 | 1.17 | 1.62 | 10.07 | -1.23 | -1.81 | 1.006 |
| 0.6 | 36.28 | 1.79 | 2.47 | 15.35 | -1.88 | -2.76 | 1.009 |
| 0.8 | 36.28 | 2.43 | 3.35 | 20.81 | -2.54 | -3.75 | 1.013 |
| 1.0 | 36.28 | 3.09 | 4.25 | 26.46 | -3.22 | -4.76 | 1.016 |

# Table 3-2 continued

| CIT Shifting Parameter (α) | CIT Revenue Loss | | Government Expenditure Savings (3) | Reduction in Consumption (VAT) Base (4) | Net CIT Loss as Percent of Primary Loss (5) | Col 4 as Percent of Preshifted VAT Base (6) | Ratio: VAT Rate with Shifting to Rate Without Shifting (7) |
|---|---|---|---|---|---|---|---|
| | Primary (1) | Secondary (2) | | | | | |
| *CIT Reduction of 90 Percent* | | | | | | | |
| 0.0 | 38.41 | 0 | 0 | 0 | 0 | 0 | 1.0 |
| 0.2 | 38.41 | 0.40 | 0.84 | 5.22 | -1.13 | -0.94 | .998 |
| 0.4 | 38.41 | 0.82 | 1.70 | 10.55 | -2.29 | -1.90 | .996 |
| 0.6 | 38.41 | 1.24 | 2.57 | 16.00 | -3.47 | -2.88 | .994 |
| 0.8 | 38.41 | 1.67 | 3.47 | 21.56 | -4.67 | -3.88 | .992 |
| 1.0 | 38.41 | 2.12 | 4.38 | 27.25 | -5.90 | -4.90 | .990 |
| *CIT Reduction of 100 Percent* | | | | | | | |
| 0.0 | 42.68 | 0 | 0 | 0 | 0 | 0 | 1.0 |
| 0.2 | 42.68 | 0 | .92 | 5.74 | -2.16 | -1.03 | .989 |
| 0.4 | 42.68 | 0 | 1.85 | 11.48 | -4.33 | -2.07 | .977 |
| 0.6 | 42.68 | 0 | 2.77 | 17.22 | -6.49 | -3.10 | .965 |
| 0.8 | 42.68 | 0 | 3.70 | 22.96 | -8.66 | -4.13 | .953 |
| 1.0 | 42.68 | 0 | 4.62 | 28.70 | -10.82 | -5.17 | .940 |

Column (1) = the first term in the numerator of equation (2-6-13).

Column (2) = the second term in the numerator of the same equation.

Column (3) = the third term in the numerator of the same equation.

Column (4) = the second term in the denominator of the same equation.

$$\text{Column (5)} = \left[ \frac{\text{column 1} + \text{column 2} - \text{column 3}}{\text{column 1}} - 1 \right] \times 100.$$

$$\text{Column (6)} = \left[ \frac{C - \text{column 4}}{C} - 1 \right] \times 100,$$

where $C$ = private domestic consumption expenditures before the tax change.

$$\text{Column (7)} = \frac{100 + \text{column 5}}{100 + \text{column 6}}, \quad \frac{\text{column 1}}{C} \times \text{column 7 and only column 7 is a function of the CIT shifting,}$$

noting that the VAT rate $(Z) = $

of the VAT rate to the degree of CIT reduction, given a specified degree of CIT shifting. Then, we examine the dependence of the VAT rate on the degree of CIT shifting, holding constant the degree of CIT reduction. This decomposition of the analysis permits a somewhat simpler exposition than would a direct focus on simultaneous variation in the CIT reduction and shifting parameters.

### 3.1.1 Sensitivity of VAT Rate to CIT Reduction

Given zero CIT shifting VAT-exclusive prices are unaffected by the CIT reduction, i.e., there is no change in either government or consumption expenditure at VAT-exclusive prices for a given bill of goods and services.

Similarly, there is no secondary CIT revenue loss since pretax profits are unaltered by the change in CIT rates. As a result, required VAT revenue is simply equal to the primary CIT revenue loss, which is proportionate to the degree of CIT reduction. Equivalently, the VAT rate is proportionate to the degree of CIT reduction. Thus, a CIT reduction of 100 percent necessitates a VAT rate of 7.68 percent and VAT revenue of $42.68 billion, equal to original CIT revenue, which is *twice* the 3.84 percent rate and $21.34 billion revenue required of the VAT if the CIT reduction were only 50 percent, or *four times* the 1.92 percent rate and $10.67 billion revenue required with a 25 percent CIT reduction. That is, the VAT rate and revenue required to compensate for CIT repeal are 100 percent and 300 percent greater than the rate and revenue required to compensate for a 50 percent CIT reduction and for a 25 percent reduction. Symbolically, $\partial^2 Z/\partial S^2 = 0$ if the CIT is not shifted, i.e., the relationship between the VAT rate and the degree of CIT removal is linear.

For any given degree of positive CIT shifting, the change in the VAT rate required to compensate for an increased degree of CIT reduction is less than proportionate to the change in CIT rates. For example, even if the CIT reduction is doubled, from 50 percent to 100 percent, the VAT rate is not fully doubled if the CIT is shifted: If the CIT is fully shifted, the VAT rate rises from 4.82 percent to 7.22 percent (the VAT rate required for CIT elimination is only 150 percent of the rate required for a 50 percent reduction in CIT rates), while a shifting parameter of 0.5 results in an increase in the VAT rate from 4.34 percent to 7.41 percent if the CIT reduction changes from 50 percent to 100 percent (in this case the latter rate is 171 percent of the former). Thus, $\partial^2 Z/\partial S^2 < 0$, if positive shifting of the CIT occurs. This reduced responsiveness of the VAT rate to changes in the degree of CIT reduction for higher values of the CIT shifting parameter is due to two reinforcing phenomena. First, as can be seen from Table 3-2, *for any given degree of shifting,* the reduction in government expenditures becomes monotonically greater in absolute value (although at a diminishing rate) as the CIT is progressively reduced. This increased expenditure savings resulting from increased CIT shifting reduces the adjustment in VAT revenue required to compensate for any increase in the degree of CIT reduction.

In addition, as the CIT is progressively reduced, the secondary CIT revenue loss, given any positive degree of CIT shifting, at first *increases at a diminishing rate.* At a CIT reduction of slightly less than 50 percent it then decreases, although it remains positive. The reason for this behavior is that the decline in taxable profit due to shifting entails less of a revenue loss the lower the *post-reduction* CIT rate (the greater the degree of CIT removal). Complete removal of the CIT obviously precludes any secondary CIT revenue loss regardless of the degree of CIT shifting, since the post-reduction CIT rate is zero.

Of course, in addition to its effect on the secondary loss and savings in government expenditure, positive CIT shifting also reduces the VAT base (consumption expenditure at VAT-exclusive prices). However, these reductions in base also proceed at a diminishing rate as CIT reduction proceeds. The base reduction is simply equal to the sum of the primary and secondary CIT revenue loss multiplied by the CIT shifting parameter, less the reduction in nominal government, investment, and export expenditure: primary loss is proportionate to the degree of CIT reduction, while secondary loss at first increases and then declines, as noted above. Thus, the decline in the VAT base proceeds at a decreasing rate with progressive CIT reduction, given any positive degree of CIT shifting. Furthermore, the change in base has very little effect on the VAT rate because the change is very small *relative to original consumption expenditure*: in all cases less than 6 percent. In absolute amount the change in VAT-exclusive consumption expenditure is second in magnitude only to the primary CIT revenue loss, but the former is a change only in tax *base*, not tax revenue.

To summarize, the required VAT rate is proportionate to the degree of CIT removal if the CIT is not shifted but is less than proportionate if the CIT is shifted. Furthermore, as demonstrated in Tables 3-1 and 3-3, the relative increase in the VAT rate required to compensate for any increase in CIT removal declines with increased CIT shifting. This phenomenon is visually portrayed in

**Table 3-3. Percentage Changes in VAT Rates and Revenues for Given Changes in CIT Reduction and Differing Degrees of CIT Shifting (percent)**

| CIT Shifting Parameter | Change in Degree of CIT Reduction (S) | | | | | |
| | From 25% to 50% | | From 50% to 75% | | From 75% to 100% | |
| | Rate | Revenue | Rate | Revenue | Rate | Revenue |
|---|---|---|---|---|---|---|
| 0.0 | 100.0 | 100.0 | 50.0 | 50.0 | 33.3 | 33.3 |
| 0.2 | 95.0 | 94.5 | 46.3 | 45.9 | 30.2 | 29.8 |
| 0.4 | 89.3 | 88.2 | 42.4 | 41.6 | 26.9 | 26.3 |
| 0.6 | 82.6 | 81.0 | 38.1 | 37.1 | 23.6 | 22.8 |
| 0.8 | 74.9 | 72.8 | 33.5 | 32.2 | 20.2 | 19.3 |
| 1.0 | 65.4 | 63.0 | 28.4 | 27.0 | 16.7 | 15.7 |

Note: Percentage changes are calculated as $\frac{\Delta Z}{Z}$ and $\frac{\Delta T_v}{T_v}$ for a given $\alpha$, where $Z$ is the VAT rate and $T_v$ is the VAT revenue.

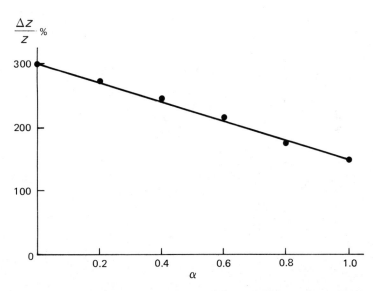

**Figure 3-1.** Relative Change in VAT Rate ($Z$) for CIT Reductions Moving from 25 Percent to 100 Percent, as Function of CIT Shifting Parameter ($\alpha$)

Figure 3-1, which contains plots of the relative change in the VAT rate, $Z$, when the degree of CIT reduction is increased from 25 percent to 100 percent, as a function of the shifting parameter, $\alpha$. The relative change in the VAT rate required to compensate for an increase in the degree of CIT removal from 25 percent to 100 per-

cent declines continuously with increase in the CIT shifting parameter: With zero CIT shifting the 300 percent increase in the degree
of CIT rate reduction implies an equivalent 300 percent increase
in the VAT rate, while with the extreme of full forward shifting of
the CIT the relative change in VAT rates is only 148 percent.

The same dependence of the CIT reduction-VAT rate association
on the degree of CIT shifting is portrayed in Figure 3–2, which relates the compensating VAT rate to the degree of CIT reduction,
holding the CIT shifting parameter constant. It is readily observed
that the curves become progressively flatter as the CIT shifting

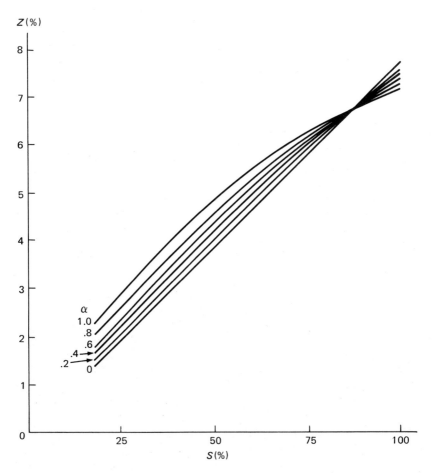

**Figure 3–2.** VAT Rate $(Z)$ as Function of Degree of CIT Reduction $(S)$, Given
CIT Shifting Parameter $(\alpha)$

parameter is increased, i.e., the rate of change of $Z$ (the VAT rate) with respect to change in $S$ (CIT reduction) is less the greater the degree of forward CIT shifting, or alternatively, $\partial^2 Z/\partial\alpha\partial S < 0$. This is more precisely indicated in Table 3-3, which contains figures for the change in the VAT rate resulting from three representative changes in the degree of CIT reduction (25 percent to 50 percent, 50 percent to 75 percent, and 75 percent to 100 percent). In each of the three cases, the percentage change in the VAT rate declines throughout with increases in CIT shifting.

It should be noted that if the CIT is shifted in any degree, the relative increase in VAT *revenue* is less than the relative increase in the VAT *rate* required to compensate for an increase in $S$ (degree of CIT removal). The change in revenue must be less than the change in rate simply because the VAT base is simultaneously reduced as the degree of CIT reduction proceeds. Thus, in the extreme case of full CIT shifting, the increase in the VAT rate (moving from $S = 25$ percent to $S = 100$ percent) is 148 percent but the increase in VAT revenue is only 139 percent. With zero CIT shifting, of course, the 300 percent increase in the VAT rate implies a corresponding 300 percent increase in VAT revenue.

### 3.1.2 Sensitivity of VAT Rate to CIT Shifting

Superficially, it might appear that an increase in shifting would necessarily require an increase in the VAT rate (and in VAT revenue), regardless of the degree of CIT reduction, simply because of the increased secondary CIT revenue loss implied by an increase in shifting. This is indeed true for low degrees of CIT removal: With a 25 percent reduction in CIT rates, zero CIT shifting requires a VAT rate of 1.92 percent while full shifting requires a rate 52 percent greater ($Z = 2.91$ percent). Thus, for sufficiently small values of $S$, $\partial Z/\partial\alpha > 0$. However, in the extreme case of full CIT removal there can be no secondary CIT revenue loss, simply because the post-tax-change CIT rate is zero. *Primary* CIT revenue loss is, of course, the same for any degree of shifting. But, any degree of positive CIT shifting will entail a *reduction* in government expenditure due to reductions in the VAT-exclusive prices of government purchases. The greater the degree of forward CIT shifting, the greater the resultant reduction in government expenditure. Thus, with complete CIT removal, *required VAT revenue* (equal to primary CIT revenue loss minus the reduction in government expenditure) *declines as the CIT shifting parameter increases.* The decline is from $42.68 billion (original CIT revenue) with zero CIT shifting to $37.91 billion (a government expenditure decline of $4.77 billion) with full shifting of the CIT. Whether the VAT rate is increased or reduced depends upon the effect of CIT shifting on the VAT base, i.e., on consumption expenditures at VAT-exclusive prices. As might be expected, the increase in CIT shifting from zero to 100 percent implies a reduction in required VAT revenue (11.2 percent) which is proportionately greater than the implied reduction in the total VAT base (less than 6 percent). As a result the VAT *rate* declines from 7.68 percent with zero shifting to 7.22 percent with full shifting, a relative reduction of 5.9 percent. Therefore, if the degree of CIT reduction is sufficiently large, an increase in CIT shifting will imply a reduction in the VAT rate, i.e. $\partial Z/\partial \alpha < 0$.

Thus, for some intermediate degree of CIT reduction, required *VAT* revenue must remain unchanged whatever the degree of CIT shifting, i.e., increases in secondary CIT revenue loss due to increased shifting must be just offset by increases in government expenditure savings resulting from the increase in shifting. For smaller CIT reductions increases in CIT shifting will require increased VAT revenues (secondary CIT revenue loss will exceed government expenditure savings) while revenue requirements will decline with increased shifting for greater CIT reductions (government expenditure savings will exceed secondary CIT revenue loss). In fact, as indicated in Table 3-1, the degree of CIT reduction for which VAT revenue is independent of shifting is in excess of 75 percent, but less than 85 percent. For $S$ = 75 percent, a CIT shifting increase from zero to unity implies a 2.3 percent increase in required VAT revenue, while at $S$ = 85 percent, required VAT revenue declines by 3.6 percent due to the change in shifting.

Note, however, the requirement that VAT revenue remain unchanged does *not* imply that the VAT rate remains unchanged as the CIT shifts. In fact, for the same reason that revenue is constant (the reduction in government expenditure due to shifted CIT savings equals the increase in secondary CIT revenue loss), the VAT rate must *increase*: the VAT base is reduced by increased CIT shifting due to the reduction in VAT-exclusive consumption prices.

The VAT *rate* will be invariant to CIT shifting only for the critical degree of CIT reduction at which the rate of decline of required VAT revenue due to CIT shifting is equal to the rate of CIT-shifting-induced decline in the VAT base. That is, there is a critical value for the degree of CIT reduction below which increases in CIT shifting imply increases in the VAT rate; either required VAT revenue rises (secondary CIT loss exceeds government expenditure savings) while the VAT base declines (due to reductions in VAT-exclusive consumption prices), or required VAT revenue declines (government ex-

Table 3-4. Percentage Changes in VAT Rates and Revenues for Given Changes in CIT Shifting and Differing Degrees of CIT Reduction (percent)

| Change in CIT Shifting Parameter (α) | Degree of CIT Reduction (S) | | | | | | | | | | | |
|---|---|---|---|---|---|---|---|---|---|---|---|---|
| | 25 Percent | | 50 Percent | | 75 Percent | | 85 Percent | | 90 Percent | | 100 Percent | |
| | Rate | Revenue | Rate | Revenue | Rate | Revenue | Rate | Revenue | Rate | Revenue | Rate | Revenue |
| From 0 to .2 | 6.5 | 6.1 | 3.8 | 3.2 | 1.3 | .4 | .3 | -.7 | -.2 | -1.2 | -1.1 | -2.2 |
| From .2 to .4 | 7.3 | 7.0 | 4.1 | 3.5 | 1.3 | .4 | .3 | -.7 | -.2 | -1.2 | -1.2 | -2.3 |
| From .4 to .6 | 8.4 | 7.9 | 4.6 | 3.8 | 1.4 | .5 | .3 | -.7 | -.2 | -1.3 | -1.2 | -2.3 |
| From .6 to .8 | 9.8 | 9.2 | 5.1 | 4.2 | 1.5 | .5 | .3 | -.8 | -.2 | -1.3 | -1.3 | -2.4 |
| From .8 to 1.0 | 11.7 | 10.9 | 5.7 | 4.7 | 1.6 | .5 | .4 | -.8 | -.2 | -1.4 | -1.3 | -2.5 |

Note: Percentage changes are calculated as $\Delta Z/Z$ and $\Delta T_U/T_U$ for a given $S$, where $Z$ is the VAT rate and $T_U$ is VAT revenues.

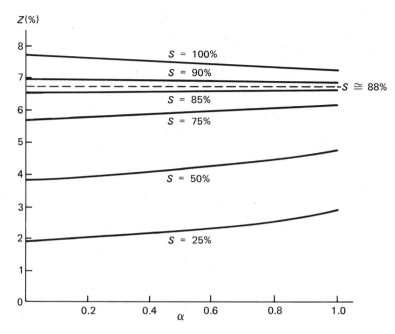

**Figure 3-3.** VAT Rate ($Z$) as Function of CIT Shifting Parameter ($\alpha$), Given Degree of CIT Reduction ($S$)

penditure savings exceed secondary CIT loss) but less rapidly than the decline in the VAT base. Above that critical degree of CIT reduction, required VAT revenue declines *more rapidly* than the VAT base, implying a *reduction* in the VAT rate with increases in shifting.

By inspection, it is clear that the critical degree of CIT reduction at which the VAT rate is independent of CIT shifting ($\partial Z / \partial \alpha$ = 0) is slightly less than 90 percent (between $S$ = 85 percent and $S$ = 90 percent). This can be seen clearly in Tables 3-1 and 3-4 and is graphically portrayed in Figures 3-3 and 3-4. In Figure 3-3 the VAT rate ($Z$) is related to the CIT shifting parameter ($\alpha$), with the CIT reduction ($S$) held constant. For CIT reductions of less than 90 percent the slopes of these curves are positive (VAT rate rises with $\alpha$), while above this level the slope is negative (the VAT rate declines with increases in $\alpha$). In Figure 3-4 the relative change in the VAT rate due to an increase in CIT shifting from zero to unity is plotted as a function of the degree of CIT reduction. Again, it is clear that the change is *positive* (moving from $\alpha$ = 0 to $\alpha$ = 1) for CIT reductions of less than 90 percent but *negative* for reductions in excess of 90 percent.

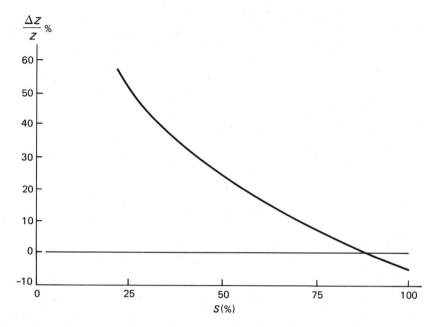

**Figure 3-4.** Relative Change in VAT Rate ($Z$) for Degrees of CIT Shifting ($\alpha$), Moving from Zero to 100 Percent, as Function of Degree of CIT Reductions ($S$)

For a CIT reduction of between 85 and 90 percent the change due to increased CIT shifting is zero. This is also precisely the point of intersection of the curves in Figure 3-2, relating the VAT rate to the degree of CIT reduction, given specified values of $\alpha$.

Determination of this VAT rate-CIT shifting invariance is significant because the degree of CIT shifting is an unknown and disputed parameter: since the sensitivity of the required VAT rate to CIT shifting is lower for larger than for smaller CIT reductions, and since the VAT rate is unchanged by CIT shifting at a CIT reduction of about 90 percent, therefore, the greater the weight placed on avoidance of unanticipated surpluses or deficits, the closer the degree of CIT reduction should be to 85-90 percent. In this range, the VAT rate would be approximately invariant to the unknown CIT shifting parameter. This conclusion is contrary to the usual predisposition toward marginal changes when uncertainty is great. Here, the almost unqualified rule is that, in order to obtain a high degree of certainty concerning the appropriate compensatory VAT rate, the degree of tax substitution must be very great.

Of course, factors other than unanticipated budgetary effects must enter a decision to substitute a VAT for the CIT, e.g., re-distributive, allocative, growth, and trade effects, but certainly significant weight must be given to aggregate demand effects.[2]

## 3.2 PRICE EFFECTS OF THE VAT-CIT SUBSTITUTION

The discussion in the preceding section of CIT-compensating VAT rates and revenues was in some sense premature. In fact, it has been impossible to discuss VAT rate determination without simultaneously considering the effects of the tax substitution, in particular of the CIT reduction, on prices. Specifically the effects of the tax substitution on the prices of government-purchased goods and services, which enter the VAT yield criterion through changes in government expenditure, and on consumption prices, which determine the magnitude of the VAT base, have entered into the determination of a compensatory VAT rate. However, in this section the price effects of the VAT-CIT substitution are examined in greater detail and more comprehensively. First, price indices by component of final demand are examined under alternative assumptions concerning the degree of CIT replacement and the extent of forward CIT shifting. Price effects are then disaggregated by modified Standard Industrial Classification two-digit industry groups. Finally, prices by commodity under the full 100-industry disaggregation are discussed.

### 3.2.1 Price Effects by Component of Final Demand

Post-tax-substitution indices by component of final demand are presented in Table 3-5 for four representative degrees of CIT reduction ($S$ = 25, 50, 75, and 100 percent) under the full range of alternative CIT shifting assumptions. As has been discussed, final consumption prices are VAT-inclusive, while investment and export prices are VAT-exclusive (full credit against final VAT liabilities is permitted for VAT invoiced on these purchases). By convention government prices are treated as VAT-exclusive, since the VAT on government purchases is both government revenue and ex-

---

2. In this conclusion, it is assumed that the imposed VAT yield criterion, an unchanged nominal government surplus or deficit, would in fact be independent of the behavior of aggregate demand. However, increases in VAT-inclusive consumption prices might serve to depress consumption demand. Offsetting this, increases in after-tax profits or reductions in investment and export prices, or both, would stimulate investment, exports, and even possibly consumption (via higher dividends and capital gains).

Table 3-5. Aggregate Price Indices, by Category of Final Demands, for Alternative Degrees of CIT Reduction and Shifting (percent)

| CIT Shifting Parameter ($\alpha$) | VAT Rate ($Z$) | $P_c$ VAT-Inc. | $P_c$ VAT-Exc. | $P_I$ | $P_R$ | $P_E$ | $P_F$ | $P_{SL}$ |
|---|---|---|---|---|---|---|---|---|
| | | | | | *Price Indices* | | | |
| | | | | *CIT Reduction of 25 Percent* | | | | |
| 0.0 | 1.92 | 101.92 | 100.00 | 100.00 | 100.00 | 100.00 | 100.00 | 100.00 |
| 0.2 | 2.04 | 101.76 | 99.73 | 99.71 | 99.76 | 99.71 | 99.71 | 99.74 |
| 0.4 | 2.19 | 101.57 | 99.39 | 99.36 | 99.48 | 99.36 | 99.37 | 99.43 |
| 0.6 | 2.38 | 101.34 | 98.98 | 98.93 | 99.15 | 98.94 | 98.96 | 99.06 |
| 0.8 | 2.61 | 101.05 | 98.48 | 98.42 | 98.75 | 98.42 | 98.44 | 98.61 |
| 1.0 | 2.91 | 100.69 | 97.84 | 97.76 | 98.24 | 97.74 | 97.79 | 98.04 |
| | | | | *CIT Reduction of 50 Percent* | | | | |
| 0.0 | 3.84 | 103.84 | 100.00 | 100.00 | 100.00 | 100.00 | 100.00 | 100.00 |
| 0.2 | 3.99 | 103.42 | 99.45 | 99.43 | 99.54 | 99.44 | 99.44 | 99.49 |
| 0.4 | 4.15 | 102.95 | 98.85 | 98.79 | 99.02 | 98.80 | 98.81 | 98.92 |
| 0.6 | 4.34 | 102.42 | 98.16 | 98.07 | 98.45 | 98.09 | 98.11 | 98.28 |
| 0.8 | 4.56 | 101.82 | 97.38 | 97.25 | 97.81 | 97.28 | 97.31 | 97.57 |
| 1.0 | 4.82 | 101.14 | 96.49 | 96.32 | 97.08 | 96.34 | 96.39 | 96.75 |
| | | | | *CIT Reduction of 75 Percent* | | | | |
| 0.0 | 5.76 | 105.76 | 100.00 | 100.00 | 100.00 | 100.00 | 100.00 | 100.00 |
| 0.2 | 5.83 | 104.99 | 99.21 | 99.16 | 99.32 | 99.18 | 99.18 | 99.25 |
| 0.4 | 5.91 | 104.18 | 98.37 | 98.28 | 98.61 | 98.30 | 98.32 | 98.46 |
| 0.6 | 6.00 | 103.32 | 97.47 | 97.34 | 97.86 | 97.38 | 97.41 | 97.63 |
| 0.8 | 6.09 | 102.41 | 96.53 | 96.36 | 97.07 | 96.41 | 96.44 | 96.75 |
| 1.0 | 6.19 | 101.45 | 95.54 | 95.31 | 96.23 | 95.37 | 95.42 | 95.83 |

**Table 3-5 continued**

| CIT Shifting Parameter (α) | VAT Rate (Z) | $P_c$ VAT-Inc. | $P_c$ VAT-Exc. | Price Indices $P_I$ | $P_R$ | $P_E$ | $P_F$ | $P_{SL}$ |
|---|---|---|---|---|---|---|---|---|
| | | | | *CIT Reduction of 100 Percent* | | | | |
| 0.0 | 7.68 | 107.68 | 100.00 | 100.00 | 100.00 | 100.00 | 100.00 | 100.00 |
| 0.2 | 7.59 | 106.48 | 98.97 | 98.91 | 99.11 | 98.93 | 98.94 | 99.03 |
| 0.4 | 7.50 | 105.28 | 97.93 | 97.82 | 98.24 | 97.86 | 97.88 | 98.05 |
| 0.6 | 7.41 | 104.08 | 96.90 | 96.73 | 97.36 | 96.79 | 96.82 | 97.08 |
| 0.8 | 7.32 | 102.88 | 95.86 | 95.64 | 96.47 | 95.72 | 95.75 | 96.10 |
| 1.0 | 7.22 | 101.68 | 94.83 | 94.55 | 95.59 | 94.65 | 94.69 | 95.13 |

Note: $P$ = aggregate price index; $C$ = personal consumption expenditures; $I$ = private nonresidential fixed investment; $R$ = private residential structures; $E$ = exports; $F$ = federal government expenditures; $SL$ = expenditures by state and local governments.

penditure, and thus cancels out. Investment is decomposed into (a) business plant and equipment and (b) private residential structures. Government is disaggregated into federal and state-local components. Finally, in a departure from conventional input-output practice, the indices represent *purchaser* prices (inclusive of trade and transportation margins) rather than *producer* prices (exclusive of trade and transportation margins).[3]

The interrelationship between degree of CIT reduction, CIT shifting, and prices is somewhat simpler than that between CIT reduction and shifting and VAT rates and revenues. Because all purchasers are assumed to face identical VAT-exclusive prices, and because the VAT is assumed to be fully shifted forward, price changes for components of final demand not ultimately subject to the VAT, i.e., all components *other than consumption*, reflect *only* the effects of the CIT reduction.[4]

The estimated price effects of tax substitution by component of final demand can be rather briefly summarized. First, regardless of the degree of CIT reduction, in the absence of CIT shifting, VAT-exclusive nonconsumption prices remain unchanged (index = 100.0), and VAT-inclusive consumption prices rise by the rate of the VAT. For example, with complete CIT removal and no CIT shifting the required VAT rate is 7.68 percent and the resultant VAT-inclusive consumption price index is 107.68.

Secondly, for any given (positive) degree of CIT reduction, VAT-exclusive prices decline continuously (VAT-inclusive prices rise by less) as forward CIT shifting increases. Again, the extreme of complete CIT elimination provides a case in point: With zero CIT shifting nonconsumption deflators are, by definition, unity; with unitary shifting, deflators for the VAT-exempt components of final demand decline to between 94.5 and 95.6. With zero shifting and CIT repeal the VAT-inclusive consumption index is 107.68, which falls with complete CIT shifting to 101.68. Note that this price decline is only marginally due to the decline in the VAT rate, which falls only from 7.68 percent (zero CIT shifting) to 7.22 percent (full CIT shifting).

---

3. Thus, trade and transportation services associated with purchases from other industries are treated as intermediate goods rather than as components of final demand.

4. As discussed previously, if the VAT were *not* assumed to be fully shifted, then introduction of the VAT would reduce *VAT-exclusive* prices of consumption goods. Since firms would find it impossible to segregate sales ultimately entering consumption from sales ultimately entering components of final demand effectively exempt from the VAT, maintenance of the assumption of identical VAT-exclusive prices for all purchasers would continue to be justified, implying a decline in the effective prices of VAT-exempt purchases, solely as a result of imposition of the (unshifted) VAT.

Even with lower degrees of CIT reduction (less than 85 to 90 percent), for which the VAT rate *rises* with increases in forward CIT shifting, the benefit of forward CIT shifting outweighs the increase in the VAT rate, resulting in a *net* decline in VAT-inclusive consumption prices as CIT shifting increases. For example, with a CIT reduction of 25 percent the VAT rate *rises* from 1.92 to 2.91 percent as CIT shifting rises from zero to 1.0, but consumption prices nonetheless *decline* from 101.9 to 100.7. Thus, the 1 percent increment in the VAT rate is more than offset by the 1.2 percent reduction in VAT-exclusive consumption prices resulting from the full forward shifting of the CIT. This differential decline occurs because consumers benefit from the shifting of both the primary and secondary CIT revenue loss, while the VAT rate rises to compensate only for the *excess* of the secondary CIT loss over the reduction in government expenditure. This increase in required VAT revenue due to CIT shifting is less than the benefit to consumers of the shifted CIT reduction but large enough relative to the now-reduced VAT base to require a significant increment in the VAT rate.

Thirdly, given any positive CIT shifting, of the exempt components of final demand, business investment in plant and equipment benefits most from the substitution of an economy-wide consumption-type VAT for the corporation-focused CIT, while net residential capital formation benefits least. In between, ranked from highest to lowest degree of price reduction, are federal government expenditures, exports, and state-local government expenditures. The relative price changes of these five exempt components are rather easily explained:

The small price reduction for residential investment reflects the combination of high labor intensity of the housing construction industry and its largely unincorporated structure. Even when contractors are incorporated, much of the work is subcontracted to unincorporated enterprises. Most of the price reduction in this sector is due to reductions in the prices of fabricated inputs, but the high degree of direct labor intensity minimizes the effect of these reductions on final output prices. Similar factors probably explain the somewhat smaller-than-average reduction in state-local government prices.

The tax substitution has a greater effect on investment than on government and export prices primarily because unincorporated enterprise is not important in either capital goods or intermediate supplier industries, and these industries have high capital-output ratios and hence high ratios of profit to value added. In general the corporate profit tax liability of the "own industry" (as opposed to intermediate supplier industries) is the most significant element in the explanation of the effect of the tax substitution on prices, and this importance appears very clearly in the case of investment in plant and equipment.

It is interesting that the greatest *VAT-exclusive* price reductions are observed in the case of private consumption. (VAT-exclusive consumption prices are obtained by dividing $P_c$ by $1 + Z$, and are approximated by subtracting the VAT rate from $P_c$.) As will be observed below, this is primarily explained by the significant CIT shifting benefits in the consumer-durable and communications industries. Of course, the imposition of the VAT liability on consumption purchases invariably (and necessarily) results in increases in VAT-inclusive prices over the level of pre-tax-substitution consumption prices. Only if the entire benefit of the CIT reduction were shifted to consumption *alone* would the aggregate consumption price index be unaffected by the tax substitution.

### 3.2.2 General Relationships Between Price Change; CIT Reduction, Shifting and Initial Rates; and Profit Shares

Before examining the actual industry and commodity price changes which can be anticipated under alternative assumptions concerning CIT reduction and shifting, the general nature of the output-price consequences of the tax substitution must be considered. Specifically, we are concerned with the general interrelationships among (a) CIT reduction, (b) CIT shifting, (c) the profit share of price, and (d) the effective CIT rate. We first consider a very simple situation, one in which there are no intermediate goods and price is determined only by value added in the given industry. Although rarefied, this simple model is formally compatible with the more general interindustry model developed in the preceding chapter (section 2.6), but it is mathematically simpler. Further, while the effects of the tax substitution on the price in one industry will in fact depend on changes in CIT rates and on CIT shifting in other industries, it will be discovered that the price effects of the tax substitution will primarily reflect changes in "own industry" CIT liabilities and shifting. Because value added contributed by the "own industry" is so predominant in virtually all cases, the simplification considered here introduces only minor violations of the true relationships. Of course, the empirical analysis employs the fully articulated interindustry model.

In contrast to the preceding discussion of aggregate indices of purchaser prices, the initial focus here is on changes in VAT-exclusive producer prices. Because it is invariably assumed that the VAT is fully shifted forward and that VAT-exclusive producer prices are identical for all purchasers, changes in these prices are due entirely to the reduction and shifting of the corporate income tax. The response of the producer prices to CIT reduction and shifting is somewhat complex, necessitating a return to the simplified model developed in section 2.4, above. In the interest of clarity, the important features of that discussion can be quickly repeated. It is assumed in the following discussion that the CIT shifting parameter, the pre-tax-substitution CIT rate, and the degree of CIT reduction are mutually independent.

It will be recalled that the CIT shifting parameter ($\alpha$) was defined as the ratio of the change in gross profit to the change in tax liability, i.e.,

$$\alpha = \frac{\pi - \pi'}{t\pi - t'\pi'} \tag{3-1}$$

where $\pi$ is gross profit, $t$ is the CIT rate, and the primes (') represent post-tax-change values. The change in profit ($\Delta\pi$) is then,

$$\Delta\pi = \pi - \pi' = \frac{\alpha}{(1 - \alpha t')}(t - t')\pi \tag{3-2}$$

Denoting the relative reduction in the CIT rate by $s(= S/100)$, i.e., $t' = (1 - s)t$, equation (3-2) can be rewritten,

$$\Delta\pi = \frac{\alpha st}{1 - \alpha(1 - s)t}\pi. \tag{3-2a}$$

If profit is expressed per unit of output, e.g., 10 cents per dollar's worth of widget; if output is measured by value at pre-tax-change prices so that the initial pre-tax-substitution price is unity by definition; and if components other than profit (e.g., the wage component) of value added (i.e., price in the absence of intermediate goods) are unaffected by the tax substitution, then the absolute change in gross profit is equal to the proportionate change in price, i.e., $\Delta\pi = \Delta P$ and $\Delta P/P = \Delta P$, since $P = 1$.[5] Thus, the basic equation, relating

---

5. The percentage change in *profit* of course depends on the initial level of profit.

the price change (absolute and relative) to CIT shifting, initial rates, and degree of reduction, becomes

$$\Delta P = \frac{\alpha st}{1 - \alpha(1 - s)t} \pi.$$

$(3-3)$

Our interest here is in the effects of $\alpha$, $s$, and $t$ on the change in price. To do so, we shall develop ten rules for evaluating the change in $\Delta P$ relative to unit changes in each of these parameters. Note that since the change in profit has been defined as $\pi - \pi'$ (gross profit before the tax substitution minus gross profit afterward), $\Delta P$ indicates a relative *decline* in price.

**Effect of Increased CIT Shifting.** An increase in the CIT shifting parameters ($\alpha$) results in an increase in the price-reduction benefits of the CIT reduction, i.e., in $\Delta P$, experessed by the partial derivative of $\Delta P$ with respect to $\alpha$:

$$\frac{\partial \Delta P}{\partial \alpha} = \frac{st\pi}{[1 - \alpha(1 - s)t]^2}$$

$(3-4)$

This expression is necessarily positive.

To determine whether the rate of increase in the price reductions is increasing or decreasing as $\alpha$(CIT shifting) increases, consider the following equation, from which two rules can be derived:

$$\frac{\partial^2 \Delta P}{\partial \alpha^2} = \frac{2St^2\pi(1 - s)}{[1 - \alpha(1 - s)t]^3}.$$

$(3-5)$

*Rule 1.* If the CIT is fully removed ($s = 1$) then the reduction in price is *proportionate* to the CIT shifting parameter $\alpha$. The change in $\Delta P$ with respect to $\alpha$ is independent of the value of $\alpha$, i.e., from equations $(3-4)$ and $(3-5)$:

$$\frac{\partial \Delta P}{\partial \alpha} = t\pi \text{ and } \frac{\partial^2 \Delta P}{\partial \alpha^2} = 0 \text{ if } s = 1.$$

$(3-6)$

*Rule 2.* If the CIT is only partially removed ($s < 1$), then the increase in price reduction is *more than proportionate* to the increase in $\alpha$, since equation $(3-5)$ is positive for values of $s$ less than unity, i.e., $(\partial^2 \Delta P / \partial \alpha^2) > 0$ if $s < 1$. Thus, $\Delta P$ increases at an increasing rate with increases in $\alpha$ if the CIT is not completely removed.

Now, consider the effect of the pre-tax-substitution effective CIT rate ($t$), which is observed to differ by industry, on the relationship between $\Delta P$ (price reduction) and CIT shifting ($a$). Rule 3 is obtained by differentiating equation (3-4) with respect to $t$:

$$\frac{\partial^2 \Delta P}{\partial t\, \partial \alpha} = \frac{s\pi(1 + \alpha t - \alpha st)}{[1 - \alpha(1 - s)t]^3} > 0. \qquad (3-7)$$

*Rule 3.* The rate of change in price with respect to CIT shifting is an *increasing function* of the initial CIT rate, i.e., the greater the initial CIT rate, the greater the price-reduction benefits of an increase in CIT shifting, regardless of the degree of CIT reduction.

Alternatively, consider the effect on the relationship between price and CIT shifting exerted by an increase in $s$ (degree of CIT removal). Rule 4 is obtained by first differentiating equation (3-4) with respect to $s$:

$$\frac{\partial^2 \Delta P}{\partial s\, \partial \alpha} = \frac{t\pi(1 - \alpha t - \alpha st)}{[1 - \alpha(1 - s)t]^3}. \qquad (3-8)$$

By inspection, (3-8) is seen to be necessarily positive for $s$ less than or equal to one. Thus;

*Rule 4.* The change in price with respect to CIT shifting is an increasing function of the degree of CIT reduction.

**Effect of Increased CIT Reduction.** From equation (3-3), the effect on prices of an increase in CIT reduction ($s$) is simply:

$$\frac{\partial \Delta P}{\partial s} = \frac{\alpha t\pi(1 - \alpha t)}{[1 - \alpha(1 - s)t]^2}, \qquad (3-9)$$

which has the following property:

$$\frac{\partial \Delta P}{\partial s} \gtreqqless 0 \text{ as } \alpha \gtreqqless 0.$$

Thus,

*Rule 5.* Reductions in the CIT, from whatever CIT level, will not affect prices if the CIT is not shifted ($\alpha = 0$).

*Rule 6.* With positive CIT shifting, price reduction will accompany any increase in CIT reduction.

Whether rate of reduction of price increases or decreases with increases in the degree of CIT reduction is less obviously determined. Specifically, from equation (3–9),

$$\frac{\partial^2 \Delta P}{\partial S^2} = -\frac{2\alpha^2 t^2 \pi (1 - \alpha t)}{[1 - \alpha(1 - s)t]^3} < 0; \qquad (3\text{–}10)$$

*Rule 7.*  Prices decline at a decreasing rate as the CIT is reduced.

Finally, consider the response of prices to a CIT reduction if, first, the degree of CIT shifting is increased, and second, initial CIT rates are increased. From equation (3–9),

$$\frac{\partial^2 \Delta P}{\partial \alpha\, \partial s} = \frac{t\pi (1 - \alpha t - \alpha st)}{[1 - \alpha(1 - s)t]^3} > 0; \qquad (3\text{–}11)$$

and

$$\frac{\partial^2 \Delta P}{\partial t\, \partial s} = \frac{\alpha \pi (1 - \alpha t - \alpha st)}{[1 - \alpha(1 - s)t]^3} > 0. \qquad (3\text{–}12)$$

Thus,

*Rule 8.*  The effect of a given CIT reduction on prices is greater the greater the degree of forward CIT shifting [equation (3–11)]; and

*Rule 9.*  The effect of a given CIT reduction on prices is greater the greater the initial CIT rate [equation 3–12)].

**Effects of Initial Profit Share of Price.**  Finally, Rule 10 is obtained by differentiating equations (3–4) and (3–9) with respect to gross profit per unit of output (or equivalently, the profit share of price):

$$\frac{\partial^2 \Delta P}{\partial \pi\, \partial \alpha} = \frac{st}{[1 - \alpha(1 - s)t]^2} > 0, \qquad (3\text{–}13)$$

and

$$\frac{\partial^2 \Delta P}{\partial \pi\, \partial s} = \frac{\alpha t(1 - \alpha t)}{[1 - \alpha(1 - s)t]^2} > 0. \qquad (3\text{–}14)$$

*Rule 10.*  The price reduction resulting from *either* an increase in CIT shifting or an increase in the degree of CIT removal is *greater* the greater the profit share of final output price.

While much of the foregoing is obvious, it is nonetheless useful to make explicit the necessary relationships between these variables. Also, although the relationships were developed under the artificial assumption that only the own-industry CIT effect mattered (on the assumption that there are no interindustry transactions), in fact the dominance of own-industry CIT liability embodied in final output price is so great that in most cases only slight violence to reality results from ignoring interindustry CIT shifting. This point is demonstrated in Table 3-6, in which own-industry CIT liability (prior to the tax change) is compared to the total direct and indirect CIT liability embodied in final output price (also prior to the tax change), for two-digit industries: in over half of the cases, the own-industry CIT accounts for over 40 percent of the total CIT liability. Thus, virtually all of the relationships developed above can be applied to individual industries on the basis merely of own-industry characteristics. Differential *relative* price effects (across industries) are almost entirely explained by differential intraindustry phenomena, and the deviations caused by interindustry effects are small enough to be disregarded.

### 3.2.3 Price Effects by Industry

To obtain a clearer understanding of the sources of these projected price effects of a VAT-CIT substitution, we developed a modified two-digit industry classification. This provides a useful intermediate level of industry and commodity disaggregation and smooths the transition to the full 100-industry disaggregation used in our input-output model.

Table 3-7 contains percentage reductions in producer prices (exclusive of VAT) for two-digit industries for different degrees of CIT reduction and shifting.[6] Because producer prices change only if the CIT is partially or fully shifted (Rule 5), the case of zero shifting is trivial and can be ignored. Attention is restricted to three representative degrees of shifting ($\alpha$ = 0.2, 0.6, and 1.0). Producer prices of imports are also disregarded, since importes are not subject to the CIT (i.e., $t$ = 0).

As indicated by Rules 3, 9, 10, the magnitude of the price reduction resulting from any degree of CIT reduction and shifting is greater the greater the initial effective CIT rate (direct and indirect, i.e., of own and intermediate supplier industries) and the greater the

---

6. The 100 industries were grouped into 34 using final demand (sales) as weights. The resultant classification is virtually the same as Aaron's.

Table 3–6.  Own- and Other-Industry CIT Liabilities as Proportions of Final-Output Price (modified two-digit industry classification)

| Industry | CIT Liabilities as Percentage of Price | | | Ratio: Col. (2) to Col. (1) (per cent) (4) |
|---|---|---|---|---|
| | Total CIT (1) | Own Industry (2) | Other Industry (3) | |
| 1 AGRICULTURE | 2.20 | 0.20 | 2.00 | 9.65 |
| 2 METAL MINING | 3.75 | 0.97 | 2.78 | 25.93 |
| 3 COAL,STONE,AND CLAY | 5.96 | 3.62 | 2.34 | 59.31 |
| 4 OIL AND GAS | 4.51 | -0.17 a | 4.70 | -4.11 |
| 5 CONSTRUCTION | 4.31 | 1.10 | 3.21 | 25.44 |
| 6 ORDNANCE | 5.14 | 1.75 | 3.39 | 34.06 |
| 7 FOOD | 4.14 | 1.26 | 2.88 | 28.87 |
| 8 TOBACCO | 9.24 | 7.40 | 1.84 | 80.13 |
| 9 TEXTILES + APPAREL | 5.80 | 1.87 | 3.93 | 32.32 |
| 10 LUMBER + WOOD PRODUCTS | 5.05 | 3.22 | 1.83 | 64.08 |
| 11 FURNITURE + FIXTURES | 5.74 | 2.36 | 3.38 | 41.34 |
| 12 PAPER + PRODUCTS | 7.16 | 4.01 | 3.15 | 56.05 |
| 13 PRINTING + PUBLISHING | 7.61 | 4.38 | 3.23 | 57.56 |
| 14 CHEM,PLAS,DRUGS, + PAINTS | 10.54 | 7.21 | 3.33 | 68.06 |
| 15 RUBBER + LEATHER | 6.42 | 3.60 | 2.82 | 56.06 |
| 16 FOOTWEAR | 4.86 | 1.73 | 3.13 | 35.55 |
| 17 PRIMARY METAL | 4.84 | 2.16 | 2.68 | 44.11 |
| 18 FABRICATED METAL | 6.45 | 3.67 | 2.78 | 56.88 |
| 19 NONELECTRICAL MACHINERY | 6.22 | 4.40 | 1.82 | 70.80 |
| 20 ELECTRICAL EQUIPMENT | 6.87 | 5.43 | 1.45 | 79.07 |
| 21 TRANS.EQUIPMENT | 6.10 | 3.55 | 2.55 | 56.58 |
| 22 INSTRUMENTS | 8.74 | 6.77 | 1.97 | 77.39 |
| 23 MISC MANUFACTURING | 5.27 | 2.02 | 3.25 | 38.37 |
| 24 TRANS + WAREHOUSING | 3.30 | 1.51 | 1.79 | 45.65 |
| 25 COMMUNICATIONS | 11.86 | 10.63 | 1.23 | 89.63 |
| 26 UTILITIES | 9.56 | 7.21 | 2.35 | 75.52 |
| 27 FINANCE + INSURANCE | 16.30 | 14.13 | 2.17 | 86.66 |
| 28 REAL ESTATE + RENTAL | 2.19 | 0.67 | 1.52 | 30.47 |
| 29 HOTELS + SERVICES | 4.34 | 0.93 | 3.41 | 21.40 |
| 30 AUTO REPAIR + SERVICES | 3.72 | 1.12 | 2.60 | 30.06 |
| 31 AMUSEMENTS | 2.82 | 0.45 | 2.37 | 15.96 |
| 32 MEDICAL,EDUCATION, + NONPROFIT ORG | 2.23 | -0.07 a | 2.31 | -3.58 |
| 33 MISCELLANEOUS | 1.08 | 0.06 | 1.01 | 5.56 |
| 34 IMPORTS | 0.00 | 0.00 | 0.00 | 0.00 |

aSee Section A.5 for explanation.

Table 3-7. Percentage Reductions in VAT-Exclusive Producer Prices, for Alternative Degrees of CIT Reduction (S) and Shifting ($\alpha$), by Two-Digit Aggregated Industry Classification[a]

| Industry | S = 25% | | | S = 50% | | | S = 75% | | | S = 100% | | |
|---|---|---|---|---|---|---|---|---|---|---|---|---|
| | $\alpha$=.2 | $\alpha$=.4 | $\alpha$=1.0 | $\alpha$=.2 | $\alpha$=.6 | $\alpha$=1.0 | $\alpha$=.2 | $\alpha$=.6 | $\alpha$=1.0 | $\alpha$=.2 | $\alpha$=.6 | $\alpha$=1.0 |
| 1 AGRICULTURE | 0.12 | 0.44 | 0.94 | 0.23 | 0.79 | 1.51 | 0.34 | 1.08 | 1.91 | 0.44 | 1.32 | 2.20 |
| 2 METAL MINING | 0.20 | 0.73 | 1.52 | 0.40 | 1.32 | 2.51 | 0.53 | 1.83 | 3.22 | 0.75 | 2.25 | 3.75 |
| 3 COAL,STN,CLAY MNG+PROD | 0.32 | 1.14 | 2.36 | 0.62 | 2.09 | 3.94 | 0.92 | 2.89 | 5.08 | 1.19 | 3.57 | 5.96 |
| 4 OIL + GAS | 0.24 | 0.83 | 1.68 | 0.47 | 1.55 | 2.85 | 0.69 | 2.16 | 3.77 | 0.90 | 2.71 | 4.51 |
| 5 CONSTRUCTION | 0.23 | 0.83 | 1.71 | 0.45 | 1.51 | 2.85 | 0.66 | 2.09 | 3.60 | 0.90 | 2.57 | 4.31 |
| 6 ORDNANCE | 0.28 | 1.01 | 2.13 | 0.54 | 1.83 | 3.49 | 0.79 | 2.51 | 4.44 | 1.03 | 3.08 | 5.14 |
| 7 FOOD | 0.22 | 0.82 | 1.75 | 0.44 | 1.48 | 2.83 | 0.64 | 2.02 | 3.53 | 0.83 | 2.48 | 4.14 |
| 8 TOBACCO | 0.51 | 1.86 | 4.11 | 0.95 | 3.36 | 6.52 | 1.43 | 4.56 | 6.11 | 1.85 | 5.55 | 9.24 |
| 9 TEXTILES + APPAREL | 0.32 | 1.14 | 2.40 | 0.61 | 2.07 | 3.94 | 0.90 | 2.84 | 5.01 | 1.16 | 3.48 | 5.80 |
| 10 LUMBER,WOOD PRODUCTS | 0.27 | 0.95 | 1.86 | 0.53 | 1.73 | 3.20 | 0.77 | 2.42 | 4.23 | 1.01 | 3.05 | 5.05 |
| 11 FURNITURE + FIXTURES | 0.31 | 1.12 | 2.34 | 0.61 | 2.03 | 3.87 | 0.88 | 2.80 | 4.94 | 1.15 | 3.45 | 5.74 |
| 12 PAPER + PRODUCTS | 0.37 | 1.39 | 2.88 | 0.76 | 2.53 | 4.78 | 1.10 | 3.49 | 6.14 | 1.43 | 4.29 | 7.16 |
| 13 PRINTING + PUBLISHING | 0.31 | 1.50 | 3.18 | 0.80 | 2.72 | 5.19 | 1.17 | 3.76 | 6.59 | 1.52 | 4.57 | 7.61 |
| 14 CHEM.,PLAST.,DRUGS+PNT | 0.58 | 2.10 | 4.49 | 1.12 | 3.78 | 7.27 | 1.62 | 5.17 | 9.17 | 2.11 | 6.33 | 10.54 |
| 15 RUBBER + LEATHER | 0.35 | 1.27 | 2.69 | 0.68 | 2.30 | 4.39 | 0.99 | 3.14 | 5.56 | 1.29 | 3.85 | 6.42 |
| 16 FOOTWEAR | 0.26 | 0.95 | 2.00 | 0.51 | 1.73 | 3.29 | 0.75 | 2.37 | 4.19 | 0.97 | 2.92 | 4.86 |
| 17 PRIMARY METAL | 0.26 | 0.93 | 1.92 | 0.51 | 1.70 | 3.20 | 0.74 | 2.34 | 4.15 | 0.97 | 2.90 | 4.34 |
| 18 FABRICATED METAL | 0.35 | 1.27 | 2.67 | 0.68 | 2.29 | 4.37 | 1.00 | 3.15 | 5.57 | 1.31 | 3.97 | 6.45 |
| 19 NONELECT. MACHINERY | 0.34 | 1.23 | 2.60 | 0.66 | 2.22 | 4.24 | 0.96 | 3.04 | 5.87 | 1.24 | 3.73 | **6.23** |
| 20 ELECTRICAL EQUIPMENT | 0.38 | 1.36 | 2.93 | 0.73 | 2.46 | 4.71 | 1.06 | 3.36 | 5.96 | 1.37 | 4.12 | 6.07 |
| 21 TRANSP. EQUIPMENT | 0.33 | 1.20 | 2.54 | 0.65 | 2.18 | 4.15 | 0.94 | 2.99 | 5.27 | 1.22 | 3.66 | 6.10 |
| 22 INSTRUMENTS | 0.47 | 1.73 | 3.68 | 0.93 | 3.13 | 5.99 | 1.35 | 4.29 | 7.75 | 1.75 | 5.24 | 8.74 |
| 23 MISC. MANUFACTURING | 0.29 | 1.03 | 2.16 | 0.56 | 1.87 | 3.55 | 0.81 | 2.57 | 4.54 | 1.05 | 3.16 | 5.27 |
| 24 TRANSP. + WAREHOUSING | 0.18 | 0.71 | 1.74 | 0.35 | 1.24 | 2.49 | 0.51 | 1.65 | 2.96 | 0.66 | 1.98 | 3.30 |
| 25 COMMUNICATIONS | 0.64 | 2.34 | 4.96 | 1.25 | 4.24 | 8.00 | 1.83 | 5.80 | 10.27 | 2.37 | 7.12 | 11.06 |
| 26 UTILITIES | 0.51 | 1.83 | 3.73 | 1.00 | 3.35 | 6.28 | 1.47 | 4.53 | 9.14 | 1.91 | 5.74 | 9.56 |
| 27 FINANCE + INSURANCE | 0.89 | 3.32 | 7.26 | 1.73 | 5.93 | 11.52 | 2.52 | 8.04 | 14.32 | 3.26 | 9.78 | 16.30 |
| 28 REAL ESTATE + RENTAL | 0.12 | 0.43 | 0.91 | 0.23 | 0.78 | 1.49 | 0.34 | 1.07 | 1.89 | 0.44 | 1.31 | 2.19 |
| 29 HOTELS + SERVICES | 0.24 | 0.85 | 1.78 | 0.46 | 1.54 | 2.93 | 0.67 | 2.12 | 3.74 | 0.87 | 2.61 | 4.34 |
| 30 AUTO REPAIR + SERVICES | 0.20 | 0.73 | 1.54 | 0.39 | 1.33 | 2.53 | 0.57 | 1.82 | 3.21 | 0.74 | 2.23 | 3.72 |
| 31 AMUSEMENTS | 0.16 | 0.59 | 1.44 | 0.30 | 1.04 | 2.06 | 0.44 | 1.40 | 2.50 | 0.56 | 1.69 | 2.82 |
| 32 MED.+ED.SERV.+NONPROF. | 0.12 | 0.44 | 0.93 | 0.23 | 0.79 | 1.22 | 0.34 | 1.09 | 1.92 | 0.45 | 1.34 | 2.23 |
| 33 MISCELLANEOUS | 0.06 | 0.21 | 0.45 | 0.11 | 0.39 | 0.73 | 0.17 | 0.53 | 0.95 | 0.22 | 0.65 | 1.03 |
| 34 IMPORTS | 0.00 | 0.00 | 0.00 | 0.00 | 0.00 | 0.00 | 0.00 | 0.00 | 0.00 | 0.00 | 0.00 | 0.00 |

Note: Reductions in prices are for all components of final demand in VAT-exclusive producer prices; if $\alpha$ = 0, there are no price changes.

[a]Industries correspond closely to the SIC two-digit classification and to that employed by Aaron.

initial level of gross-of-tax profits (also direct and indirect). Thus, in comparing industries the relative price reduction will be greater the larger the total initial CIT component of output price (first column of Table 3–6), regardless of the degree of CIT reduction and (positive) shifting.

In general, the dominant *own-industry* CIT coefficient will depend upon gross-of-tax profit as a proportion of value added in the industry, which will in turn depend upon:

1. The capital intensity of the industry and the rate of capital turnover (or equivalently, the capital-output ratio);
2. The rate of return to capital in the industry;
3. The extent of incorporation in the industry, as measured, e.g., by the corporate proportion of industry sales or of industry value added (gross product originating); and
4. The CIT rate (affected by the special corporate tax treatment given to some industries, e.g., oil depletion allowances).

These characteristics of supplier industries similarly serve to determine the "other-industry" component of the total CIT coefficient.

The largest price reductions are observed, then, in those industries which are most highly incorporated and capital-intensive. Assuming CIT repeal and complete forward CIT shifting, the largest price reductions are found in communications (11.9 percent), chemicals (10.5 percent), utilities (9.6 percent), and tobacco processing (9.2 percent), all noted for both extreme incorporation and relatively large profit shares of value added (capital intensity).[7] Correspondinly, the smallest price reductions occur in unincorporated, relatively labor-intensive industries: real estate and rental (2.2 percent), agriculture (2.2 percent), medical, educational, and related services (2.2 percent), and amusements (2.8 percent). The real estate industry may in addition be subject to preferential CIT treatment (depreciation, capital gains, etc.); the small price effect may then represent an artifically low effective CIT rate, even considering the degree of incorporation.

As has been explained, if the CIT is repealed, the percentage price reduction in any industry is simply proportionate to the CIT shifting parameter (Rule 1). A fivefold increase in shifting (from $\alpha = 0.2$ to $\alpha = 1$) then implies a fivefold increase in the percentage price reduction. For example, agricultural prices decline by 0.44

---

7. The largest reduction, 16.3 percent in finance and insurance, is primarily due to the definition of gross product originating; see Appendix A.

percent if the CIT is shifted only 20 percent ($\alpha$ = 0.2), but by 2.2 percent if the CIT is fully shifted. Communications prices, on the other hand, decline by 2.37 percent under 20 percent shifting but by 11.86 percent in the case of full CIT shifting.

If the CIT is not completely repealed, however, the change in price is more than proportionate to the change in CIT shifting (Rule 2). For example, with a 50 percent reduction in CIT rates a change in $\alpha$ (the CIT shifting parameter) from 0.2 to 1 (a 400 percent increase in the degree of CIT shifting) results in a 557 percent increase in the magnitude of the agricultural price reduction; in communications, the figure is 548 percent. The *absolute* price reduction is, of course, greater in communications than in agriculture (6.85 percentage points vs. 1.28 points), since the effective CIT rate is higher and the profit share of value added is larger in the former industry than in the latter (see Rules 3 and 10).

Similarly, the effect of an increase in the degree of CIT shifting is observed to be greater the greater the reduction in effective CIT rates (Rule 4). Communications again provides a case in point: The absolute increase in the magnitude of price reduction resulting from an increase in the degree of CIT shifting from 0.2 to 1 is 6.85 percentage points if effective CIT rates are halved ($S$ = 50 percent), but 9.49 percentage points if the CIT is completely repealed.

That price reductions are greater the greater the degree of CIT reduction (Rule 6) should be obvious. Thus, assuming full shifting of the CIT, a 50 percent reduction in CIT rates results in a price reduction of 1.5 percent in agriculture, while CIT repeal reduces prices in this industry by 2.2 percent. In communications, under similar assumptions, the respective reductions are 8.1 percent and 11.9 percent. Note, however, that the increased degree of price reduction is less than proportionate to the percentage increase in the CIT reduction (Rule 7): in both agriculture and communications, doubling the CIT reduction (from 50 percent to complete repeal) increases the price reduction only by about 46 percent.

That an increase in $S$ reduces prices more when shifting is great (Rule 8) is apparent in the communications industry: with a shifting parameter of 0.2, prices decline by 1.25 percent when CIT rates are reduced by 50 percent; if the CIT is repealed, prices decline by 2.37 percent. The percentage point increment due to the increase in $S$ is thus about 1.12 percent. However, with full CIT shifting, this increment increases to 3.8 percentage points (price reduction rises from 8.1 percent to 11.9 percent as a result of the increase in $S$). In agriculture, similarly, this percentage point increment due to a move from 50 percent CIT reduction to repeal is less than 0.2 percent if the shifting parameter is 0.2 (price reductions of 0.23 percent versus 0.44 percent) but 0.7 percent (price reductions of 1.5 percent versus 2.2 percent) if the CIT is fully shifted. The smaller magnitude of the price reduction in agriculture than in communications reflects the less important role of corporate profits and the lower effective (direct and indirect) CIT rate in the agricultural sector.

Producer price reductions by input-output sector (104 industries), under the alternative CIT reduction and shifting assumptions, are given in Table 3–8. A comparison of the price changes by input-output sector and by two-digit industry indicates that very little information is lost by restricting discussion to the higher level of aggregation. Of course, variations in producer price reductions (assuming, e.g., full CIT reduction and shifting) are observed within a two-digit classification. For example, the average price reduction of 6.2 percent in the nonelectrical machinery industry is the result of ten individual industry price reductions ranging from 5.9 percent (special industrial machinery) to 8 percent (machine shop products). Similarly, price reductions in foods range from 3.1 percent (meat products) to 5.2 percent (beverages), with a weighted average of 4.1 percent. However, the two-digit aggregation in general more than compensates in comprehensibility for its loss of detail. Nevertheless, variation within two-digit classifications is certainly significant in particular cases.

Although the producer prices discussed above exclude trade and transportation margins, these are relatively minor components of final purchase prices facing government, investment, and export purchasers. Thus, producer price reductions provide close approximations of purchaser price reductions for those components of final demand which are not subject to a net VAT liability. Of course, the two-digit indices would differ somewhat for each of the three final demand components due to differences in the weights applied to the individual industries.

Consumption, however, must be treated separately. First, markups (trade and transportation margins) are a much more important component of final sale price. More importantly, these purchases alone are subject to a full VAT liability, not offset by rebates or credits. Thus, on both counts, final VAT-inclusive consumption prices will necessarily diverge from VAT-exclusive producer prices.

Percentage consumer price *increases* (VAT-inclusive), under alternative CIT reduction and shifting assumptions, are displayed by

## Table 3-8. Percentage Reductions in VAT-Exclusive Producer-Prices, for Alternative Degrees of CIT Reduction (S) and Shifting (α), by Industry

| Industry | S = 25% α=.2 | S = 25% α=.6 | S = 25% α=1.0 | S = 50% α=.2 | S = 50% α=.6 | S = 50% α=1.0 | S = 75% α=.2 | S = 75% α=.6 | S = 75% α=1.0 | S = 100% α=.2 | S = 100% α=.6 | S = 100% α=1.0 |
|---|---|---|---|---|---|---|---|---|---|---|---|---|
| 1 LIVESTOCK | 0.14 | 0.53 | 1.13 | 0.28 | 0.95 | 1.32 | 0.41 | 1.30 | 2.30 | 0.53 | 1.60 | 2.66 |
| 2 OTHER AGRICLTURE | 0.11 | 0.40 | 0.86 | 0.21 | 0.73 | 1.39 | 0.31 | 0.99 | 1.76 | 0.41 | 1.22 | 2.03 |
| 3 FOREST + FISHERY | 0.13 | 0.47 | 1.03 | 0.25 | 0.85 | 1.64 | 0.36 | 1.16 | 2.05 | 0.47 | 1.41 | 2.35 |
| 4 AG ETC SERVICE | 0.16 | 0.58 | 1.25 | 0.30 | 1.03 | 2.00 | 0.44 | 1.40 | 2.50 | 0.57 | 1.71 | 2.86 |
| 5 IRON MINING | 0.21 | 0.75 | 1.58 | 0.41 | 1.37 | 2.60 | 0.60 | 1.89 | 3.33 | 0.78 | 2.33 | 3.88 |
| 6 NONFERROUS MINING | 0.19 | 0.70 | 1.45 | 0.38 | 1.27 | 2.40 | 0.55 | 1.75 | 3.08 | 0.78 | 2.16 | 3.60 |
| 7 COAL MINING | 0.23 | 0.79 | 1.59 | 0.44 | 1.46 | 2.71 | 0.65 | 2.04 | 3.56 | 0.85 | 2.54 | 4.23 |
| 8 CRUDE PETROLEUM-GAS | 0.35 | 1.19 | 2.32 | 0.69 | 2.22 | 4.05 | 1.01 | 3.14 | 5.45 | 1.32 | 3.97 | 6.62 |
| 9 STONE-CLAY MINING | 0.23 | 0.81 | 1.63 | 0.46 | 1.51 | 2.79 | 0.67 | 2.11 | 3.68 | 0.88 | 2.64 | 4.39 |
| 10 CHEMICAL ETC MINERALS | 0.24 | 0.85 | 1.72 | 0.47 | 1.56 | 2.90 | 0.69 | 2.18 | 3.81 | 0.90 | 2.71 | 4.52 |
| 11 RESIDENTIAL BUILDING | 0.24 | 0.85 | 1.76 | 0.46 | 1.55 | 2.92 | 0.68 | 2.14 | 3.77 | 0.88 | 2.64 | 4.41 |
| 12 PRIVATE INDUST BUILD | 0.23 | 0.84 | 1.74 | 0.45 | 1.52 | 2.88 | 0.66 | 2.10 | 3.70 | 0.86 | 2.59 | 4.32 |
| 13 OTHER PRI NON-RES BUILD | 0.24 | 0.87 | 1.80 | 0.47 | 1.58 | 2.99 | 0.69 | 2.18 | 3.85 | 0.90 | 2.70 | 4.50 |
| 14 OTHER PRIVATE CONST | 0.21 | 0.74 | 1.54 | 0.40 | 1.35 | 2.55 | 0.59 | 1.87 | 3.29 | 0.77 | 2.31 | 3.85 |
| 15 PUBLIC NON-RES BUILDINGS | 0.26 | 0.91 | 1.87 | 0.50 | 1.66 | 3.12 | 0.73 | 2.30 | 4.04 | 0.95 | 2.84 | 4.74 |
| 16 HIGHWAYS | 0.22 | 0.78 | 1.60 | 0.43 | 1.43 | 2.68 | 0.63 | 1.99 | 3.48 | 0.82 | 2.46 | 4.11 |
| 17 OTHER PUBLIC CONST | 0.23 | 0.80 | 1.64 | 0.44 | 1.46 | 2.74 | 0.64 | 2.03 | 3.56 | 0.84 | 2.51 | 4.18 |
| 18 MAINT-REPAIR CONST | 0.21 | 0.74 | 1.52 | 0.41 | 1.36 | 2.54 | 0.60 | 1.88 | 3.30 | 0.78 | 2.33 | 3.88 |
| 19 ORDNANCE AND ACCESS | 0.28 | 1.01 | 2.13 | 0.54 | 1.83 | 3.49 | 0.79 | 2.51 | 4.44 | 1.03 | 3.08 | 5.14 |
| 20 MEAT PRODUCTS | 0.17 | 0.62 | 1.33 | 0.33 | 1.12 | 2.15 | 0.48 | 1.54 | 2.72 | 0.63 | 1.88 | 3.14 |
| 21 DAIRY PRODUCTS | 0.22 | 0.81 | 1.73 | 0.43 | 1.47 | 2.81 | 0.63 | 2.01 | 3.55 | 0.82 | 2.46 | 4.10 |
| 22 CANNING AND PRESERVING NON-MEATS | 0.24 | 0.88 | 1.89 | 0.47 | 1.60 | 3.06 | 0.69 | 2.18 | 3.86 | 0.89 | 2.67 | 4.46 |
| 23 GRAIN MILL PROD | 0.24 | 0.87 | 1.86 | 0.46 | 1.56 | 3.00 | 0.67 | 2.13 | 3.78 | 0.87 | 2.61 | 4.36 |
| 24 BAKERY PRODUCTS | 0.27 | 1.00 | 2.13 | 0.53 | 1.81 | 3.46 | 0.78 | 2.47 | 4.38 | 1.01 | 3.03 | 5.05 |
| 25 SUGAR | 0.18 | 0.65 | 1.39 | 0.35 | 1.17 | 2.24 | 0.50 | 1.60 | 2.84 | 0.65 | 1.96 | 3.27 |

**Table 3-8 continued**

| Industry | 1 | 2 | 3 | 4 | 5 | 6 | 7 | 8 | 9 | 10 | 11 | 12 |
|---|---|---|---|---|---|---|---|---|---|---|---|---|
| 26 CONFECTIONARY PROD | 0.24 | 0.86 | 1.83 | 0.46 | 1.55 | 2.97 | 0.67 | 2.12 | 3.76 | 0.87 | 2.63 | 4.34 |
| 27 BEVERAGE INDUSTRIES | 0.28 | 1.03 | 2.18 | 0.55 | 1.86 | 3.55 | 0.80 | 2.54 | 4.50 | 1.02 | 3.12 | 5.29 |
| 28 MISC FOODS | 0.23 | 0.84 | 1.78 | 0.45 | 1.51 | 2.89 | 0.65 | 2.07 | 3.66 | 0.85 | 2.54 | 4.23 |
| 29 TOBACCO MANUFACTURE | 0.51 | 1.88 | 4.11 | 0.98 | 3.36 | 6.52 | 1.43 | 4.56 | 8.11 | 1.85 | 5.55 | 9.24 |
| 30 FABRICS,YARN,THREAD MILLS | 0.35 | 1.26 | 2.69 | 0.67 | 2.28 | 4.37 | 0.98 | 3.11 | 5.53 | 1.28 | 3.83 | 6.38 |
| 31 MISC TEXTILE-FLOOR COVERINGS | 0.35 | 1.26 | 2.68 | 0.67 | 2.27 | 4.35 | 0.98 | 3.11 | 5.52 | 1.27 | 3.81 | 6.34 |
| 32 APPAREL | 0.31 | 1.12 | 2.35 | 0.60 | 2.03 | 3.86 | 0.88 | 2.78 | 4.91 | 1.14 | 3.41 | 5.69 |
| 33 MISC FABRICATED TEXTILES | 0.31 | 1.17 | 2.47 | 0.62 | 2.12 | 4.04 | 0.92 | 2.91 | 5.14 | 1.19 | 3.58 | 5.96 |
| 34 LUMBER-WOOD PROD,EXC CONTAINER | 0.27 | 0.92 | 1.84 | 0.52 | 1.71 | 3.16 | 0.76 | 2.39 | 4.18 | 1.00 | 2.99 | 4.99 |
| 35 WOODEN CONTAINERS | 0.30 | 1.04 | 2.06 | 0.59 | 1.93 | 3.55 | 0.86 | 2.70 | 4.70 | 1.13 | 3.38 | 5.63 |
| 36 HOUSEHOLD FURNITURE | 0.29 | 1.16 | 2.42 | 0.57 | 2.10 | 3.99 | 0.91 | 2.89 | 5.10 | 1.19 | 3.56 | 5.93 |
| 37 OTHER FURNITURE-FIXTURES | 0.29 | 1.05 | 2.20 | 0.57 | 1.91 | 3.63 | 0.83 | 2.63 | 4.64 | 1.08 | 3.24 | 5.39 |
| 38 PAPER-ALLIED PROD,EXC CONTAINER | 0.38 | 1.38 | 2.86 | 0.75 | 2.51 | 4.74 | 1.09 | 3.46 | 6.09 | 1.42 | 4.26 | 7.10 |
| 39 PAPERBOARD CONTAINERS | 0.32 | 1.50 | 3.12 | 0.82 | 2.74 | 5.18 | 1.19 | 3.70 | 6.65 | 1.55 | 4.66 | 7.77 |
| 40 PRINTING-PUBLISHING | 0.32 | 1.50 | 3.18 | 0.80 | 2.72 | 5.19 | 1.18 | 3.72 | 6.59 | 1.52 | 4.57 | 7.61 |
| 41 CHEMICALS-SEL PROD | 0.61 | 2.22 | 4.75 | 1.18 | 4.00 | 7.69 | 1.72 | 5.46 | 9.09 | 2.23 | 6.69 | 11.14 |
| 42 PLASTICS AND SYNTHETIC MAT | 0.63 | 2.31 | 4.94 | 1.23 | 4.16 | 7.99 | 1.79 | 5.68 | 10.07 | 2.32 | 6.95 | 11.55 |
| 44 DRUGS-CLEANING-TOILET PREP | 0.56 | 2.03 | 4.34 | 1.08 | 3.66 | 7.03 | 1.57 | 5.00 | 10.09 | 2.04 | 6.12 | 10.29 |
| 45 PAINTS AND ALLIED PROD | 0.61 | 2.21 | 4.73 | 1.18 | 3.99 | 7.86 | 1.71 | 5.45 | 9.66 | 2.22 | 6.09 | 10.20 |
| 46 PETROLEUM REFINING, ETC | 0.24 | 0.83 | 1.68 | 0.47 | 1.55 | 2.86 | 0.69 | 2.16 | 3.77 | 0.90 | 2.71 | 4.91 |
| 47 RUBBER AND MISC PLASTIC PROD | 0.35 | 1.27 | 2.69 | 0.68 | 2.30 | 4.39 | 0.99 | 3.14 | 5.26 | 1.28 | 3.85 | 6.42 |
| 48 LEATHER TANNING-INDUST LEATHER | 0.26 | 1.28 | 2.72 | 0.69 | 2.32 | 4.43 | 1.00 | 3.18 | 5.62 | 1.30 | 3.90 | 6.49 |
| 49 FOOTWEAR AND OTHER LEATHER PROD | 0.37 | 0.95 | 2.00 | 0.51 | 1.73 | 3.29 | 0.75 | 2.37 | 4.19 | 0.97 | 2.92 | 6.85 |
| 50 GLASS AND GLASS PRODUCTS | 0.37 | 1.33 | 2.75 | 0.72 | 2.42 | 4.57 | 1.05 | 3.33 | 5.89 | 1.37 | 4.10 | 6.07 |
| 51 STONE AND CLAY PRODUCTS | 0.21 | 0.95 | 1.94 | 0.52 | 1.73 | 3.25 | 1.06 | 3.34 | 4.21 | 1.37 | 4.21 | 4.74 |
| 52 PRIMARY IRON-STEEL MAN | 0.29 | 0.76 | 1.58 | 0.42 | 1.39 | 2.63 | 0.61 | 1.92 | 3.38 | 0.79 | 2.37 | 5.96 |
| 53 COPPER MANUFACTURE | 0.24 | 1.04 | 2.16 | 0.57 | 1.60 | 3.60 | 0.76 | 2.63 | 4.63 | 1.08 | 3.25 | 5.42 |
| 54 ALUMINUM MANUFACT | 0.36 | 0.88 | 1.82 | 0.48 | 1.60 | 3.02 | 0.83 | 2.20 | 3.78 | 0.91 | 2.72 | 4.23 |
| 55 OTHER NONFERROUS MANUFACT | 0.36 | 1.31 | 2.76 | 0.71 | 2.34 | 4.53 | 0.70 | 2.27 | 3.78 | 1.34 | 4.02 | 6.71 |
| 56 METAL CONTAINERS | 0.35 | 1.29 | 2.72 | 0.70 | 2.34 | 4.46 | 1.03 | 3.22 | 4.63 | 1.32 | 3.96 | 6.59 |
| 57 HEATING-PLUMBING-STRUCT METAL PROD | 0.34 | 1.28 | 2.69 | 0.69 | 2.31 | 4.41 | 1.02 | 3.17 | 5.69 | 1.30 | 3.90 | 6.50 |
| 58 STAMPING,SCREWMACHINE PROD,BOLTS | 0.35 | 1.23 | 2.59 | 0.66 | 2.23 | 4.25 | 1.00 | 3.06 | 5.61 | 1.25 | 3.76 | 6.27 |
| 59 OTHER FABRICATED METAL PRODUCTS | 0.33 | 1.26 | 2.67 | 0.67 | 2.28 | 4.35 | 0.97 | 3.12 | 5.41 | 1.28 | 3.83 | 6.38 |
| 60 ENGINES AND TURBINES | 0.35 | 1.20 | 2.59 | 0.64 | 2.23 | 4.25 | 0.98 | 3.06 | 5.52 | 1.28 | 3.66 | 6.10 |
| 61 FARM MACHINERY-EQUIPMENT | 0.34 | 1.26 | 2.67 | 0.68 | 2.28 | 4.15 | 0.98 | 2.98 | 5.57 | 1.29 | 3.87 | 6.45 |
| 62 CONSTRUCTION-MINING-OIL FIELD MACH | 0.34 | 1.27 | 2.69 | 0.68 | 2.30 | 4.39 | 0.99 | 3.15 | 5.39 | 1.25 | 3.74 | 6.24 |
| 63 MATERIALS HANDLING EQUIPMENT | 0.32 | 1.23 | 2.60 | 0.66 | 2.22 | 4.24 | 0.96 | 3.05 | 5.33 | 1.24 | 3.73 | 6.22 |
| 64 METALWORKING MACHINERY | 0.34 | 1.16 | 2.45 | 0.62 | 2.10 | 4.00 | 0.91 | 2.87 | 5.08 | 1.18 | 3.53 | 5.86 |
| 65 SPECIAL INDUSTRY MACHINERY | 0.32 | 1.28 | 2.70 | 0.68 | 2.30 | 4.41 | 1.00 | 3.16 | 5.08 | 1.29 | 3.88 | 6.47 |
| 66 GENERAL INDUSTRIAL MACHINERY | 0.43 | 1.57 | 3.32 | 0.84 | 2.84 | 5.42 | 1.23 | 3.89 | 5.59 | 1.59 | 4.77 | 6.45 |
| 67 MACHINE SHOP PRODUCTS | 0.57 | 1.20 | 2.54 | 0.64 | 2.17 | 4.14 | 0.93 | 2.96 | 5.38 | 1.21 | 3.63 | 7.95 |
| 68 OFFICE,COMPUTING,ACCOUNTING MACH | 0.53 | 1.20 | 2.54 | 0.64 | 2.17 | 4.14 | 0.93 | 2.96 | 5.24 | 1.21 | 3.63 | 6.06 |

**Table 3-8 continued**

| | | | | | | | | | | | | |
|---|---|---|---|---|---|---|---|---|---|---|---|---|
| 68 SERVICE INDUST MACHINES | 0.35 | 1.26 | 2.66 | 0.67 | 2.28 | 4.35 | 0.98 | 3.12 | 5.52 | 1.28 | 3.83 | 6.39 |
| 69 ELECTRICAL EQUIP | 0.35 | 1.29 | 2.74 | 0.69 | 2.33 | 4.46 | 1.00 | 3.19 | 5.65 | 1.30 | 3.91 | 6.52 |
| 70 HOUSEHOLD APPLIANCES | 0.37 | 1.35 | 2.87 | 0.72 | 2.45 | 4.68 | 1.06 | 3.35 | 5.93 | 1.37 | 4.11 | 6.86 |
| 71 ELECTRIC LIGHTING-WIRING EQUIP | 0.39 | 1.41 | 2.99 | 0.75 | 2.54 | 4.87 | 1.10 | 3.48 | 6.16 | 1.42 | 4.26 | 7.11 |
| 72 RADIO,TV,COMMUNICATION EQUIPMENT | 0.39 | 1.41 | 3.00 | 0.75 | 2.54 | 4.87 | 1.09 | 3.47 | 6.16 | 1.42 | 4.26 | 7.09 |
| 73 ELECTRIC COMPONENTS AND ACCESS | 0.39 | 1.41 | 3.01 | 0.75 | 2.55 | 4.89 | 1.10 | 3.49 | 6.18 | 1.42 | 4.27 | 7.12 |
| 74 MISC ELECTRICAL MACHINERY | 0.31 | 1.12 | 2.37 | 0.60 | 2.02 | 3.86 | 0.87 | 2.76 | 4.88 | 1.13 | 3.38 | 5.63 |
| 75 MOTOR VEHICLES-EQUIPMENT | 0.37 | 1.34 | 2.84 | 0.72 | 2.43 | 4.63 | 1.05 | 3.33 | 5.88 | 1.36 | 4.08 | 6.80 |
| 76 AIRCRAFT AND PARTS | 0.27 | 0.98 | 2.07 | 0.53 | 1.78 | 3.39 | 0.77 | 2.44 | 4.31 | 1.00 | 3.00 | 5.00 |
| 77 OTHER TRANSPORT EQUIPMENT | 0.27 | 0.96 | 2.01 | 0.52 | 1.74 | 3.31 | 0.75 | 2.39 | 4.22 | 0.98 | 2.94 | 4.89 |
| 78 SCIENTIFIC-CONTROL INSTRUMENTS | 0.46 | 1.68 | 3.58 | 0.90 | 3.04 | 5.82 | 1.31 | 4.16 | 7.37 | 1.70 | 5.10 | 8.50 |
| 79 OPTICAL,OPHTHALMI,-PHOTO EQUIP | 0.50 | 1.83 | 3.90 | 0.98 | 3.31 | 6.34 | 1.42 | 4.53 | 8.02 | 1.85 | 5.54 | 9.24 |
| 80 MISC MANUFACTURING | 0.29 | 1.03 | 2.16 | 0.56 | 1.87 | 3.55 | 0.81 | 2.57 | 4.54 | 1.05 | 3.16 | 5.27 |
| 81 TRANSPORTATION-WAREHOUSING | 0.18 | 0.71 | 1.74 | 0.35 | 1.24 | 2.49 | 0.51 | 1.65 | 2.96 | 0.66 | 1.98 | 3.30 |
| 82 COMMUNICATIONS,EXC RADIO-TV | 0.64 | 2.34 | 4.96 | 1.25 | 4.24 | 8.10 | 1.83 | 5.80 | 10.27 | 2.37 | 7.12 | 11.86 |
| 83 RADIO-TV BROADCASTING | 0.42 | 1.54 | 3.35 | 0.81 | 2.77 | 5.34 | 1.18 | 3.77 | 6.69 | 1.53 | 4.60 | 7.67 |
| 84 ELECTRIC UTILITIES | 0.52 | 1.84 | 3.78 | 1.01 | 3.37 | 6.34 | 1.47 | 4.65 | 8.19 | 1.92 | 5.76 | 9.59 |
| 85 GAS UTILITIES | 0.52 | 1.85 | 3.74 | 1.02 | 3.39 | 6.34 | 1.50 | 4.72 | 8.27 | 1.95 | 5.86 | 9.77 |
| 86 WATER AND SANITARY SERVICES | 0.48 | 1.72 | 3.53 | 0.94 | 3.14 | 5.91 | 1.38 | 4.34 | 7.64 | 1.79 | 5.37 | 8.95 |
| 87 WHOLESALE-RETAIL TRADE | 0.23 | 0.82 | 1.66 | 0.45 | 1.50 | 2.80 | 0.66 | 2.08 | 3.65 | 0.86 | 2.58 | 4.30 |
| 88 FINANCE AND INSURANCE | 0.89 | 3.32 | 7.26 | 1.73 | 5.93 | 11.52 | 2.52 | 8.04 | 14.32 | 3.26 | 9.78 | 16.30 |
| 89 REAL ESTATE AND RENTAL | 0.12 | 0.43 | 0.91 | 0.23 | 0.78 | 1.49 | 0.34 | 1.07 | 1.89 | 0.44 | 1.31 | 2.19 |
| 90 HOTELS,PERSONAL-REPAIR SERVICES | 0.23 | 0.83 | 1.74 | 0.45 | 1.51 | 2.86 | 0.66 | 2.08 | 3.66 | 0.85 | 2.56 | 4.26 |
| 91 BUSINESS SERVICES | 0.25 | 0.90 | 1.91 | 0.48 | 1.64 | 3.12 | 0.71 | 2.24 | 3.96 | 0.92 | 2.75 | 4.59 |
| 92 RESEARCH AND DEVELOPMENT | 0.20 | 0.72 | 1.49 | 0.39 | 1.31 | 2.48 | 0.57 | 1.80 | 3.18 | 0.74 | 2.22 | 3.71 |
| 93 AUTO REPAIR SERVICES | 0.20 | 0.73 | 1.54 | 0.39 | 1.33 | 2.53 | 0.57 | 1.82 | 3.21 | 0.74 | 2.23 | 3.72 |
| 94 AMUSEMENTS | 0.16 | 0.59 | 1.44 | 0.30 | 1.04 | 2.06 | 0.44 | 1.40 | 2.50 | 0.56 | 1.69 | 2.82 |
| 95 MEDICAL,EDUCATIONAL,NONPROFIT ORG | 0.12 | 0.44 | 0.93 | 0.23 | 0.79 | 1.52 | 0.34 | 1.09 | 1.92 | 0.45 | 1.34 | 2.23 |
| 96 FEDERAL GOV'T ENTERPRISES | 0.07 | 0.25 | 0.54 | 0.13 | 0.44 | 0.85 | 0.19 | 0.60 | 1.07 | 0.24 | 0.73 | 1.22 |
| 97 ST & LO GOV'T ENTERPRISES | 0.11 | 0.38 | 0.79 | 0.21 | 0.70 | 1.31 | 0.30 | 0.96 | 1.69 | 0.40 | 1.19 | 1.98 |
| 98 GROSS IMPORTS | 0.00 | 0.00 | 0.00 | 0.00 | 0.00 | 0.00 | 0.00 | 0.00 | 0.00 | 0.00 | 0.00 | 0.00 |
| 99 BUSI TRAVEL, ENTERTAI'T & GIFTS | 0.15 | 0.57 | 1.26 | 0.30 | 1.02 | 1.97 | 0.43 | 1.38 | 2.46 | 0.56 | 1.69 | 2.81 |
| 100 OFFICE SUPPLIES | 0.40 | 1.46 | 3.08 | 0.78 | 2.65 | 5.04 | 1.15 | 3.63 | 6.42 | 1.49 | 4.46 | 7.44 |
| 104 HOUSEHOLD INDUSTRY | 0.00 | 0.00 | 0.00 | 0.00 | 0.00 | 0.00 | 0.00 | 0.00 | 0.00 | 0.00 | 0.00 | 0.00 |

Note: Reductions in prices are for all components of final demand in VAT-exclusive producer prices; if $\alpha = 0$, there are no price changes.

two-digit industry in Table 3-9 and by disaggregated input-output sector in Table 3-10. With zero CIT shifting, of course, VAT-*exclusive* consumption prices are unaffected by the tax substitution, and VAT-*inclusive* prices rise across the board by the VAT *rate* (1.9, 3.8, 5.8, and 7.7 percent with 25, 50, 75, and 100 percent CIT removal, respectively; see Table 3-1). VAT-exclusive consumption prices respond to forward CIT shifting in the same manner as the producer prices previously discussed. In all cases it is assumed that the VAT is fully shifted forward, and VAT-inclusive prices are simply VAT-exclusive prices previously discussed multiplied by 1 plus the VAT rate.

Overall, consumption prices must rise as a result of the tax substitution. However, although these prices rise on average, individual prices may rise by more or less than the average, depending on the pre-tax substitution CIT liability incorporated in final consumption prices. In some cases VAT-inclusive prices actually fall if the CIT is shifted, e.g., tobacco, chemicals and communications. All variation around the average is necessarily explained by the shifted CIT reduction. Those indust· ies in which CIT liabilities, relative to sales, are greatest exhibit the smallest price increases (greatest price reductions) when the VAT replaces the CIT and the reduction in the latter is shifted forward to the benefit of purchasers.

With full CIT shifting (regardless of the degree of CIT reduction), five two-digit industries exhibit price *reductions*: tobacco (a VAT-inclusive consumer price change of –0.9 percent when the CIT is fully removed), chemicals (–1 percent), utilities (–3 percent), communications (–6 percent), and finance and insurance (–10.3 percent). With CIT shifting of 0.6 only two industries exhibit such price reductions: communications (–0.2 percent with full CIT reduction) and finance and insurance (–3.1 percent). With CIT shifting of only 0.2, there are no price reductions, and this is also true for the 100-industry classifications.

Similarly, the *largest* consumer price increases are observed in those industries which benefit *least* from the CIT reduction. With full CIT shifting and CIT removal ($S$ = 100 percent and $\alpha$ = 1), the required VAT rate is 7.2 percent, while the aggregate VAT-inclusive consumer price index (Table 3-5) rises by 1.7 percent (less than the VAT rate due to the CIT-shifting-induced decline in VAT-exclusive producer prices). However, in the five industries exhibiting the biggest price increases (Table 3-9, ignoring "miscellaneous" and "imports"), these increases are all more than *twice* the average: real estate and rental (a 4.9 percent price increase with full CIT removal and shifting); medical, educational, and related services

Table 3-9. Percentage Increases in VAT-Inclusive Consumer Prices, for Alternative Degrees of CIT Reduction (S) and Shifting (α), by Two-Digit Aggregated Industry Classification[a]

| Industry | S = 25% | | | S = 50% | | | S = 75% | | | S = 100% | | |
|---|---|---|---|---|---|---|---|---|---|---|---|---|
| | α=.2 | α=.6 | α=1.0 | α=.2 | α=.6 | α=1.0 | α=.2 | α=.6 | α=1.0 | α=.2 | α=.6 | α=1.0 |
| 1 AGRICULTURE | 1.87 | 1.76 | 1.59 | 3.64 | 3.19 | 2.62 | 5.33 | 4.38 | 3.34 | 6.92 | 5.40 | 3.87 |
| 3 COAL,STN,CLAY MNG+PROD | 1.75 | 1.32 | 0.70 | 3.40 | 2.37 | 1.08 | 4.96 | 3.23 | 1.31 | 6.44 | 3.95 | 1.46 |
| 4 OIL + GAS | 1.81 | 1.54 | 1.19 | 3.51 | 2.77 | 1.87 | 5.31 | 3.77 | 2.28 | 6.65 | 4.60 | 2.55 |
| 6 ORDNANCE | 1.78 | 1.42 | 0.92 | 3.46 | 2.58 | 1.46 | 5.05 | 3.53 | 1.82 | 6.56 | 4.33 | 2.09 |
| 7 FOOD | 1.81 | 1.54 | 1.17 | 3.52 | 2.79 | 1.88 | 5.15 | 3.82 | 2.36 | 6.69 | 4.70 | 2.70 |
| 8 TOBACCO | 1.62 | 0.82 | -0.45 | 3.15 | 1.50 | -0.68 | 4.60 | 2.06 | -0.80 | 5.97 | 2.54 | -0.87 |
| 9 TEXTILES + APPAREL | 1.76 | 1.34 | 0.73 | 3.41 | 2.41 | 1.15 | 4.98 | 3.26 | 1.43 | 6.47 | 4.05 | 1.63 |
| 10 LUMBER+WOOD PRODUCTS | 1.79 | 1.47 | 1.08 | 3.47 | 2.64 | 1.66 | 5.07 | 3.59 | 1.97 | 6.58 | 4.37 | 2.16 |
| 11 FURNITURE + FIXTURES | 1.71 | 1.35 | 0.75 | 3.41 | 2.42 | 1.18 | 4.99 | 3.31 | 1.45 | 6.47 | 4.05 | 1.64 |
| 12 PAPER + PRODUCTS | 1.71 | 1.17 | 0.40 | 3.32 | 2.10 | 0.57 | 4.85 | 2.85 | 0.65 | 6.28 | 3.48 | 0.68 |
| 13 PRINTING + PUBLISHING | 1.68 | 1.07 | 0.15 | 3.27 | 1.92 | 0.19 | 4.77 | 2.61 | 0.21 | 6.19 | 3.20 | 0.21 |
| 14 CHEM.,PLAST.,DRUGS,PNT | 1.62 | 0.84 | -0.35 | 3.15 | 1.51 | -0.62 | 4.59 | 2.04 | -0.80 | 5.95 | 2.50 | -0.95 |
| 15 RUBBER + LEATHER | 1.74 | 1.26 | 0.56 | 3.37 | 2.27 | 0.87 | 4.92 | 3.11 | 1.09 | 6.39 | 3.84 | 1.24 |
| 16 FOOTWEAR | 1.79 | 1.46 | 1.00 | 3.48 | 2.64 | 1.59 | 5.08 | 3.61 | 1.98 | 6.60 | 4.43 | 2.26 |
| 17 PRIMARY METAL | 1.79 | 1.46 | 1.00 | 3.43 | 2.63 | 1.58 | 5.08 | 3.59 | 1.96 | 6.59 | 4.41 | 2.22 |
| 18 FABRICATED METAL | 1.74 | 1.28 | 0.61 | 3.38 | 2.30 | 0.93 | 4.93 | 3.14 | 1.14 | 6.40 | 3.84 | 1.29 |
| 19 NONELECT. MACHINERY | 1.73 | 1.24 | 0.52 | 3.36 | 2.24 | 0.84 | 4.91 | 3.07 | 1.00 | 6.37 | 3.91 | 1.15 |
| 20 ELECTRICAL EQUIPMENT | 1.71 | 1.19 | 0.41 | 3.34 | 2.15 | 0.64 | 4.87 | 2.95 | 0.79 | 6.33 | 3.62 | 0.90 |
| 21 TRANSP. EQUIPMENT | 1.71 | 1.16 | 0.33 | 3.32 | 2.09 | 0.51 | 4.84 | 2.85 | 0.63 | 6.29 | 3.50 | 0.71 |
| 22 INSTRUMENTS | 1.69 | 1.11 | 0.26 | 3.29 | 2.00 | 0.36 | 4.80 | 2.73 | 0.41 | 6.23 | 3.34 | 0.44 |
| 23 MISC. MANUFACTURING | 1.78 | 1.42 | 0.92 | 3.46 | 2.57 | 1.45 | 5.05 | 3.51 | 1.80 | 6.55 | 4.30 | 2.05 |
| 24 TRANSP. + WAREHOUSING | 1.86 | 1.65 | 1.13 | 3.62 | 3.05 | 2.21 | 5.29 | 4.25 | 3.04 | 6.88 | 5.29 | 3.69 |
| 25 COMMUNICATIONS | 1.39 | -0.01 | -2.18 | 2.58 | -0.07 | -3.61 | 3.90 | -0.15 | -4.71 | 5.04 | -0.22 | -5.49 |
| 26 UTILITIES | 1.52 | 0.51 | -0.92 | 2.94 | 0.85 | -1.67 | 4.28 | 1.08 | -2.45 | 5.54 | 1.25 | -3.02 |
| 27 FINANCE + INSURANCE | 1.13 | -0.02 | -4.56 | 2.19 | -1.85 | -7.25 | 3.17 | -2.53 | -9.01 | 4.09 | -3.09 | -10.26 |
| 28 REAL ESTATE + RENTAL | 1.92 | 1.94 | 1.97 | 3.75 | 3.53 | 3.26 | 5.48 | 4.86 | 4.18 | 7.12 | 6.00 | 4.88 |
| 29 HOTELS + SERVICES | 1.81 | 1.52 | 1.10 | 3.51 | 2.75 | 1.78 | 5.13 | 3.77 | 2.25 | 6.67 | 4.64 | 2.59 |
| 30 AUTO REPAIR + SERVICES | 1.84 | 1.63 | 1.32 | 3.58 | 2.96 | 2.17 | 5.23 | 4.07 | 2.78 | 6.79 | 5.01 | 3.23 |
| 31 AMUSEMENTS | 1.99 | 1.77 | 1.43 | 3.67 | 3.26 | 2.66 | 5.37 | 4.52 | 3.54 | 6.99 | 5.59 | 4.20 |
| 32 MED.,ED.SERV.+NONPROF. | 1.92 | 1.93 | 1.96 | 3.74 | 3.51 | 3.23 | 5.47 | 4.84 | 4.14 | 7.11 | 5.98 | 4.84 |
| 33 MISCELLANEOUS | 2.02 | 2.29 | 2.73 | 3.94 | 4.18 | 4.52 | 5.76 | 5.78 | 5.80 | 7.50 | 7.14 | 6.76 |
| 34 IMPORTS | 1.96 | 2.08 | 2.29 | 3.82 | 3.78 | 3.77 | 5.58 | 5.21 | 4.81 | 7.26 | 6.43 | 5.59 |

Notes: Changes in prices are for private consumption expenditures at VAT-inclusive purchaser prices (i.e., producer price plus transportation and trade margins). VAT is assumed to be fully shifted for alternative combinations of S and α. If α = 0, percentage price changes are the same for all industries, and are equal to the VAT rate: 1.92 percent for S = 25 percent, 3.84 percent for S = 50 percent, 5.76 percent for S = 75 percent, and 7.68 percent for S = 100 percent.

[a] Industries correspond closely to the SIC two-digit classification and to that used by Aaron.

Table 3-10. Percentage Increases in VAT-Inclusive Consumer Prices, for Alternative Degrees of CIT Reduction (S) and Shifting (α), by Industry

| Industry | S = 25% | | | S = 50% | | | S = 75% | | | S = 100% | | |
|---|---|---|---|---|---|---|---|---|---|---|---|---|
| | α=.2 | α=.6 | α=1.0 | α=.2 | α=.6 | α=1.0 | α=.2 | α=.6 | α=1.0 | α=.2 | α=.6 | α=1.0 |
| 1 | 1.88 | 1.77 | 1.61 | 3.65 | 3.22 | 2.67 | 5.34 | 4.43 | 3.41 | 6.94 | 5.46 | 3.97 |
| 2 | 1.87 | 1.75 | 1.58 | 3.64 | 3.17 | 2.59 | 5.32 | 4.36 | 3.30 | 6.91 | 5.37 | 3.82 |
| 3 | 1.88 | 1.77 | 1.60 | 3.65 | 3.22 | 2.66 | 5.34 | 4.43 | 3.42 | 6.94 | 5.47 | 3.99 |
| 7 | 1.82 | 1.58 | 1.22 | 3.54 | 2.85 | 1.99 | 5.17 | 3.91 | 2.51 | 6.72 | 4.79 | 2.87 |
| 9 | 1.81 | 1.55 | 1.23 | 3.52 | 2.79 | 1.92 | 5.13 | 3.79 | 2.33 | 6.66 | 4.62 | 2.58 |
| 10 | 1.81 | 1.54 | 1.14 | 3.52 | 2.78 | 1.87 | 5.14 | 3.81 | 2.34 | 6.67 | 4.66 | 2.65 |
| 19 | 1.78 | 1.42 | 0.92 | 3.46 | 2.58 | 1.46 | 5.05 | 3.53 | 1.82 | 6.56 | 4.33 | 2.09 |
| 20 | 1.84 | 1.63 | 1.36 | 3.57 | 2.95 | 2.19 | 5.22 | 4.05 | 2.76 | 6.78 | 4.98 | 3.17 |
| 21 | 1.81 | 1.54 | 1.17 | 3.53 | 2.79 | 1.88 | 5.15 | 3.83 | 2.36 | 6.69 | 4.70 | 2.71 |
| 22 | 1.80 | 1.51 | 1.10 | 3.51 | 2.74 | 1.77 | 5.13 | 3.75 | 2.23 | 6.66 | 4.61 | 2.56 |
| 23 | 1.81 | 1.52 | 1.12 | 3.51 | 2.75 | 1.80 | 5.13 | 3.78 | 2.27 | 6.67 | 4.64 | 2.60 |
| 24 | 1.79 | 1.46 | 0.98 | 3.48 | 2.63 | 1.57 | 5.08 | 3.60 | 1.96 | 6.59 | 4.42 | 2.24 |
| 25 | 1.83 | 1.62 | 1.33 | 3.57 | 2.93 | 2.14 | 5.21 | 4.02 | 2.70 | 6.77 | 4.93 | 3.10 |
| 26 | 1.91 | 1.52 | 1.13 | 3.52 | 2.76 | 1.81 | 5.13 | 3.78 | 2.28 | 6.67 | 4.64 | 2.61 |
| 27 | 1.79 | 1.46 | 1.01 | 3.48 | 2.64 | 1.60 | 5.08 | 3.62 | 1.99 | 6.60 | 4.43 | 2.27 |
| 28 | 1.81 | 1.53 | 1.15 | 3.52 | 2.78 | 1.84 | 5.14 | 3.80 | 2.32 | 6.68 | 4.64 | 2.66 |
| 29 | 1.62 | 0.82 | -0.46 | 3.15 | 1.50 | -0.69 | 4.60 | 2.06 | -0.81 | 5.97 | 2.54 | -0.88 |
| 30 | 1.75 | 1.33 | 0.72 | 3.41 | 2.40 | 1.13 | 4.98 | 3.28 | 1.39 | 6.46 | 4.02 | 1.59 |
| 31 | 1.73 | 1.33 | 0.72 | 3.41 | 2.41 | 1.14 | 4.99 | 3.29 | 1.41 | 6.47 | 4.04 | 1.61 |
| 32 | 1.76 | 1.35 | 0.76 | 3.42 | 2.43 | 1.19 | 4.99 | 3.33 | 1.48 | 6.48 | 4.08 | 1.68 |
| 33 | 1.72 | 1.21 | 0.44 | 3.35 | 2.18 | 0.69 | 4.89 | 2.99 | 0.87 | 6.34 | 3.67 | 0.99 |
| 34 | 1.79 | 1.34 | 0.74 | 3.47 | 2.64 | 1.66 | 5.07 | 3.59 | 1.97 | 6.58 | 4.37 | 2.16 |
| 36 | 1.76 | 1.34 | 0.74 | 3.41 | 2.41 | 1.16 | 4.98 | 3.47 | 1.60 | 6.46 | 4.03 | 1.60 |
| 37 | 1.78 | 1.44 | 0.94 | 3.47 | 2.59 | 1.50 | 5.06 | 3.55 | 1.87 | 6.57 | 4.35 | 2.13 |
| 38 | 1.71 | 1.17 | 0.41 | 3.32 | 2.11 | 0.58 | 4.84 | 2.86 | 0.66 | 6.28 | 3.49 | 0.70 |
| 39 | 1.69 | 1.10 | 0.26 | 3.28 | 1.96 | 0.31 | 4.78 | 2.66 | 0.31 | 6.20 | 3.24 | 0.28 |
| 40 | 1.68 | 1.07 | -0.15 | 3.27 | 1.92 | 0.19 | 4.77 | 2.61 | 0.21 | 6.19 | 3.20 | 0.21 |
| 41 | 1.58 | 0.41 | -0.68 | 3.07 | 1.25 | -1.13 | 4.48 | 1.69 | -1.44 | 5.81 | 3.06 | -1.67 |
| 42 | 1.51 | 0.85 | -1.31 | 2.92 | 1.72 | -2.16 | 4.25 | 0.97 | -2.74 | 5.51 | 1.17 | -3.17 |
| 43 | 1.62 | 0.78 | -0.49 | 3.15 | 1.52 | -0.60 | 4.60 | 2.06 | -0.78 | 5.88 | 2.52 | -0.92 |
| 44 | 1.60 | 0.49 | 0.56 | 3.11 | 1.39 | 0.87 | 4.54 | 1.88 | 1.10 | 6.65 | 2.30 | 2.55 |
| 45 | 1.81 | 1.54 | 1.19 | 3.51 | 2.77 | 1.87 | 5.31 | 3.77 | 1.98 | 6.39 | 4.60 | 1.24 |
| 46 | 1.74 | 1.26 | 0.56 | 3.37 | 2.27 | 0.87 | 4.92 | 3.11 | 1.09 | 6.60 | 3.82 | 2.26 |
| 48 | 1.79 | 1.46 | 1.00 | 3.48 | 2.64 | 1.59 | 5.08 | 3.61 | 0.95 | 6.60 | 4.43 | 1.02 |
| 49 | 1.73 | 1.24 | 0.55 | 3.35 | 2.22 | 0.80 | 4.89 | 3.02 | 2.02 | 6.35 | 3.69 | 1.04 |
| 50 | 1.73 | 1.24 | 0.54 | 3.36 | 2.22 | 0.80 | 4.90 | 3.03 | 1.60 | 6.35 | 3.70 | 2.29 |
| 51 | 1.79 | 1.47 | 1.02 | 3.48 | 2.66 | 1.62 | 5.01 | 3.63 | 2.17 | 6.50 | 4.45 | 1.79 |
| 53 | 1.77 | 1.38 | 0.85 | 3.50 | 2.49 | 1.31 | 5.11 | 3.39 | 0.60 | 6.60 | 4.15 | 2.48 |
| 54 | 1.80 | 1.51 | 1.10 | 3.25 | 2.72 | 1.75 | 4.84 | 3.72 | 2.17 | 6.64 | 4.56 | 0.67 |
| 56 | 1.71 | 1.15 | 0.33 | 3.32 | 2.08 | 0.50 | 4.90 | 2.84 | 0.60 | 6.28 | 3.48 | 0.67 |

**Table 3-10 continued**

| | | | | | | | | | | | | |
|---|---|---|---|---|---|---|---|---|---|---|---|---|
| 57 | 1.29 | 3.84 | 6.40 | 1.14 | 3.14 | 4.93 | 0.93 | 2.30 | 3.38 | 0.61 | 1.28 | 1.74 |
| 58 | 1.35 | 3.88 | 6.41 | 1.20 | 3.17 | 4.94 | 0.97 | 2.32 | 3.39 | 0.63 | 1.29 | 1.74 |
| 59 | 0.75 | 3.52 | 6.29 | 0.65 | 2.87 | 4.85 | 0.52 | 2.10 | 3.32 | 0.33 | 1.16 | 1.71 |
| 60 | 1.24 | 3.82 | 6.39 | 1.09 | 3.11 | 4.92 | 0.87 | 2.27 | 3.37 | 0.55 | 1.26 | 1.74 |
| 63 | 1.00 | 3.67 | 6.34 | 0.87 | 2.99 | 4.89 | 0.70 | 2.19 | 3.35 | 0.45 | 1.21 | 1.72 |
| 64 | 1.54 | 3.99 | 6.45 | 1.35 | 3.26 | 4.97 | 1.80 | 2.38 | 3.40 | 0.69 | 1.32 | 1.75 |
| 67 | 1.62 | 5.04 | 6.47 | 1.42 | 3.30 | 4.98 | 1.14 | 2.41 | 3.41 | 0.73 | 1.34 | 1.76 |
| 68 | 1.15 | 3.76 | 6.37 | 1.01 | 3.07 | 4.91 | 0.82 | 2.24 | 3.36 | 0.52 | 1.24 | 1.73 |
| 69 | 0.75 | 3.52 | 6.29 | 0.65 | 2.87 | 4.85 | 0.52 | 2.10 | 3.32 | 0.33 | 1.16 | 1.71 |
| 70 | 0.97 | 3.66 | 6.34 | 0.86 | 2.98 | 4.88 | 0.70 | 2.18 | 3.35 | 0.45 | 1.21 | 1.72 |
| 71 | 0.74 | 3.52 | 6.28 | 0.65 | 2.87 | 4.83 | 0.53 | 2.10 | 3.31 | 0.35 | 1.16 | 1.71 |
| 72 | 0.66 | 3.47 | 6.27 | 0.57 | 2.83 | 4.83 | 0.46 | 2.06 | 3.31 | 0.30 | 1.14 | 1.70 |
| 73 | 0.65 | 3.46 | 5.50 | 0.57 | 2.82 | 5.01 | 0.46 | 2.06 | 3.43 | 0.30 | 1.14 | 1.70 |
| 74 | 1.78 | 4.14 | 6.24 | 1.54 | 3.37 | 4.81 | 1.23 | 2.46 | 3.04 | 0.77 | 1.36 | 1.76 |
| 75 | 0.48 | 3.36 | 6.53 | 0.43 | 2.74 | 5.03 | 0.35 | 2.01 | 3.04 | 0.24 | 1.11 | 1.70 |
| 76 | 1.92 | 4.22 | 6.58 | 1.66 | 3.44 | 5.06 | 1.31 | 2.51 | 3.44 | 0.82 | 1.38 | 1.77 |
| 77 | 2.16 | 4.37 | 6.21 | 1.88 | 3.56 | 4.79 | 1.50 | 2.60 | 3.47 | 0.93 | 1.44 | 1.78 |
| 78 | 0.34 | 3.27 | 6.26 | 0.32 | 2.68 | 4.72 | 0.28 | 1.96 | 3.28 | 0.21 | 1.09 | 1.69 |
| 79 | 0.56 | 3.41 | 6.55 | 0.52 | 2.79 | 4.82 | 0.45 | 2.05 | 3.31 | 0.31 | 1.14 | 1.70 |
| 80 | 2.05 | 4.30 | 6.88 | 1.80 | 3.51 | 5.05 | 1.45 | 2.57 | 3.46 | 0.92 | 1.42 | 1.78 |
| 81 | 3.69 | 5.29 | 5.04 | 3.04 | 4.25 | 5.29 | 2.21 | 3.05 | 3.62 | 1.19 | 1.65 | 1.86 |
| 82 | 5.50 | 0.23 | 5.53 | 4.72 | 1.06 | 3.90 | 1.72 | 0.08 | 2.68 | 2.19 | 0.02 | 0.39 |
| 84 | 3.06 | 1.12 | 5.49 | 2.51 | 1.00 | 4.27 | 1.72 | 0.80 | 2.94 | 0.98 | 0.49 | 0.52 |
| 85 | 3.25 | 1.64 | 5.67 | 1.92 | 1.39 | 4.25 | 1.38 | 1.06 | 2.92 | 0.94 | 0.49 | 0.51 |
| 86 | 2.37 | 3.09 | 4.09 | 9.01 | 2.53 | 4.38 | 7.25 | 1.85 | 2.01 | 0.72 | 0.62 | 0.55 |
| 88 | 10.26 | 10.00 | 7.12 | 4.18 | 4.86 | 3.17 | 3.26 | 3.53 | 2.19 | 4.56 | 0.02 | 0.13 |
| 89 | 4.88 | 6.00 | 6.68 | 2.30 | 4.86 | 5.48 | 1.82 | 3.75 | 3.75 | 0.97 | 0.94 | 0.92 |
| 90 | 2.65 | 4.67 | 6.61 | 2.78 | 3.62 | 5.14 | 1.55 | 2.63 | 3.52 | 1.13 | 1.53 | 1.81 |
| 91 | 2.31 | 4.66 | 6.79 | 3.54 | 4.07 | 5.09 | 2.17 | 2.96 | 3.48 | 0.94 | 1.45 | 1.79 |
| 93 | 3.23 | 5.01 | 6.99 | 4.14 | 4.52 | 5.23 | 2.66 | 3.26 | 3.58 | 1.32 | 1.63 | 1.84 |
| 94 | 4.20 | 5.59 | 7.11 | 5.06 | 4.84 | 5.37 | 3.23 | 3.51 | 3.67 | 1.43 | 1.77 | 1.99 |
| 95 | 4.84 | 5.98 | 7.33 | 4.39 | 4.98 | 5.47 | 3.93 | 3.88 | 3.74 | 1.96 | 1.93 | 1.92 |
| 96 | 5.91 | 6.62 | 7.17 | 4.81 | 5.36 | 5.63 | 3.45 | 3.62 | 3.85 | 2.36 | 2.13 | 1.98 |
| 97 | 5.10 | 6.14 | 7.26 | 5.21 | 4.98 | 5.51 | 3.77 | 3.78 | 3.82 | 2.10 | 1.99 | 1.94 |
| 98 | — | 6.43 | — | 4.81 | 5.21 | 5.58 | — | — | — | 2.29 | 2.08 | 1.96 |
| 104 | 7.22 | 7.41 | 7.59 | 6.19 | 6.00 | 5.83 | 4.82 | 4.34 | 3.99 | 2.91 | 2.38 | 2.04 |

Note: Same as Table 3-9.

(4.8 percent); amusements (4.2 percent); agricultural produce (3.9 percent); and transportation and warehousing (3.7 percent).

With full CIT removal the *range* of consumer price changes with full shifting is from a 6.8 percent increase (miscellaneous) to a 10.3 percent reduction (finance and insurance), with an average increase of 1.7 percent. However, with CIT shifting of 0.6 and CIT repeal the range is from 7.1 to –3.1 percent, the higher average price increase of 4.1 percent explained by the higher VAT rate required for partial compared to full shifting. With shifting of 0.2 this consumer price range is from 7.5 to 4.1 percent with an average of 6.5 percent. And, of course, zero shifting of the CIT implies that prices inclusive of VAT will rise by 7.7 percent (the VAT rate) in all industries.

For a CIT reduction of less than 85 to 90 percent, *reductions* in the degree of CIT shifting imply *reductions* in the VAT rate. In consequence, the largest price increases decline and the smallest increases rise, relative to the mean, thus necessarily reducing the range in consumer price variation resulting from the tax substitution.

In summary, consumer prices (VAT inclusive) are highly sensitive to CIT reduction and shifting. This sensitivity is compounded by the relationships between CIT reduction and shifting, on the one hand, and the compensating VAT rate on the other. With a high degree of CIT shifting, relative (intercommodity) consumer prices are significantly changed, and these relative price changes are greater the greater the degree of CIT removal.

*Chapter 4*

# Income Distribution: Differential Incidence of the VAT-CIT Substitution

Because consumption expenditure as a proportion of income declines as income increases, a VAT applied at a uniform rate to all consumer purchases is obviously regressive in its apparent distribution of tax liabilities over income classes. However, the important question of VAT incidence does not relate to this nominal distribution of VAT liabilities but to the change in the distribution of disposable income which results from the introduction of the VAT and the simultaneous, compensating changes in other tax or governmental expenditure and transfer programs. Specifically, the issue here is the *differential* incidence of the VAT-CIT substitution. A very different differential incidence could result from other programs of substitution incorporating the VAT, e.g., revenue-sharing grants (financed by the VAT) replacing local property tax support of education.

The incidence of a VAT-CIT substitution is determined by other elements besides nominal VAT incidence. Real incomes will be altered by changes in factor earnings and by changes in the prices of goods and services, resulting both from the reduction in the CIT and from the compensating imposition of the VAT.

Apart from exceptional cases, the prices of consumption goods do not change equiproportionally, as discussed previously. Hence, the effects of the price adjustments on *real* household income will depend on the composition of consumer expenditures. Families whose consumption is dominated by commodities experiencing relatively large price increases will be most adversely affected. It is certainly not unreasonable to expect that the composition as well as the level of family consumption expenditure will be a function of income, and that this relationship will significantly affect the incidence of the tax substitution. Thus, it is necessary to utilize information concerning the composition of consumer expenditures by income class in order to assess the distributional effects of the tax substitution.

Furthermore, unless the CIT savings are fully shifted forward, the CIT reduction will imply increases in some or all nominal factor incomes. In the short run it is not unreasonable to assume that these changes in income will accrue to owners of capital, as has been assumed implicitly in the treatment of CIT shifting and revenue yield. The full distributional effects of the tax change will then incorporate increases in the after-tax incomes of capital owners, who can reasonably be expected to be concentrated at the upper end of the income distribution. To quantify this effect, it is necessary to determine the level of wealth and the portfolio composition of each income class.[1]

Finally, in addition to increases in prices of consumption goods and in the nominal incomes of owners of securities, any degree of forward CIT shifting will bring about reductions in the price of investment goods. These price reductions will not be offset by imposition of the VAT since investment purchases are not themselves subjected to a consumption-type VAT. Initially at least, this reduction in capital goods prices implies that the original, pre-tax-substitution level of capital earnings can be maintained with a smaller rate of nominal investment; the cost of the fixed bill of real investment purchases (as defined by the original investment final demand vector) will have been reduced. The benefit to investors in physical capital is simply this reduction in the nominal cost of the given net investment bundle.

For example, assume that corporate enterprises were investing $1,000,000 per year in capital goods prior to the tax substitution and earning $200,000 in profits before paying the CIT at a 50 percent rate, leaving $100,000 in after-tax profits. If the CIT is repealed and if the CIT reduction is shifted forward through lower VAT-exclusive prices, there is in the short run no consequent change in net profit income. However, if investment goods prices decline

---

1. Part of the increase in after-tax corporate profits will, of course, benefit foreign holders of stock in U.S. corporations. This has, however, been ignored in the distribution of after-tax profits by income class. Although this introduces a bias into the analysis because it increases the apparent regressivity of the tax substitution by overstating the nominal income gains of domestic owners of stocks, the magnitude of this bias is expected to be small enough to be disregarded.

by 10 percent, the enterprises need spend only $900,000 to acquire the same physical volume of capital goods. The savings of $100,000 represents unused funds, not obtainned at the sacrifice of capital earnings. At least in the short run, under present assumptions, this reduction in the cost of the fixed bill of capital goods purchases must be treated as an increase in the real incomes of owners of capital, since they will not suffer any offsetting reductions in their income from capital. On the other hand, in the longer run, if the CIT reduction is allowed to stimulate investment demand without being offset by stringent monetary policy and increased interest rates, the medium-short-run effect may be a rise in the price of investment goods in response to increased demand and limited supply.

In the classical case of zero forward shifting of the CIT, implying that capital earnings are indeed quasi-rents, capital goods prices are unaffected and no benefit accrues in the form of a reduction in the nominal cost of the prespecified gross investment vector (net investment plus depreciation). Instead, the owners of capital goods benefit from an increase in earnings on a given real investment. In the nonclassical cases, i.e., some degree of forward CIT shifting, capital consumption (depreciation) has been considered as an intermediate good, with the benefits of price reductions (more than offset, however, by imposition of the VAT) flowing to consumers. But in these cases, it has been argued (section 2.4.4), that capital earnings can no longer be viewed as quasi-rents, and net earnings of capital enter into price formation. In this event, capital owners can anticipate receiving an unchanged flow of *net* earnings on the basis of a smaller level of nominal investment (unchanged physical investment). Thus, the benefit to investors of a decline in capital goods prices is the reduction in the nominal cost of the original bill of *net* investment purchases. This benefit must be distributed over households according to their participation in the purchase of capital goods. Thus, owners of unincorporated enterprises benefit directly from reduced nominal investment costs, while owners of corporate stock benefit indirectly via either higher current dividends, or higher future earnings (capital gains). This contrasts with the classical case of zero CIT shifting in which the entire (short-run) benefit accrues to owners of *corporate* wealth in the form of increased after-tax corporate profits.

In this chapter, changes in the cost of living for each income class are computed by combining the previously estimated price changes of consumption goods and services with information on the level and composition of consumer expenditure by income class, on the assumption that real consumption expenditure (level and composition) is unaffected by the tax substitution. Actually, of course, the shifting of consumption to the new basket that is optimal at the new relative prices will provide some opportunity for gain, indicating that the burden of the shift will have been slightly overestimated. Similarly, unshifted CIT savings are allocated to income classes on the basis of the share of wealth and portfolio composition (common stock versus other assets) unique to each income class. Finally, the benefits derived from the reductions in capital goods prices and hence in the nominal cost of net investment purchases are distributed on the same basis as the benefits of unshifted CIT savings; that is, ownership of corporate wealth is taken as a proxy for participation in current capital expenditure.[2] The sum of these effects, i.e., the increase in nominal consumption expenditure less (a) the increase in income, and (b) the reduction in investment cost, relative to income then represents the differential incidence of the tax substitution by income class. This information is further summarized by computing a Gini-coefficient, or index of concentration, which permits an (albeit somewhat arbitrary) assessment of the change in the overall degree of inequality in income distribution which results from the VAT-CIT substitution.

In almost all actual cases of VAT imposition, a system of multiple rates has been set up to mitigate the obvious regressivity of the tax by partially or wholly exempting some consumer goods deemed to be "necessities." We shall assess the implications of these dual rate systems, and we suggest and evaluate alternative means of reducing the regressivity of tax systems that incorporate the VAT.

To simplify matters the analysis is restricted to the extreme cases of complete repeal of the CIT under the polar assumptions of full or zero forward CIT shifting. These extremes most clearly delimit and exemplify the range of redistributive consequences of a VAT-CIT substitution.

Since the tax substitution analysis is based on data relating to input-output relationships, final demands, and corporate income tax liabilities observed in 1969, it is necessary for consistency to use the 1969 level and distribution of consumption expenditure by income class. These 1969 income-consumption relationships have been estimated from 1960–61 data, which are the most recent that

---

2. In principle, ownership of corporate wealth, weighted by the corporate share of net investment, plus ownership of noncorporate physical capital, weighted by the noncorporate share of net investment, would be employed to distribute these benefits, However, the required information is not readily available by income class, and it is likely that the distribution of corporate wealth would be highly correlated with the weighted distribution of total physical wealth particularly because of the predominance of net corporate capital formation (in excess of 75 percent of the total).

are sufficiently disaggregated [U.S. Bureau of Labor Statistics]. Two alternative assumptions concerning the responses of consumption patterns to the relative price changes which occurred between 1960 and 1969 have been used to convert 1960 consumption patterns to 1969 prices:

a. The *percentage distribution of nominal expenditures* over consumption commodities for a given 1969 income class is assumed to be identical to that of the 1960–61 income class having the same real income. This is implied by *unitary relative-price elasticity of demand*. The adjustment of real levels of consumption of each good and service to relative price changes is just sufficient to maintain the budgetary shares, for a given income class, for each commodity.

b. Alternatively, it can be assumed that the *level of real consumption* of each good and service for a 1969 income class will be identical to that of the 1960–61 income class having the same real income. This would be implied by *zero relative price elasticity of demand*. In this case, the *share of expenditure* accounted for by the goods and services with above-average price increases would be greater in 1969 than in 1960, while the share of expenditure accounted for by those with below-average price increases (relative price reductions) would decline.

The computations of the redistributive results are made under both price-elasticity assumptions. However, since the estimated incidence of the tax substitution is relatively insensitive to the elasticity assumptions, the discussion is confined to the less extreme case of unitary elasticity. But, it should be understood that the alternative elasticity assumptions have been employed only in converting 1960–61 consumer budget composition to 1969 consumer prices. Zero elasticity is assumed in both cases in the assessment of the redistributive effects of the tax-substitution-induced price changes, i.e., the composition of real 1969 consumption is assumed to be unaltered by the price changes resulting from the tax substitution. Real consumption patterns have not been permitted to respond to these price changes for the sake of simplicity and of consistency with the input-output assumption of a fixed vector of final consumption demands. The data underlying the incidence analysis are presented in Table 4–1.

## 4.1 INCOME REDISTRIBUTION WITH FULL CIT SHIFTING

Consider first the impact of the VAT-CIT substitution on income redistribution under the assumption of full CIT shifting. Since the

**Table 4-1. Underlying Data for Personal Income Distribution, 1960–1961 and 1968**

| Income Class | 1960–1961 | | Average Propensity to Consume [(2) ÷ (1)] | No. of Families & Individuals | 1968 | | | Aggregate Common Stock Distrib. |
| | Mean Income (1) | Mean Expenditure (2) | (3) | (4) | Mean Income (5) | Percentage of Aggregate Income (6) | | (7) |
|---|---|---|---|---|---|---|---|---|
| Less than $3,000 | $ 1,810 | $ 2,140 | 1,182 | 12,394 | $ 1,780 | 4.0% | | 2.1% |
| $3,000–$4,999 | 4,240 | 4,140 | 0.976 | 8,720 | 4,000 | 6.4 | | 4.4 |
| $5000–7,499 | 6,150 | 5,860 | 0.953 | 11,502 | 6,240 | 13.1 | | 2.3 |
| $7,500–$9,999 | 8,550 | 7,680 | 0.898 | 10,706 | 8,660 | 17.0 | | 12.3 |
| $10,000–14,999 | 11,720 | 9,900 | 0.845 | 13,318 | 12,110 | 29.5 | | 31.4 |
| $15,000 and more | 21,930 | 15,090 | 0.688 | 7,660 | 21,300 | 29.9 | | 47.3 |
| | | | | | | 100.00 | | 100.0 |

*Source:*

Columns (1) and (2): Based on U.S. Bureau of Labor Statistics (Report 237–93 and Supplements, Table 1A).

Columns (4) and (5): Based on U.S. Bureau of the Census (1969, Tables 2 and 4).

Column (6): From columns (4) and (6).

Column (7): From Katona (1970, Table 6–15).

benefits of CIT repeal are fully shifted forward in the form of lower prices, there will be no changes in nominal income, i.e., net-of-tax profits and other factor incomes are unaffected. As indicated in the preceding chapter, the CIT-compensating VAT rate in this case is 7.22 percent. VAT-inclusive consumer prices rise on average by about 1.70 percent. However, because of differing initial corporate tax liabilities, consumer prices will not move uniformly. The tax substitution implies VAT-inclusive price increases in excess of 3 percent in such important, but relatively unincorporated, sectors as foods and services. The most important price decreases occur in the capital-intensive and highly incorporated utilities and communications sectors (decreases of 3 percent or more). The effect on consumption expenditure will then clearly be sensitive to the composition of the consumption budget.

The percentage increases in overall consumption costs by income class, as indicated in Table 4-2, are 2.3 percent and 2.5 percent for the lowest income classes, 2.5 percent for the highest, and 2.1 percent for the middle. The above-average increase for the lowest income class is accounted for by the substantial price increases for food, housing, and medical care, which collectively account for about 57 percent of household expenditure at this income level. The importance of these three items declines continuously with increases in income. The below-average increases in the middle income range are primarily accounted for by the decline in the price of private transportation, which takes a greater share of the budget at these income levels than at any others.

These changes in consumption expenditures effectively represent net changes in tax burden on consumption account, i.e., reductions in real disposable income resulting from the tax substitution. In addition, households will benefit, directly or indirectly, from the reduction in capital goods prices resulting from forward CIT shifting, a benefit *not* offset by the imposition of a VAT liability. The *aggregate* benefit of capital goods price changes is simply the reduction in the nominal cost of the fixed level of real net investment. To distribute these benefits over income classes the distribution of corporate common stockholdings is used as a proxy for direct participation in net capital formation. For a given income class, its benefit per dollar of income (benefit as a percentage of income) due to the reduction in capital prices is obtained as follows: the total share of common stock held by individuals in the income class (the ratio of the total value of common stock held by individuals in the income class to the total value of common stock held by individuals of all income classes) is multiplied by aggregate savings on net in-

Table 4-2. Incidence of Income Redistribution, Assuming CIT Repeal and Full CIT Shifting

| 1960-61 Income Class | Reduction in Investment Cost ($\Delta I/Y$) | Increase in Consumption Cost | | | | Net Incidence ($\Delta C/Y - \Delta I/Y$) | |
|---|---|---|---|---|---|---|---|
| | | $A1^a$ | | $A2^b$ | | $A1^a$ | $A2^b$ |
| | | $\Delta C/C$ | $\Delta C/Y$ | $\Delta C/C$ | $\Delta C/Y$ | | |
| Less than $3,000 | .007 | 0.023 | 0.027 | 0.024 | 0.028 | 0.019 | 0.020 |
| $3,000-$4,999 | .009 | 0.021 | 0.021 | 0.022 | 0.022 | 0.011 | 0.012 |
| $5,000-$7,499 | .002 | 0.021 | 0.020 | 0.022 | 0.021 | 0.017 | 0.018 |
| $7,500-$9,999 | .009 | 0.021 | 0.019 | 0.022 | 0.020 | 0.009 | 0.010 |
| $10,000-$14,999 | .016 | 0.022 | 0.019 | 0.023 | 0.020 | 0.003 | 0.004 |
| $15,000 and more | .024 | 0.025 | 0.017 | 0.026 | 0.018 | -0.007 | -0.006 |

Note: Gini coefficient ($g$) = 0.374 before tax substitution and 0.380 after substitution. The investment price index ($P_I$) = 0.9455; the export price index ($P_E$), 0.9465; original exports ($E$), $47.49 billion; gain to rest of world from lowered export prices ($\Delta E$), $2.54 billion.

aUnitary price elasticity assumed for adjusting consumption in 1960–61 to 1969 prices.

bZero price elasticity assumed for adjusting consumption in 1960–61 to 1969 prices.

vestment purchases and divided by aggregate income of the class. The distribution of stock ownership is shown in Table 4-1, column 6, and the resultant investment cost savings as a proportion of income are in Table 4-2, column 1.

Presumably because of the concentration of retired rentiers in the lowest income class, net investment savings *as a percentage of income* are as high or higher in the two lowest income classes as in the next higher classes. Not surprisingly, the gain is greatest for the highest income group (income in excess of $15,000), although average family stockholdings in this class were probably understated. The percentage gain ranges from a low of 0.2 percent for the $5,000–$7,499 income class to 2.4 percent at incomes about $15,000 (with incomes expressed in 1960-61 dollars).

The resultant total net incidence of the tax substitution, with CIT repeal and full shifting, is simply the algebraic sum of the increases in consumption expenditures plus reductions in investment expenditures, expressed as a percentage of income. For this purpose, the change in consumption expenditure must be expressed as a percentage of income, rather than of expenditure itself. This is done simply by multiplying by the pre-tax-substitution ratio of expenditure to income (the average propensity to consume) by the percentage increase in consumption expenditure, i.e.,

$$\frac{\Delta C}{Y} = \left(\frac{\Delta C}{C}\right)\left(\frac{C}{Y}\right),$$

where $\Delta C$ is the change in consumption expenditure and $C$ and $Y$ are the original (presubstitution) levels of expenditure and income, respectively. The incidence of net investment savings (investment cost reduction) is already expressed as a percentage of income. Thus, the full net incidence is given by the sum of the two components:

$$- \frac{\Delta Y}{Y} = \frac{\Delta C}{Y} - \frac{\Delta I}{Y} = \frac{\Delta C - \Delta I}{Y},$$

where $\Delta I$ is the *reduction* in net investment expenditure; and it is displayed in the last two columns of Table 4-2.

Not surprisingly, since the average propensity to consume declines with income, while stock ownership rises with income class, the tax substitution with full CIT shifting is generally regressive: The net incidence declines from 1.9 percent at the lowest income class to approximately zero at incomes of $10,000–$14,999, and is negative about $15,000. Thus, even under the most favorable assumption of full forward shifting of the CIT savings, the effect of the VAT-CIT substitution is to redistribute income from lower to higher income classes.

To quantify this effect, Gini coefficients, or indices of concentration, were computed for the original income distribution and for the income distribution resulting from the tax substitution. This coefficient effectively measures the degree to which the full distribution diverges from income equality. A Gini coefficient of zero would imply absolute family-income equality; the most extreme inequality would result in a coefficient of unity. The pre-tax-substitution Gini coefficient for the disposable income distribution had a value of 0.374; the tax substitution increases the coefficient to only 0.380, suggesting that the tax substitution results in only marginal changes in relative incomes.[3]

It should be pointed out that the first-round aggregate effect of the tax substitution, in an open economy, is to increase taxes paid by citizens of the government imposing the tax. The aggregate burden on U.S. taxpayers would increase simply because part of the advantage of the CIT reduction would redound to the benefit of foreign purchasers of U.S. exports. The aggregate benefit of the substitution to the rest of the world (or aggregate burden on domestic taxpayers), under the present assumption of full CIT removal and full forward shifting, would be in fact approximately $2.54 billion, on the basis of original export sales of $47.49 billion and a reduction in export prices of 5.35 percent.

## 4.2 INCOME REDISTRIBUTION WITH ZERO CIT SHIFTING

Under the classical assumption of zero CIT shifting, it is somewhat simpler to assess the effects of the VAT-CIT substitution on income redistribution. First, because export prices are unaffected, no benefit

---

3. The arbitrary nature of the Gini coefficient should be recognized in interpreting it as a measure of change in the degree of distributional inequality resulting from a public policy measure, e.g., the VAT-CIT substitution. As Vickrey has pointed out, very different patterns of income distribution are consistent with a particular value of the Gini coefficient: a concept of distributive justice may distinguish very clearly between two income-distributional policies which generate virtually identical measures of inequality. Specifically, in the present case, peculiarities in the relationship between tax burden and income at very low levels of income (less than $5,000 or $7,500) may disguise the significant regressivity of the tax substitution over the bulk of the income range, i.e., above $5,000. For a further discussion, see Shoup [1970, pp. 580–581].

accrues to the rest of the world: the weighted average domestic incidence of the tax change is zero. Secondly, capital goods prices do not change, implying no benefit on net investment account. Thus, it is necessary to consider only changes in consumption expenditure and the distribution of the increase in net-of-tax profits.

The increase in net corporate profits is simply the original CIT revenue ($42.68 billion). This increase can be distributed over income classes the same way as were net investment cost savings: the aggregate change in profit is multiplied by the share of aggregate common stock held by a particular income class, and the result is divided by the aggregate income of that class, giving the relative benefit of the profit increase as a proportion of income of the average family in that income class, as reflected in increased stock dividends or capital gains or both.

Not surprisingly, the profit effect with zero CIT shifting is significantly greater than investment savings with full CIT shifting. The aggregate benefit from investment savings (the change in investment goods prices times original net investment) was only $6.82 billion, compared to the $42.68 billion increase in net profit. Thus, regressivity with zero shifting should be much greater than with full shifting.

The ratio of increase in net profits to income ($\Delta P/Y$), by income class, is shown in Table 4-3. Again, because of the distribution of stock ownership, the benefit is greater below an income of $5,000 (3.4 percent for the lowest income class and 4.4 percent for the next higher one) than for the $5,000 to $7,499 class (1.1 percent). The

**Table 4-3. Incidence of Income Redistribution, Assuming CIT Repeal and Zero CIT Shifting**

| *1960-61*<br>*Income Class* | *Profit*<br>*Increase*<br>*($\Delta P/Y$)* | *Consumption Expenditure*<br>*Increase* | | *Net Incidence*<br>*($\Delta C/Y - \Delta P/Y$)* |
|---|---|---|---|---|
| | | *$\Delta C/C$* | *$\Delta C/Y$* | |
| Less than $3,000 | .034 | .0768 | .091 | .057 |
| $3,000–$4,999 | .044 | .0768 | .075 | .031 |
| $5,000–$7,499 | .011 | .0768 | .074 | .063 |
| $7,500–$9,999 | .043 | .0768 | .069 | .026 |
| $10,000–$14,999 | .072 | .0768 | .065 | –.007 |
| $15,000 and more | .102 | .0768 | .053 | –.049 |

$\Delta P$ = profit increase (= Original CIT Revenue) = $42.68 billion. The VAT rate ($Z$) = 7.68 percent and the consumption price index ($P_C$) = 1.0768. Note: Gini coefficient ($g$) = 0.374 before tax substitution and 0.397 after substitution.

greatest increase in nominal income (10.2 percent) was in the highest income group.

To the gain on profit account must be added the effect of the price changes on consumption expenditure. With zero CIT shifting this effect is also somewhat simpler: all consumption prices rise by exactly the rate of the VAT, 7.68 percent. Obviously, then, the expenditure required to purchase any prespecified bill of consumption goods will rise by an equivalent amount. To specify the change in expenditure, by income class, as a proportion of income, it is only necessary to multiply the VAT rate (rate of expenditure increase) by the average propensity to consume. Because the average propensity to consume declines continuously with income, the increase in consumption expenditure relative to income also declines throughout, from 9.1 percent at the lowest levels of income to only 5.3 percent at the highest (15,000 and above).[4]

The net incidence (burden) of the VAT-CIT substitution is then simply the increase in relative expenditure less the gain in relative profit:

$$- \frac{\Delta Y}{Y} = \frac{\Delta C}{Y} - \frac{\Delta P}{Y} \, .$$

Computed in this manner, the net incidence (burden) with zero CIT shifting (Table 4–3) ranges from 6.3 percent at incomes from $5,000 to $7,499 to a –4.9 percent for families with incomes in excess of $15,000. The incidence for the lowest income group is 5.7 percent.

The pre-tax-substitution Gini-coefficient is 0.374; the post-tax value is 0.397. Thus, the increase in inequality is much greater with zero shifting of the CIT than with unitary CIT shifting, for which the post-tax-substitution coefficient increased to only 0.380. This substantive increase in the coefficient for zero shifting reflects a significant divergence from proportionality. Zero shifting implies a marked redistribution from low income families, who lose as much as 5.7 percent, and from middle income families, who lose 6.3 percent, to high income families, whose incomes actually increase by about 5 percent.

To summarize, the degree of regressiveness of a VAT-CIT substitution depends on assumptions concerning CIT shifting. As ex-

---

4. The increase in consumption expenditure relative to income for the lowest income class exceeds the VAT rate because, on average, households in this income class dissave.

pected, the most severe regressivity is observed if, in accordance with classical theory, the CIT is not shifted and the CIT savings accrue entirely to owners of capital (at least in the short run).

## 4.3 DUAL RATES

In response to this observed regressivity of the VAT-CIT substitution, or to more superficial conceptions of the "absolute" regressivity of the VAT, governments have in practice usually exempted some selected commodities from taxation at the full rates, paralleling the policy applied in imposing sales taxes.

Because the main objective of such "dual rate" systems is the reduction of regressivity, that bill of goods which would necessarily result in the greatest such reduction was selected for analysis. Specifically, in order to minimize the burden of the VAT on the lower income groups, all commodity classes exhibiting an income elasticity of less than 1 were given VAT preference. The resultant commodity classes are: food (elasticity of 0.59), tobacco (0.34), housing (0.60), utilities (0.45), supplies for household operation and personal care (0.42), and medical care and education (0.76), where the elasticities are weighted average elasticities computed from income class data [U.S. Bureau of Labor Statistics]. This is obviously *not* the bill of goods conventionally exempted from state retail sales taxes.[5] In the aggregate, these commodity classes account for approximately 54 percent of consumer expenditures.

The aggregate VAT-inclusive consumer price index is not affected by the imposition of dual rates; what is saved on a preferred commodity is made up in the aggregate via increased VAT liabilities on nonexempted commodities. Thus, the differential incidence effects depend entirely on differences in the composition of consumption budgets between income classes. Hence, the exemption

---

5. Four reasons for this divergence of conventional exemption practice from that which most effectively mitigates regressivity can be suggested. First, the choice of commodities selected for exemption may be guided by other objectives besides mitigation. For example, externality considerations or moral judgments concerning the social desirability of some types of consumption may enter, as in the decision not to exempt tobacco or alcoholic beverages.

Secondly, as will become very clear, the use of dual rate schemes may create severe distortions in the price structure, resulting in significant inefficiencies of allocation as households attempt to minimize their tax burdens (legal tax avoidance achieved by shifting consumption patterns toward exempted commodities) and potentially leading to tax evasion: the development of black markets and other methods of illegal tax avoidance.

Thirdly, and related to the second, many items in income inelastic demand are also *price inelastic*, and as is well known, the allocative inefficiency (excess

of income-inelastic items minimizes the regressivity of a dual-rate VAT as a replacement for the CIT.

It should be noted that the exemption of, e.g., tobacco sales to consumers from the VAT does not mean that retail tobacconists are exempted from the VAT network. To exempt value added completely at all stages of production ultimately embodied in consumer purchases of tobacco it would be necessary not only to exempt the tobacconist but also to provide the retailer with a refund of all VAT invoiced on his purchases. Similarly, if it were desired to tax a preferred commodity at one-half the regular VAT rate, the net VAT liability of the retailer would be one-half the VAT rate times all preferred sales, less *all* VAT invoiced (at full rates) on his intermediate purchases. In general, a dual-rate system under the invoice method requires only that the final sale be identified as subject to a preferred rate, with the usual full credit of the VAT invoiced on intermediate purchases.

To examaine the sensitivity of incidence to the degree of exemption, two cases are considered: (a) the application of one-half the "normal" (non-exempt-commodity) rate to items in income-inelastic demand, and (b) the complete exemption of (application of a zero rate to) income-inelastic items. The results are again assessed for the extreme cases of complete CIT removal with full and zero forward CIT shifting. The differential incidence of the VAT-CIT substitution for the three cases of full-rate, half-rate, and zero-rate VAT preferences is presented in Tables 4-4 (full CIT shifting) and 4-5 (zero CIT shifting).

In the case of CIT repeal and full forward CIT shifting, the introduction of preferential treatment for income-inelastic commodities increases the normal VAT rate from 7.22 percent to 9.89 percent with half-exemption and to 15.69 percent, more than double the single rate, with full exemption. The benefit received on purchases of exempted commodities is the reduction in the effective VAT rate

---

burden) imposed by an excise tax is less the more price inelastic the demand. Thus, on allocative grounds it is desirable to subject these commodities to special *higher* rather than lower rates. The fundamental point, ultimately, is that the rate structure of ad valorem taxes should be determined on the basis of criteria other than income distributional effects, with undesirable consequences in the latter dimension compensated by other simultaneous changes in the tax system, e.g., rebatable credits against income taxes or an appropriately structured system of transfers (negative taxes).

Finally, as a means of enhancing progressivity, exemptions under existing ad valorem taxes may be "nonoptimal" because they are attempts to make the taxes *appear* progressive without significantly altering the incidence of a basically regressive tax system.

Table 4-4. Incidence[a] of Dual VAT Rates, Assuming CIT Repeal and Full CIT Shifting

| 1960-61 Income Class | Investment Cost Reduction ($\Delta I/Y$) | Consumption Expenditure Increase | | | | | | Net Incidence ($\Delta C/Y - \Delta I/Y$) | | |
|---|---|---|---|---|---|---|---|---|---|---|
| | | Single Rate | | Half Rate | | Zero Rate | | Single Rate | Half Rate | Zero Rate |
| | | $\Delta C/C$ | $\Delta C/Y$ | $\Delta C/C$ | $\Delta C/Y$ | $\Delta C/C$ | $\Delta C/Y$ | | | |
| Less than $3,000 | .007 | .023 | 0.027 | .018 | .021 | 0.004 | .004 | .019 | .014 | .003 |
| $3,000-$4,999 | .009 | .021 | 0.021 | .020 | .020 | 0.015 | .015 | .011 | .011 | .006 |
| $5,000-7,499 | .002 | .021 | 0.020 | .021 | .020 | 0.019 | .018 | .017 | .018 | .016 |
| $7,500-$9,999 | .009 | .021 | 0.019 | .022 | .020 | 0.023 | .021 | .009 | .011 | .012 |
| $10,000-$14,999 | .016 | .022 | 0.019 | .024 | .021 | 0.028 | .023 | .003 | .005 | .007 |
| $15,000 and more | .024 | .025 | 0.017 | .028 | .019 | 0.034 | .023 | -.007 | -.005 | -.001 |

| VAT Rates | Nonexempt | Exempt |
|---|---|---|
| Single rate | 7.22% | 7.22% |
| Half rate | 9.89 | 4.95 |
| Zero rate | 15.69 | 0 |

| | Gini Coefficients |
|---|---|
| Single rate | .380 |
| Half rate | .377 |
| Zero rate | .377 |
| Pre-VAT | .374 |

Note: Consumption price index independent of exemption ($P_C$) = 1.0168.

[a]Unitary relative price elasticity assumed for adjusting consumption in 1960-61 to 1969 prices.

Table 4-5.  Incidence[a] of Dual VAT Rates, Assuming CIT Repeal and Zero CIT Shifting

| 1960-61 Income Class | Profit Increase ($\Delta P/Y$) | Consumption Expenditure Increase | | | | | | Net Incidence ($\Delta C/Y - \Delta P/Y$) | | |
|---|---|---|---|---|---|---|---|---|---|---|
| | | Single Rate | | Half Rate | | Zero Rate | | Single Rate | Half Rate | Zero Rate |
| | | $\Delta C/C$ | $\Delta C/Y$ | $\Delta C/C$ | $\Delta C/Y$ | $\Delta C/C$ | $\Delta C/Y$ | | | |
| Less than $3,000 | .034 | .0768 | .091 | .0697 | .082 | .0543 | .064 | .057 | .048 | .030 |
| $3,000-$4,999 | .044 | .0768 | .075 | .0742 | .072 | .0687 | .067 | .031 | .028 | .023 |
| $5,000-7,499 | .011 | .0768 | .074 | .0755 | .072 | .0727 | .069 | .063 | .061 | .058 |
| $7,500-$9,999 | .043 | .0768 | .069 | .0768 | .069 | .0768 | .069 | .026 | .026 | .026 |
| $10,000-$14,999 | .072 | .0768 | .065 | .0782 | .066 | .0813 | .069 | -.007 | -.006 | -.003 |
| $15,000 and more | .102 | .0768 | .053 | .0798 | .055 | .0861 | .059 | -.049 | -.047 | -.043 |

| VAT Rates | | |
|---|---|---|
| | Nonexempt | Exempt |
| Single rate | 7.68% | 7.68% |
| Half rate | 10.48 | 5.24 |
| Zero rate | 16.48 | 0.00 |

| | Gini Coefficients |
|---|---|
| Single rate | .397 |
| Half rate | .395 |
| Zero rate | .394 |
| Pre-VAT | .374 |

Note: Consumption price index independent of exemption ($P_C$) = 1.0768.

[a]Unitary relative price elasticity assumed for adjusting consumption in 1960-61 to 1969 prices.

applied to these purchases: from 7.22 percent to 4.95 percent (half-rate) or to 0 percent (zero rate, or full exemption).[6]

As can be seen from the estimates of net incidence, the half-rate benefits families with income below about $3,000 at the expense of those with incomes above $15,000. With full exemption, those below $7,500 benefit at the expense of those above $10,000. However, the effect for the overall redistribution is marginal. The post-substitution Gini-coefficient is reduced from 0.380 (no exemption), to 0.377 (half *and* total exemption). Thus, either dual-rate system moves back only halfway to the presubstitution coefficient of 0.374. Under either dual-rate system the VAT-CIT substitution is still markedly regressive above an income of $5,000. However, families at the lowest income levels (below $5,000) do derive significant benefits from exemption, in the extreme (below $3,000) an increase of 2.3 percent in disposable income (the difference between $\Delta C/Y$ for the single rate and the zero rate).

In the case of zero CIT shifting, the absolute magnitudes of the redistributive effects of dual rates are similar. Again, the benefits of both full and partial exemptions are concentrated among those with an income below $7,500. Full exemption, for example, would increase the disposable income of the lowest income group by 2.7 percent, compared to a single-rate VAT (although the net tax burden

---

6. Note that the "half-rate," 4.95 percent, is more than one-half the "single rate," 7.22 percent, simply because the full rate applied to nonexempt commodities, 9.89 percent, must be above the single rate to compensate for the lower rate applied to preferentially treated commodities, and the half rate is one-half this full rate. In general the relationship between the degree of exemption, the full rate, and the "exemption rate" is given by

$$Z_f = \frac{R}{C(1 + \rho e - \rho)}$$
$$Z_e = eZ_f$$

where    $Z_f$ is the full rate,

$Z_e$ is the rate applied to preferential commodities,

$e$ is the ratio of the preferential to the full rate,

$C$ is total personal consumption expenditure (the *VAT base*),

$\rho$ is the proportion of expenditure accounted for by preferential commodities, and

$R$ is the required VAT revenue yield.

In the present case with $\rho = 0.54$ and $R/C = 0.0722$ (the single VAT rate, i.e., in the absence of exemptions; assuming full CIT repeal and shifting), the relationship between $e$ and the VAT rate is

of this group would still rise by 3.0 percent in comparison to the presubstitution level of disposable income). However, because the substitution with zero CIT shifting is so much more steeply regressive (through the effect of increased profits), the dual-rate systems are also significantly more regressive compared to the pretax-substitution condition. Without exception, the Gini coefficient is increased by the tax substitution from 0.374 to 0.397; half-exemption reduces it only to 0.395, and full exemption has the almost unnoticeable marginal effect of an 0.001 reduction (to 0.394). But to achieve these relatively minor improvements in incidence it is necessary to increase the normal VAT rate from 7.68 percent (no exemption) to 10.48 percent (half exemption) and 16.48 percent (full exemption), respectively.

If dual rates only mitigated regressivity, even marginally, they might be justified. However, apart from their marginal redistributive effectiveness, they can be expected to have a significant adverse impact on other dimensions of the economic structure. Note particularly the radical rate differences which are implied by dual-rate systems: full rates of about 10 percent versus half rates of 5 percent or full rates in excess of 15 percent with total exemption of preferred commodities. The allocative effects of such substantial rate differentials can certainly be expected to be noticeable and are

---

$$Z_f = \frac{0.0722}{(0.46 + 0.54e)}$$

and

$$Z_e = \frac{0.0722e}{(0.46 + 0.54e)}.$$

or graphically

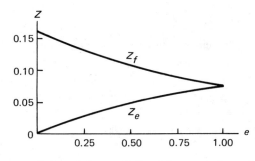

The general characteristics of these relationships are independent of the specific values of the variables $C$, $R$, and $\rho$.

necessarily adverse. With such staggering rate differentials it is hard to believe that consumer budget composition would not be altered in an attempt to minimize the burden of the tax. Thus, a dual rate VAT could entail substantial excess burdens, i.e., losses in welfare due solely to the peculiarities of the tax system.

In brief, dual rates minimally reduce the regressivity of the VAT-CIT substitution, but only by sacrificing the major claim which can be made for the VAT: its allocative neutrality. Even if other benefits can validly be claimed for the substitution, e.g., growth and trade advantages (the validity of which will be discussed in succeeding sections), or elimination of biases against equity financing, these could be achieved much more efficiently by other means, e.g., investment credits and devaluation or various forms of integration of personal and corporate income taxes, without incurring either the adverse allocative or redistributive effects of dual- or single-rate VAT systems.

However, alternatives to dual rate systems can be suggested to offset the regressivity of the substitution, and render it redistributively neutral or desirable. These can only be discussed here briefly. The least radical means would be to permit *VAT liabilities to be credited against federal personal income tax liabilities.* For this method to work it would be necessary, first, that net credits, i.e., the excess of gross credits for the VAT over gross personal income tax liabilities, be refunded to the taxpayer, and second, that the *degree* of credit depend upon income, declining as income rises.[7] Under this method either the VAT rate would have to be increased, so that reduced income tax revenues would be compensated by increased VAT revenues, implying VAT rates significantly higher than those discussed here, *or* changes in the *level and structure* of income tax rates would have to be introduced to compensate for the aggregate *net* income tax revenue loss resulting from the VAT credit. In either case, the net incidence of the change in tax structure would result from compensating changes in *three* tax instruments: the VAT, the CIT, and the personal income tax. Changes in the structure and yield of the latter would have to be explicitly incorporated into the analysis if the consequences of the tax substitution were to be assessed.

A more substantial change in tax structure which could also

---

7. Note that the use of rebatable credits would require that all households file income tax returns, even those whose income is so low that they are not otherwise subject to the income tax. This would involve a quantum leap in the administrative burden of the income tax, particularly since the tax reform act of 1969.

serve to offset the regressivity of the VAT-CIT substitution would be the simultaneous introduction of a *progressive expenditures tax* (PET) [Kaldor].[8] At one extreme, the PET could be designed so that, by applying appropriate negative and positive PET rates, the net incidence of the PET-augmented VAT-CIT substitution would be reduced to zero on average for any income class (or to a positive constant, i.e., a tax liability proportionate to income, if the CIT were shifted forward, since that would imply a net increase in domestic tax liabilities due to the benefit accruing to the rest of the world in the form of lower export prices).

At the other extreme, it would be possible to dispense with the VAT completely, relying only on the PET to compensate for CIT removal. In that case, any desired degree of progressivity could be built into the substitution simply by manipulating the PET rate structure. Of course, much the same effects could be obtained by using the personal income tax to compensate for corporate tax removal, e.g., by integrating corporate and personal income taxation and by introducing appropriate simultaneous changes in the rate structure of the latter. However, the two alternatives are *not* indentical. In terms of consumption and savings effects major differences could be expected. Thus, the personal income tax and the PET offer basically different alternatives for replacement of the CIT or mitigation of VAT regressivity. In terms of incentive effects, it might be noted, the PET would more closely approximate the VAT than would the personal income tax, particularly with reference to the trade and investment effects discussed in the following chapters.

---

8. Administration of the progressive expenditures tax entails certain difficulties, although these are not insurmountable. In a regime already employing an income tax, introduction of PET would require in addition only the computation of annual flows into or out of investment, or to or from gifts and bequests.

✳ *Chapter 5*

# Capital Stock and Investment Effects of the VAT-CIT Substitution

Standing virtually on a par with the alleged adverse international trade effects of the corporate income tax, examined in the following chapter, is the damping effect which the CIT is claimed to exert on economic growth through reduction in the rate of investment. Two views of this adverse investment effect have been advanced.

The first rests upon the relation of corporate liquidity to investment. With fixed or limited debt-equity ratios, the rate of net investment is constrained by the rate of growth of the equity base. The CIT enters this process by eroding one of the most important sources of nondebt finance: corporate retained earnings. A CIT reduction that was not fully shifted forward in the form of lower prices would result in an increase in after-tax corporate profits. Some fraction of this profit increase would presumably be translated into increased dividends, but the remainder, representing an increase in retained earnings, could be used to finance a net increase in corporate investment. And even if the CIT were shifted forward, the CIT reduction would increase the level of *real* net profits and hence investment because prices of capital goods would fall as a result of reductions and shifts of the CIT and of the simultaneous imposition of a consumption-type VAT which exempted capital goods purchases from tax. Thus, the liquidity theory of investment would predict an increase in the rate of investment in response to the VAT-CIT substitution, regardless of the degree of CIT shifting.

An alternative to this financial or cash-flow view of investment is the neoclassical theory of the determinants of real rates of investment [Hall and Jorgenson; Jorgenson and Siebert].

In the neoclassical theory, the process of investment determination is decomposed into two distinct phases: (1) determination of the *optimal capital stock* and (2) determination of the *rate of investment* over time by which the optimal capital stock is to be realized. In this context, the VAT-CIT substitution alters the rate of investment primarily through its effects on the optimal capital stock. Application of the CIT reduces the net rate of return to capital relative to the gross rate; this results in a reduction of the optimal capital stock. Therefore, reduction or repeal of the CIT would, ceteris paribus, raise the net rate of return to capital and hence increase the optimal capital stock.

The fundamental assumption of neoclassical theory is that the behavior of firms is profit-maximizing. Thus, the theory is applicable only to the case of zero CIT shifting, in which capital earnings in the short run represent quasi-rents. Application of the neoclassical model under the assumption of any degree of short-run forward shifting of a profits tax involves either assuming a highly elastic supply of foreign capital or the analysis of a farily complex and dynamic set of reactions if internal contradictions which would render the exercise of little value are to be avoided. Even in the classical case of zero CIT shifting the neoclassical theory relies upon assumptions concerning production functions which are much more rigorous than, and in formal contradiction to, those imposed by an input-output model.

Because of these incompatibilities between the neoclassical theory of investment and the model underlying our study of the VAT-CIT substitution, the analysis in this chapter of the investment effects of the tax substitution is limited to applications of the liquidity theory of investment. On the basis of previous analyses of investment behavior the effect of the VAT-CIT substitution on cumulative *gross* investment and short-term investment demand are assessed. These investment effects are projected first under the classical assumption of zero CIT shifting and then under the polar assumption of full forward shifting, assuming in both cases that the CIT is completely repealed. Estimates of the investment effects are developed for a selected set of individual manufacturing industries, for all manufacturing, and for all industries.

The liquidity theory of investment effectively explains real gross investment in the current period as a function of real cash flow in past periods. As originally formulated by Meyer and Glauber, whose estimates by industry are most consistent with the present application, real gross investment in period $t(I_t)$, is determined by

$$I_t = a_0 + a_1 (T - V)_{t-1} + a_2 c_{t-1} + a_3 r_{t-3}$$

$$+ a_4 \Delta SP_{t-1} + a_5 I_{t-2}, \tag{5-1}$$

where $T$ is real profit plus depreciation; $V$ is real dividends; $T - V$ represents real *net* cash flow (net profit plus depreciation minus dividends); $c$ is an index of capital utilization; $r$ is a market interest rate; and $SP$ is an index of stock prices. Because of the inclusion of lagged investment as a determinant of current investment, investment in the current period is a function of a stream of past cash flows. Thus, under the Meyer-Glauber formulation, an increase in cash flow in period $t$ will then influence investment in periods $t + 1, t + 3,$ $t + 5, \ldots$. This cumulative (undiscounted) increment in gross investment demand resulting from a unit change in current cash flow is simply

$$\text{Cum } I = \sum_{s=1}^{\infty} \frac{\Delta I_{t+s}}{\Delta (T - V)_t} = \frac{a_1}{1 - a_5}, \tag{5-2}$$

where $a_1$ is the coefficient of net cash flow and $a_5$ is the coefficient of lagged investment in equation (5-1). Estimates of these coefficients have been derived by Meyer and Glauber for eleven manufacturing industries [p. 155].

To project the cumulative increase in gross investment due to an increase in cash flow it is necessary first to predict what fraction of that increase in cash flow would be siphoned off by higher dividends. The liquidity theory of investment does not itself explain corporate dividend behavior. To project the consequences of increased gross cash flows for the level of dividends we made use of Brittain's estimates of the determinants of corporate dividend behavior. In Brittain's analysis, dividends or, equivalently, retained earnings, are explained by the levels of profit and depreciation, and by the effect of the tax system on the desirability of capital gains relative to current dividend income. The basic dividend relationship proposed by Brittain is simply

$$D = b_0 + b_1 P + b_2 A + b_3 t_{25} P + (1 - b_4) D_{-1}, \tag{5-3}$$

Where $D$ is the level of nominal dividend payments; $P$ is nominal net-of-tax profit; $A$ is the nominal depreciation charge; and $t_{25}$ is a "tax shelter" variable (marginal rate of personal income tax at the highest quartile of the distribution of dividend income, reflecting the relative desirability of capital gains over current income).

Equation (5–3) provides a basis for estimating dividends in *nominal* dollar terms. That is, a given change in *nominal* net-of-tax profit induces a change in *nominal* dividends. The change in real cash flow net of dividends is then the nominal change in net cash flow (change in net profit less change in dividends) deflated by a relevant price index. It is this change in real cash flow which serves to alter future investment behavior in the Meyer-Glauber model. For projecting investment behavior by industry the change induced in nominal net cash flow by tax substitution is deflated by an industry-specific index of investment goods prices. The index is obtained by applying interindustry capital flows as weights to tax-substitution-induced changes in individual capital goods prices.

## 5.1 INVESTMENT EFFECTS WITH ZERO SHIFTING

Under the classical assumption of zero CIT shifting, the supply schedule for capital goods will be unaffected by the tax substitution, though the effective price may rise as a result of increased demand for these goods, at least in the short run. However, if the CIT is repealed, after-tax profits increase by the full amount of original CIT liabilities. These initial CIT liabilities, or profit increases by industry, are presented in the first column of Table 5–1. Estimates of the change in dividends, based on Brittain's industry-specific estimates of the net profit-dividend relationship, are contained in the second column. The change in net cash flow (column 3) is simply the increase in profit less the increase in dividends. This represents the real net cash flow effect of the tax substitution, under the assumptions of CIT repeal, zero CIT shifting, and unchanged capital goods prices.

The *long-run investment effect* of this change in real net cash flow is then determined via the gross investment parameters estimated by Meyer and Glauber, again on an industry-specific basis. These investment effects represent undiscounted sums of the effects of the current-year increase in the net cash flow on investment in all future years.

For all manufacturing and for all industries these cumulative investment effects are approximately 1 1/3 times the increase in net cash flow. Compared to the original CIT liability, the cumulative

Table 5-1. Investment Effects of the Tax Substitution, Cash-Flow Approach; Assuming CIT Repeal and Zero CIT Shifting (dollars in millions)

| Industry | CIT Liability (= Profit Increase) (1) | Dividend Increase (2) | Increase in Real Net Corporate Cash Flow (3) | Cumulative Increase in Corporate Gross Investment (4) | Short-run Investment Effect (5) |
|---|---|---|---|---|---|
| Food and tobacco | $ 1,727 | $ 592 | $ 1,135 | $ 212 | 4.8% |
| Textiles and apparel | 964 | 282 | 682 | 483 | 10.3 |
| Paper and allied products | 873 | 250 | 623 | 1,450 | 26.9 |
| Chemicals | 3,182 | 954 | 2,228 | 1,226 | 5.6 |
| Petroleum and coal | 692 | 207 | 485 | 638 | 3.1 |
| Rubber | 454 | 64 | 390 | 293 | 11.4 |
| Stone, clay, and glass | 630 | 190 | 440 | 543 | 9.2 |
| Iron and steel | 818 | 314 | 504 | 496 | 2.2 |
| Nonferrous metals | 257 | 99 | 158 | 530 | 7.3 |
| Machinery, except electrical | 2,446 | 939 | 1,507 | 2,263 | 22.6 |
| Electrical machinery | 2,182 | 838 | 1,344 | 2,753 | 8.6 |
| Manufacturing | 21,923 | 6,351 | 15,572 | 20,580 | 11.5 |
| All industries | 42,680 | 18,429 | 24,251 | 32,050 | 5.3 |

Notes:
Column 1: Estimated by Milton L. Godfrey of Cybermatics, Inc. See Appendix A.
Column 2: Estimation is based on Table 27 and equation (4–10), Corporate Dividend Policy, J. A. Brittain.
Column 3: Column 1 less Column 2.
Column 4: Estimation is based on [Meyer and Glauber, Table VII–5 and eq. (1), Table VII–2].
Column 5: Percent increase in gross investment is computed by means of (short-run) cash-flow elasticity indicated in [Meyer and Glauber, Table VII–6]. Cash flow = net profits less dividends plus depreciation.

increase in the investment activity of manufacturing industries is about equal to the CIT liability, while for all industry the investment effect is only about four-fifths the CIT liability. In both cases, however, the investment effects are certainly significant. As percentages of actual 1969 investment the tax-substitution-induced increases are 20 percent and 8 percent for manufacturing and for all industries, respectively. Recall, however, that these effects would in fact be distributed over future periods rather than being concentrated in the current period.

In fact, the persistence of these gross investment effects over the long term renders their interpretation somewhat difficult. The Meyer and Glauber short-run elasticities of investment with respect to net cash flow, which ignore the lagged investment effects, provide an alternative basis for projecting the investment stimulus of the tax substitution. The estimated short-run effects can be more directly interpreted as predictions of the initial consequences of the tax substitution. Short-run percentage increases in gross investment, as presented in column 5 of Table 5-1, were obtained by multiplying the short-run cash flow elasticity (from Meyer and Glauber) by the percentage increase in real net cash flow prior to the tax substitution. In the short run, the repeal of the CIT, assuming zero CIT shifting, is estimated to increase investment by 12 percent in manufacturing and by 5 percent in all industries.

The investment stimulus of the tax substitution is observed to vary significantly over individual manufacturing industries. The cumulative investment expansion ranges from 20 percent to 350 percent of the increase in net cash flow (initial CIT liability less increase in dividends), with food and tobacco at the low end of the spectrum and nonferrous metals at the high end. Relative to the original CIT liabilities, the gross investment effects fall between 12 percent (food and tobacco) and 206 percent (nonferrous metals).

In terms of short-run investment elasticities a very different distribution of industries emerges. The estimated percentage increase in investment is only 2 percent in iron and steel and 3 percent in petroleum and coal, versus 23 percent in nonelectrical machinery and 27 percent in paper and allied products. In these short-run terms, nonferrous metals and food and tobacco, which represented the high and low cumulative investment extremes, are much closer, with 7 percent and 5 percent investment increases respectively.

These anticipated short-run investment responses are particularly significant when it is considered that they reflect only the first-year effects of the tax substitution. While further rounds of factor and output-market price adjustments would be expected to alter (probably erode) the very long-term effects of the substitution, the short-run responses can more realistically be interpreted as actual projections. The cumulative investment responses, on the other hand, must be interpreted primarily as indices of the degree of required future adjustment. However, the estimates of long-term, cumulative investment responses are uniquely interesting nonetheless. As the interindustry differences between cumulative and short-run effects indicate, those industries which are ultimately most significantly affected by the tax substitution are not necessarily those showing the most marked immediate responses. Those industries which, primarily for technological reasons, exhibit low short-run investment elasticities, may yet exhibit the most substantial longer term responses to the change in tax structure. Alternatively, equivalent short-run responses to the tax substitution need not imply that two industries will not be differentially affected by the tax substitution in the longer run.

## 5.2 INVESTMENT EFFECTS WITH FULL SHIFTING

For the polar case of full forward shifting of the CIT, the analysis is somewhat simpler. Obviously, nominal net cash flow is unaffected by the tax substitution since after-tax profits are unchanged, and dividends, in Brittain's analysis, are determined only by *nominal* net profit. Thus, the investment effects stem entirely from changes in capital goods prices and hence in *real* net cash flow, given the pre-tax-substitution level of *nominal* net cash flow. The unchanged nominal net cash flow is given in the first column of Table 5-2. The relative reduction in capital goods prices (column 2) differs very little over industries, ranging from 5.3 to 5.9 percent with a mean for manufacturing and for all industries of about 5.5 percent.

Given the increase in real net cash flow (column 3), the cumulative gross investment effect (column 4) is then obtained via equation (5-2). For manufacturing, the induced expansion of investment is about $2.7 billion or about 13 percent of the cumulative investment effect under the assumption of zero CIT shifting. However, the $9 billion all-industry effect is relatively greater, at about 30 percent of the zero-shifting stimulus, reflecting the greater importance of unincorporated enterprise in sectors other than manufacturing when full shifting, rather than zero shifting, is assumed. That is, under the latter assumption no investment stimulus was felt in the unincorporated sector, since only corporate cash flows were increased and capital goods prices were unaffected. However, under the as-

Table 5-2. Investment Effects of the Tax Substitution, Cash-Flow Approach, Assuming CIT Repeal and Full CIT Shifting (dollars in millions)

| Industry | Corporate Cash Flow (1) | Reduction in Price of Investment Goods (2) | Increase in Real Net Corporate Cash Flow (3) | Cumulative Increase in Corporate Gross Investment (4) | Cumulative Increase in Total Gross Investment (5) | Short-run Investment Effect (6) |
|---|---|---|---|---|---|---|
| Food and tobacco | $ 3,819 | 5.95% | $ 242 | $ 45 | $ 57 | 1.3% |
| Textiles and apparel | 1,614 | 5.42 | 93 | 66 | 68 | 1.5 |
| Paper and allied products | 1,917 | 5.32 | 108 | 251 | 251 | 4.7 |
| Chemicals | 4,614 | 5.81 | 284 | 156 | 160 | 0.7 |
| Petroleum and coal | 395 | 5.26 | 220 | 289 | 307 | 1.5 |
| Rubber | 946 | 5.72 | 57 | 43 | 43 | 1.7 |
| Stone, clay, and glass | 1,416 | 5.78 | 87 | 107 | 112 | 1.9 |
| Iron and Steel | 2,903 | 5.75 | 177 | 174 | 175 | 0.8 |
| Nonferrous metals | 915 | 5.60 | 54 | 182 | 182 | 2.5 |
| Machinery except electrical | 3,792 | 5.52 | 221 | 332 | 343 | 3.4 |
| Electrical machinery | 2,845 | 5.71 | 172 | 353 | 356 | 1.1 |
| Manufacturing | 33,995 | 5.50 | 1,979 | 2,615 | 2,672 | 1.5 |
| All industries | 73,627 | 5.45 | 4,244 | 5,609 | 8,980 | 1.5 |

Notes:
Column 1: Estimated by Milton L. Godfrey of Cybermatics, Inc.
Column 2: Estimation is based on Table 3–8 and 1969 capital flows as estimated by Milton L. Godfrey, Cybermatics, Inc.
Column 3: Column 1 subtracted from [column 1 ÷ (1 − column 2/100)].
Column 4: Same as for column 4, Table 5–1.
Column 5: Increase in total gross investment (corporate and noncorporate) as approximated by multiplying the increase in corporate gross investment by 1 plus the ratio between depreciation in the two sectors.
Column 6: Same as for column 5, Table 5–1.

sumption of full CIT shifting the source of the investment stimulus is identical in both incorporated and unincorporated sectors. In both sectors the investment expansion derives entirely from the tax-substitution-induced reductions in capital goods prices.

For all industries, the cumulative increase in gross investment ($9 billion) is more than twice the increase in real corporate cash flow ($4.2 billion) but only about 23 percent of original CIT liabilities ($42.7 billion). For manufacturing, the $2.7 billion cumulative investment effect is about 125 percent of the increase in real cash flow ($2 billion) but only 12 percent of initial CIT liabilities ($21.9 billion).

Individual manufacturing industries again exhibit wide variations, with a cumulative investment response of only 25 percent of the increase in real cash flow in food and tobacco versus an investment expansion in excess of 300 percent of the increased real cash flow in nonferrous metals. The mean cumulative investment effect for this selected group of industries is somewhat in excess of the manufacturing average of 125 percent of the cash flow increase.

The gross investment effects, computed as before from short-run elasticities (Meyer and Glauber), are closely grouped around 1.5 percent (manufacturing and all industries). Iron and steel is again relatively low (0.8 percent), although the lowest estimated increase is in chemicals (0.7 percent). The greatest short-run investment stimulus is observed in paper and allied products (4.7 percent).

Thus, under either extreme assumption for CIT shifting, investment would be significantly stimulated by the tax substitution. However, the investment expansion would be much greater, particularly in the short run, if the CIT were not shifted (a 5.3 percent increase in gross investment for all industry) than if the CIT were fully shifted (a 1.5 percent investment increase). In either event, the investment claims for the tax substitution are broadly substantiated, at least in the short run.

✳ *Chapter 6*

# The Tax Substitution and
# International Trade

Of the debates concerning the potential effects of a value
added tax, none have been more confused than those concerning international trade. Because the VAT would be
rebated on exports and imposed as a border tax on imports, it is
often alleged that it would therefore *stimulate* exports and *restrict*
imports.

These effects are corollaries to the asserted discriminatory consequences for the U.S. balance of trade of the recent European ex-
tensions of the value added tax. Common Market countries have
been replacing previously existing indirect business taxes with value
added taxes as part of the tax harmonization efforts of the EEC,
and similar moves toward value added taxes have been taken in the
rest of Europe. These developments have often been cited as a
significant contributing cause of the deterioration over the last
decade of the U.S. trade position.

There are, in fact, two related questions to ask about the trade
effects of a VAT: First, what are the consequences of a VAT-CIT
substitution for a country's international trade position? And,
second, given these consequences (if any), is this tax substitution the
most desirable means of achieving trade objectives?

The question of the trade consequences of a VAT is simultaneously simple and complex. Most simply stated, there are no trade
effects of a VAT per se. Whether changes in export and import
patterns will accompany the introduction of a VAT depends upon
the relative price consequences of the menu of change in the VAT
and in other taxes. If the only consequence of the VAT and simul-

taneous changes in other taxes and government expenditures (or deficits) is to increase VAT-inclusive prices by the amount of the VAT and leave VAT-exclusive prices unchanged, then no trade consequences unique to the tax substitution can be expected. VAT-exclusive export prices will be unchanged, and VAT-inclusive import prices will rise by the same amount as the prices of import-competing goods. More generally, changes in exports will depend upon changes in export prices relative to world market prices, and imports will be affected only if import prices are affected differently than the prices of import-competing goods. Of course, even if these relative prices are unaffected by the tax substitution, imports and exports may be affected if the policy change alters the aggregate level of economic activity and hence demands for both domestic *and* foreign products, or if the composition of aggregate demand is altered.[1] But these effects of a change in fiscal policy could in general be achieved by means other than a tax substitution.

If the VAT is fully shifted forward, its effect on export prices relative to world prices and import prices relative to prices of domestic import-competing goods will be neutral. Relative price changes can then only result from other fiscal changes which accompany the introduction of the VAT. This means that the source of any change in the level and composition of the trade balance must be found in price changes resulting from the reduction *and* shifting of the corporate profits tax. The U.S. trade balance will be favorably affected by the tax substitution only if export prices are reduced by shifting some fraction of the benefits of the CIT reduction to foreign purchasers, as discussed in Chapter 4, or if import-competing prices rise by less than the VAT rate due to forward shifting of the CIT savings. Thus, just as in the case of relative price changes generally, the causal burden of changes in the balance of trade is on the CIT reduction rather than on the VAT imposition.

The answer to the second question—the relative desirability of the VAT as a means of achieving trade objectives—is somewhat simpler. Briefly put, any *trade* effects which can be achieved via a VAT, e.g., as a substitute for a forward-shifted CIT, can be as easily achieved via a one-time change in exchange rates. In consequence, trade effects would not seem to provide a compelling reason for introducing a VAT. However, it should be noted that while the consequences of a VAT-CIT substitution on the *balance of trade* might be equivalent to a corresponding devaluation, differential effects of these alternative policies for the *composition of trade* and for

---

1. These issues and the general subject of the trade consequences of the VAT are discussed in greater detail by Stout.

*international capital flows* and the *balance of payments* render the devaluation a less-than-perfect alternative to the VAT-CIT substitution. This point, and a further discussion of the effects on U.S. trade of the European value added taxes, will be considered in somewhat more detail at the conclusion of this chapter.

## 6.1 EFFECT OF VAT-CIT SUBSTITUTION ON EXPORTS

To repeat, the export consequences of the tax substitution depend only upon price changes resulting from the shifted CIT reduction. Given any export price changes it is then possible to determine what the resultant increase in exports will be. First, consider the definitional relationships between the *value* of exports ($V_x$), the *quantity* of exports ($x$), and relative export prices ($P_x/P_w$), where $P_x$ is the domestic price of exports and $P_w$ is an index of world prices:

$$V_x = xP_x. \tag{6-1}$$

The quantity of exports is related to domestic export prices and to world market prices via a demand function of foreign purchasers for domestic exports, i.e.,

$$x = f(P_x/P_w). \tag{6-2}$$

For present purposes the essential information conveyed by this demand function can be summarized in terms of the *price elasticity* of the demand for exports, $\epsilon_x$. Setting the indices of world prices and of pre-tax-substitution domestic export prices equal to unity, and assuming world prices to be unaffected by changes in domestic export prices ($dP_w = 0$), this elasticity is defined as

$$\epsilon_x = \left[\frac{dx}{d(P_x/P_w)}\right]\frac{P_x/P_w}{x} = \frac{dx}{dP_x}\frac{P_x}{x}. \tag{6-3}$$

Then, by differentiating equation (6-1) with respect to $P_x$, the consequences for the *value* of exports of any change in export prices, can be determined:

$$\frac{dV_x}{dP_x} = x + P_x\left(\frac{dx}{dP_x}\right) = x + x\left(\frac{dx}{dP_x}\right)\left(\frac{P_x}{x}\right) = x(1 + \epsilon_x), \tag{6-4}$$

or alternatively, the resultant change in export value is

$$dV_x = x(dP_x)\ (1 + \epsilon_x) = V_x\left(\frac{dP_x}{P_x}\right)(1 + \epsilon_x), \qquad (6\text{-}5)$$

since $x = V_x/P_x$.

Equation (6-5) provides the basis for estimating the hypothetical consequences of any tax-substitution-induced changes in prices for the value of U.S. exports. Estimates are already available for all the elements entering this equation except the price elasticity of export demand $(\epsilon_x)$: $V_x$ simply represents aggregate exports prior to the tax substitution, i.e., for present purposes actual exports in 1969; and estimates of the percentage change in export prices, $(dP_x/P_x)$, resulting from the tax substitution are contained in Table 3-5. A value of -1.24 for $\epsilon_x$, which has been estimated statistically by Houthakker and Magee, underlies the basic analysis. To assess the sensitivity of the export expansion and the improvement in the balance of trade resulting from the tax substitution, the absolutely higher elasticity of -2 is used as an alternative estimate. This higher value, although arbitrary, is consistent with the conventional conception of export demand as relatively price elastic.

The export expansions, or increases in the value of exports, corresponding to alternative stipulations concerning the degee of CIT reduction and shifting are presented in Table 6-1. The case of zero CIT shifting is clearly trivial: $dP_x = 0$, and no change in either the value or physical volume of exports is observed in the short run. With positive CIT shifting the increase in export value is proportionate to the percentage reduction in export prices, with $1 + \epsilon_x$ providing the factor of proportionality. Thus, the difference in export value under the alternative elasticity assumptions is greater than the difference between the elasticities [= -2 - (-1.24)]: If $\epsilon_x = -1$, then $V_x$ is independent of export price, i.e., $dV_x = 0$. Thus, the estimated expansion under the higher elasticity is always 4.17 [= (-2 + 1)/(-1.24 + 1)] times that under the lower elasticity.

Even under the assumption of full CIT removal and shifting the export effects are disappointingly small. With an elasticity of -2, the $2.3 billion increase in exports is only 5.3 percent of original export sales ($43.5 billion). The basic Houthakker-Magee elasticity of -1.24 implies an even more marginal increase in exports of less than $0.6 billion, or 1.3 percent of original export sales. However, with the higher elasticity, the export expansion alone would be sufficient to move the balance of trade from a deficit of $0.7 billion

**Table 6-1. Hypothetical Changes in U.S. Trade Balance, 1969 (dollars in billions)**

| CIT Shifting Parameter ($\alpha$) | Export Price Reduction $\left(-\dfrac{\Delta P_x}{P_x}\right)$ | Import Competing Price Reduction $\left(-\dfrac{\Delta P_d}{P_d}\right)$ | Assuming Houthakker-Magee Elasticities ($\epsilon_x = -1.24; \epsilon_x = -0.88$) | | | | Assuming Higher Elasticities ($\epsilon_x = -2.00; \epsilon_m = -1.00$) | | | |
|---|---|---|---|---|---|---|---|---|---|---|
| | | | Increase in Exports ($\Delta V_x$) | Export-Induced Imports ($\Delta V_m{'}$) | Reduction in Imports ($-\Delta V_m$) | Change in Trade Balance ($\Delta V$) | Increase in Exports ($\Delta V_x$) | Export-Induced Imports ($\Delta V_m{'}$) | Reduction in Imports ($-\Delta V_m$) | Change in Trade Balance ($\Delta V$) |
| | | | *CIT Reduction of 25 Percent* | | | | | | | |
| 0.2 | 0.29% | 0.31% | $0.030 | $.007 | $0.121 | $0.144 | $0.126 | $.011 | $0.137 | $0.252 |
| 0.6 | 1.06 | 1.14 | .111 | .025 | 0.443 | 0.529 | 0.461 | .041 | 0.504 | 0.924 |
| 1.0 | 2.26 | 2.39 | .236 | .053 | 0.930 | 1.113 | 0.983 | .086 | 1.056 | 1.953 |
| | | | *CIT Reduction of 50 Percent* | | | | | | | |
| 0.2 | 0.56 | 0.61 | .058 | .013 | 0.237 | 0.282 | 0.244 | .022 | 0.270 | 0.492 |
| 0.6 | 1.91 | 2.06 | .199 | .045 | 0.801 | 0.955 | 0.831 | .073 | 0.911 | 1.669 |
| 1.0 | 3.66 | 3.92 | .382 | .085 | 1.525 | 1.822 | 1.592 | .137 | 1.733 | 3.188 |
| | | | *CIT Reduction of 75 Percent* | | | | | | | |
| 0.2 | 0.82 | 0.89 | .086 | .020 | 0.346 | 0.412 | 0.357 | .032 | 0.393 | 0.718 |
| 0.6 | 2.62 | 2.83 | .274 | .062 | 1.101 | 1.313 | 1.140 | .099 | 1.251 | 2.292 |
| 1.0 | 4.63 | 5.00 | .483 | .107 | 1.945 | 2.321 | 2.014 | .171 | 2.210 | 4.053 |
| | | | *CIT Reduction of 100 Percent* | | | | | | | |
| 0.2 | 1.07 | 1.16 | .112 | .026 | 0.451 | 0.537 | 0.465 | .041 | 0.513 | 0.937 |
| 0.6 | 3.21 | 3.48 | .335 | .075 | 1.354 | 1.614 | 1.396 | .121 | 1.538 | 2.813 |
| 1.0 | 5.35 | 5.81 | .559 | .122 | 2.260 | 2.697 | 2.327 | .196 | 2.568 | 4.699 |

Notes to Table 6-1

$V_x$ = exports of goods and services exclusive of investment income = $43.5 billion in 1969; $V_m$ = imports of goods and services exclusive of investment income = $44.2 billion in the same year.

$$\Delta V_x = V_x \frac{\Delta P_X}{P_x}(1 + \epsilon_x),$$

**where** $\Delta P_x$ = change in export price, and $\epsilon_x$ = relative price elasticity of exports.

$$\Delta V_m = -V_m \frac{\Delta P_d}{P_d} \epsilon_m,$$

where $\Delta P_d$ = change in import price, and $\epsilon_m$ = relative price elasticity of imports.

$$\Delta V_m{}' = \gamma \left(V_x \frac{\Delta P_x}{P_x} \epsilon_x\right)\left(1 - \frac{\Delta P_d}{P_d} \epsilon_m\right)$$

where $\Delta V_m{}'$ = induced imports due to exports and $\gamma$ = total import coefficient per unit of exports = .0447.

$$\Delta V = \Delta V_x - \Delta V_m - \Delta V_m{}'.$$

Changes in aggregated price indices $\Delta P_x$ and $\Delta P_d$ are obtained by weighting changes in pre-VAT producer price by 1969 exports and imports, respectively.

to a surplus of $1.6 billion, while under the Houthakker-Magee elasticity the deficit would decline to $0.1 billion. The export consequences are, of course, correspondingly less for lower degrees of CIT reduction and CIT shifting.

## 6.2 EFFECT OF THE VAT-CIT SUBSTITUTION ON IMPORTS

The effects of the VAT-CIT substituion on imports can be approached in a similar manner. The value of imports $(V_m)$ is simply the product of their quantity $(m)$ and import prices $(P_m)$:

$$V_m = mP_m. \qquad (6\text{-}6)$$

The quantity of imports demanded can be expressed as a function of the price of imports relative to the prices of import-competing domestic commodities $(P_d)$. These prices can be viewed as VAT-exclusive since both domestic and imported commodities are subject to VAT (if at all), and the VAT $(Z)$ does not itself affect price relatives, i.e., $P_m(1 + Z)/P_d(1 + Z) = P_m/P_d$. Thus, the import demand function can be written as

$$m = g\left(\frac{P_m}{P_d}\right). \qquad (6\text{-}7)$$

Assuming again that domestic tax changes do not affect VAT-exclusive world market prices, i.e., that $P_m$ is a constant, then import demand can only be affected by changes in $P_d$. The price elasticity of demand for imports is simply defined as

$$\epsilon_m = \frac{dm}{d\left(\dfrac{P_m}{P_d}\right)} \left(\frac{P_m/P_d}{m}\right) \qquad (6\text{-}8)$$

and since $d P_m = 0$ $(P_m$ is constant),[2]

---

2. Note that

$$d\left(\frac{P_m}{P_d}\right) = \frac{1}{P_d}\, d P_m - \frac{P_m}{P_d{}^2}\, d P_d$$

and with $d P_m = 0$,

$$d\left(\frac{P_m}{P_d}\right) = -\left(\frac{P_m}{P_d}\right)\left(\frac{d P_d}{P_d}\right)$$

$$\epsilon_m = -\left(\frac{dm}{dP_d}\right)\left(\frac{P_d}{r}\right). \tag{6-8a}$$

Then differentiating the value of imports with respect to $P_d$ (the domestic import-competing price), we obtain

$$\frac{dV_m}{dP_d} = P_m\left(\frac{dm}{dP_d}\right) = P_m\left(\frac{m}{P_d}\right)\left(\frac{dm}{dP_d}\right)\left(\frac{P_d}{m}\right) = -\frac{V_m}{P_d}\epsilon_m. \tag{6-9}$$

Finally, the relative change in the value of imports is:

$$\frac{dV_m}{V_m} = -\frac{dP_d}{P_d}\epsilon_m \tag{6-10}$$

i.e., the product of the relative change in the price of import-competing goods and the price elasticity of import demand.

An index of percentage changes in the prices of import-competing goods resulting from the VAT-CIT substitution was obtained by weighting final producer prices in each industry by the quantity of imports. As in the case of exports, two alternative stipulations concerning $\epsilon_m$ have been used, the Houthakker-Magee estimate of $-0.88$ and the commonly assumed value of $-1$. The reduction in the value of imports due to the tax-substitution-induced change in prices of import-competing commodities is presented in Table 6-1 for the range of alternative CIT reduction and shifting assumptions.

## 6.3 AGGREGATE EXPORT-IMPORT EFFECTS

For imports as for exports, the trade consequences of the tax substitution follow entirely from the shifting of the CIT. If the CIT is not shifted ($\alpha = 0$), then VAT-exclusive price of domestic import-competing commodities will be unchanged by the tax substitution. VAT-inclusive (consumption) prices of both imports and domestically produced commodities will rise by the VAT rate, implying unchanged relative (domestic-to-import) prices. However, if the CIT reduction is shifted forward in the form of lower prices, then domestic prices will decline relative to prices on imports, which do not benefit from the CIT reduction. The relative reduction in imports is the product of the relative reduction in import-competing prices and the relative price elasticity of imports. Thus, the import contraction under the lower (Houthakker-Magee) elasticity of $-0.88$ is always 88 percent of the import contraction implied by the unitary elasticity assumption. With complete CIT repeal and full CIT shifting the import decline is projected to be $2.3 billion under the Houthakker-Magee elasticity and $2.6 billion under the unitary elasticity assumption. These import contractions, 5.1 percent and 5.8 percent of actual 1969 imports, respectively, would alone have been sufficient to move the United States trade position from a deficit of $0.7 billion to a surplus of either $1.6 billion or $1.9 billion. As always, smaller effects are observed in the case of lower degrees of CIT reduction and shifting.

One final trade effect of the tax substitution must be incorporated before the short-run consequences to the net balance of trade can be projected. This relates to the import effect of the export expansion. From the definition of the relative price elasticity of export demand, equation (6-3), the change in the *quantity* of exports resulting from the export price reduction is

$$dx = \epsilon_x \left( \frac{d\,P_x}{P_x} \right) x \ . \tag{6-11}$$

At prices prevailing prior to the tax substitution the quantity of imports absorbed in each unit of exports is given by the *total* import coefficient per unit of exports, $\gamma$, and the increase in imports due to export expansion is simply $\gamma dx$. However, if it is assumed that the response of export producers to the tax-substitution-induced change in the prices of import-competing goods is consistent with the aggregate relative price elasticity of imports, $\epsilon_m$, then a fraction $\frac{dP_d}{P_d} \epsilon_m$ of this initially induced increase in imports will be displaced by domestic production. Thus, the net increase in imports in response to the induced increase in exports, denoted $dV_{m'}$, is

$$d V_{m'} = \gamma \left[ x \left( \frac{dP_x}{P_x} \right) \epsilon_x \right] \left[ 1 - \left( \frac{d\,P_d}{P_d} \right) \epsilon_m \right] . \tag{6-12}$$

We evaluated this expression for both pairs of elasticity assumptions and for the alternative stipulations concerning CIT reduction and shifting, employing our observed (pre-tax-substitution) value of the total import coefficient of exports, $\gamma = 0.0447$.[3]

---

3. Note that $x$, the quantity of exports prior to the tax substitution, measured at pre-tax substitution prices, is simply $V_x$, i.e., $x = V_x$.

Under the lower (Houthakker-Magee) export and import elasticity assumptions, the export-induced increase in the value of imports is approximately 22 percent of the increase in the *value* of exports, while under the higher elasticities less than 9 percent of the export expansion is offset by induced imports.

The net change in the balance of trade is then simply the algebraic sum of these three components: the export expansion, the import contraction, and the export-induced increase in imports, i.e.,

$$dV = dV_x - dV_m - dV_{m'}. \qquad (6\text{--}13)$$

Changes in the balance of trade implied by the tax substitution are also indicated in Table 6–1. Under the most favorable assumptions of CIT repeal and full forward CIT shifting the balance of trade is improved by $2.7 billion assuming the lower (Houthakker-Magee) elasticities and by $4.7 billion assuming the higher elasticities. In all cases, the improvement is 74 percent greater using the higher elasticities.

In all cases the contribution of import contraction $(-dV_m)$ is greater than that of export expansion (either $dV_x$ or $dV_x - dV_{m'}$). With the higher elasticities, for which the export elasticity, disregarding signs, is 1 plus the import elasticity, the gross increase in export value $(dV_x)$ would just equal the reduction in imports $(-dV_m)$ if the relative reduction in export prices were equal to the relative reduction in the prices of domestic import-competing goods. However, the relative decline in the latter is approximately 8 percent greater than the relative reduction in export prices in all cases, i.e. $(dP_m/P_m) \cong 1.08 \ (dP_x/P_x)$, due primarily to the importance of agricultural exports, and this price difference generates a reduction in imports slightly greater than the gross increase in the value of exports. Because of the export-induced increase in imports (even adjusted for the reduction in import-competing prices), the decline in imports would be greater than the net increase in exports $(dV_x - dV_{m'})$ even if $|\epsilon_x| = 1 + |\epsilon_m|$.

The Houthakker-Magee elasticities, –1.24 for exports and –0.88 for imports, shift even more of the burden of the balance-of-trade improvement to imports. Even if prices of both exports and import-competing domestic goods changed proportionately, the import contraction would be 3.67 times greater than the gross expansion in the value of exports $-dV_m/dV_x = \epsilon_m/(1 + \epsilon_x) = 0.88/0.24$. Because import-competing prices decline relatively more than export prices, the import contraction is more than 3.7 times greater than the gross export expansion.

At this point a serious qualification is in order: There exists a fundamental contradiction between the aggregate export and import elasticities, on the one hand, and the export and import-competing price changes, on the other. Specifically, implicit in the estimation of the aggregate elasticities is the assumption that the *structure* of individual export (or import-competing) prices is unchanged, that is, all export (import-competing) prices must be assumed to change proportionately; only the level of these prices varies relative to world market prices. But the essential characteristic of the VAT-CIT substitution, under the assumption of forward shifting of the CIT, is that the structure of relative prices is altered. In particular, as discussed in Chapter 3, relative prices decline in those industries which are highly incorporated and capital intensive. Thus, the foregoing application of the aggregate elasticities is in contradiction to the assumptions underlying their estimation and interpretation. In the present context, in which relative prices are changing in response to the reduction and shifting of the CIT, trade effects can be legitimately projected only on a disaggregated basis. Because no reliable estimates of export and import elasticities by industry have been available, a somewhat compromising recourse has been to use estimates of aggregate elasticities. Since it is unlikely that the elasticities are identical for all industries, that procedure can at best be viewed as only an approximation.

In addition to its questionable legitimacy, the use of aggregate export and import elasticities obscures one of the most interesting dimensions of the trade consequences of the VAT-CIT substitution: the differential interindustry effects of the export and import-competing expansion. On the export side these balance-of-trade effects can be partially traced back to individual domestic industries by examining each industry's relative direct and indirect contribution of value added to total export sales. To precisely attribute the export expansion effects to individual industries it would, of course, be necessary to apply commodity-specific export price elasticities, information on which is generally nonexistent. However, export shares, in conjunction with relative price changes, are at least indicative of these differential interindustry effects.

## 6.4 INTERINDUSTY BALANCE-OF-TRADE EFFECTS

Table 6-2 indicates the distribution of export value added over producer industries. Those industries which make the greatest contributions to the value of exports and experience the greatest price re-

Table 6-2. Export Composition and Exports and Imports Relative to Industry Value Added, Two-Digit Aggregated Industries, 1969

| | Industry Share of Total Exports | Ratio to Value Added of Exports | Ratio to Value Added of Imports | Producer Price Reduction[a] |
|---|---|---|---|---|
| 1 AGRICULTURE | 7.68% | .1168 | .0681 | 2.20% |
| 2 METAL MINING | 0.55 | .2354 | .7975 | 3.75 |
| 3 COAL,STN,CLAY MNG&PROD | 2.40 | .0931 | .0615 | 5.96 |
| 4 OIL & GAS | 1.23 | .0548 | .2673 | 4.51 |
| 5 CONSTRUCTION | 1.62 | .0131 | .0000 | 4.31 |
| 6 ORDNANCE | 1.15 | .1603 | .1175 | 5.14 |
| 7 FOOD | 1.47 | .0318 | .1415 | 4.14 |
| 8 TOBACCO | 0.09 | .0251 | .0063 | 9.24 |
| 9 TEXTILES & APPAREL | 0.95 | .0271 | .1596 | 5.80 |
| 10 LUMBER,WOOD PRODUCTS | 1.17 | .0858 | .1968 | 5.05 |
| 11 FURNITURE & FIXTURES | 0.08 | .0100 | .0522 | 5.74 |
| 12 PAPER & PRODUCTS | 2.12 | .0981 | .1599 | 7.16 |
| 13 PRINTING & PUBLISHING | 1.61 | .0605 | .0104 | 7.61 |
| 14 CHEM.,PLAST.,DRUGS,PNT | 8.58 | .1876 | .0532 | 10.54 |
| 15 RUBBER & LEATHER | 1.28 | .0817 | .0768 | 6.42 |
| 16 FOOTWEAR | 0.03 | .0082 | .2483 | 4.86 |
| 17 PRIMARY METAL | 5.67 | .1289 | .1412 | 4.84 |
| 18 FABRICATED METAL | 5.28 | .0900 | .0234 | 6.45 |
| 19 NONELECT. MACHINERY | 9.33 | .1510 | .0686 | 6.23 |
| 20 ELECTRICAL EQUIPMENT | 5.67 | .1056 | .0821 | 6.87 |
| 21 TRANSP. EQUIPMENT | 6.47 | .1047 | .1972 | 6.10 |
| 22 INSTRUMENTS | 1.42 | .1114 | .0822 | 8.74 |
| 23 MISC. MANUFACTURING | 0.48 | .0557 | .2357 | 5.27 |
| 24 TRANSP. & WAREHOUSING | 9.50 | .1342 | .0775 | 3.30 |
| 25 COMMUNICATIONS | 1.18 | .0302 | .0000 | 11.86 |
| 26 UTILITIES | 1.24 | .0336 | .0029 | 9.56 |
| 27 FINANCE & INSURANCE | 1.41 | .0228 | .0140 | 16.30 |
| 28 REAL ESTATE & RENTAL | 4.41 | .0288 | b | 2.19 |
| 29 HOTELS & SERVICES | 6.66 | .0804 | b | 4.34 |
| 30 AUTO REPAIR & SERVICES | 0.62 | .0286 | b | 3.72 |
| 31 AMUSEMENTS | 0.17 | .0155 | b | 2.82 |
| 32 MED.,ED.SERV.&NONPROF. | 0.15 | .0019 | b | 2.23 |
| 33 WHOLESALE & RETAIL | 8.27 | .0341 | b | 1.08 |

Source: Milton L. Godfrey, Cybermatics, Inc. (See Appendix A, below.)
[a]Assuming complete CIT repeal ($S$ = 200 percent) and full forward shifting ($\alpha$ = 1).
[b]No Imports.

ductions due to shifting of the CIT can be anticipated to be most affected by the tax-substitution-induced stimulation of exports. Conversely, those with minimal direct and indirect contributions of value added to exports and exhibiting the most marginal reductions in prices would be only marginally affected by the export expansion per se, although they might be significantly affected by indirect factor and commodity price reactions to the increase in exports.

The industries which make the greatest contributions to exports are transportation and warehousing (9.5 percent of export value), wholesale trade (8.3 percent), agriculture (7.7 percent), chemicals (8.6 percent), nonelectrical machinery (9.3 percent), transportation equipment (6.5 percent), primary metals (5.7 percent), fabricated metals (5.3 percent), hotels and services (6.7 percent) and electrical equipment (5.7 percent). Together these ten industries account for about 73 percent of the value added embodied in exports.

However, five of these industries exhibit price reductions, assuming CIT repeal and full shifting, significantly smaller than average: wholesale trade (a 1.1 percent price reduction), agriculture (2.2 percent), transportation and warehousing (3.3 percent), hotels and services (4.3 percent) and primary metals (4.8 percent). Of these, wholesale trade, transportation and warehousing, and hotels and services would probably benefit significantly from the export expansion in any event, simply because of the nature of these industries, e.g., the role of trade and transportation in other export sales. Agriculture, on the other hand, would probably experience only a marginal export expansion, while the implications for primary metals would depend critically on the industry's own export elasticity and indirect embodiment in the exports of other industries, in particular fabricated metals, transportation equipment, and electrical and nonelectrical machinery.

The other five industries exhibit major price reductions (still assuming CIT repeal and full shifting): chemicals (10.5 percent), electrical equipment (6.9 percent), fabricated metals (6.5 percent), nonelectrical machinery (6.2 percent), and transportation equipment (6.1 percent). These industries would be expected to experience the most marked stimulus as a result of the export expansion.

At the other end of the spectrum are the industries whose contributions to export sales are negligible: furniture (0.1 percent); footwear (0.03 percent), tobacco (0.1 percent), and miscellaneous manufacturing (0.5 percent) industries. However, they might yet experience some stimulus from the export expansion as a result of price reductions, several of which are significant: tobacco (a 9.2 percent price reduction), furniture (5.7 percent), miscellaneous manufacturing (5.3 percent), and footwear (4.9 percent).

By ranking industries in the order of price reduction and then comparing their export shares, an alternative view is obtained of industries which might be expected to contribute significantly to the export expansion. Consider those industries experiencing the greatest price reductions: finance and insurance (a price reduction of 16.3 percent versus an export share of 1.4 percent), communications

(11.9 percent versus 1.2 percent), chemicals (10.5 percent versus 8.6 percent), utilities (9.6 percent versus 1.2 percent), tobacco (9.2 percent versus 0.1 percent), and instruments (8.7 percent versus 1.4 percent). Even those with relatively small export shares might yet gain significantly in export sales because of the decline in their selling prices.

Conversely, of industries exhibiting the smallest price reductions, even those with large shares of total export sales might be only marginally affected. Minimal price reductions are observed for wholesale and retail trade (1.1 percent price reduction versus 8.3 percent export share), real estate and rental (2.2 versus 4.4 percent), agriculture (2.2 versus 7.7 percent), medical and other services (2.2 versus 0.2 percent), amusements (2.8 versus 0.2 percent), auto repair and services (3.7 versus 0.6 percent), and metal mining (3.8 and 0.6 percent). Of these, only wholesale trade and real estate and rental could be expected to contribute significantly (indirectly) to the export expansion.

The foregoing discussion has concerned the probable contributions of different industries to the aggregate export expansion. A very different issue concerns those industries which *themselves* would be most markedly affected by increases in exports. As an indication of this potential intraindustry effect of the export expansion, estimates of value added embodied in exports as a ratio to total value added in the industry are also shown in Table 6-2.

## 6.5 VALUE ADDED AND EXPORT SUBSTITUTION

Not surprisingly, certain industries which account for a very small proportion of total exports nonetheless contribute a substantial proportion of their own value added to export sales. Most noteworthy is the case of metal mining: This industry accounts for only 0.6 percent of total exports, but 24 percent of the industry's value added is ultimately exported. The ordnance industry, accounting for 1.2 percent of exports but with exports absorbing 16 percent of total ordnance value added, provides another extreme example. With a below-average price reduction (3.8 percent), metal mining might not be markedly affected by a tax substitution, although one would also expect the relative export price elasticity to be quite high for this industry. Conversely, ordnance exhibits a more substantial price reduction, 5.1 percent, but is export price elasticity is probably much lower.

The two industries which would probably be most substantially affected internally by any export expansion are chemicals and nonelectrical machinery. Not only do these industries account for large shares of aggregate exports (8.6 and 9.3 percent, respectively) and experience relatively large price reductions if the CIT is repealed and shifted (10.5 and 6.2 percent, respectively), but exports also account for a substantial share of their own values added (18.8 percent for chemicals and 15.1 percent for nonelectrical machinery).

At the other extreme industries such as tobacco and textiles not only contribute only small shares of aggregate exports (0.1 and 1.0 percent, respectively), but exports also account for only marginal proportions of their own values added (2.5 percent for tobacco and 2.7 percent for textiles). Thus, even though they would experience significant price reductions if the CIT were repealed and fully shifted (9.2 percent for tobacco and 5.8 percent for textiles), it is still unlikely that these industries would participate in any aggregate export expansion resulting from the tax substitution.

Finally, an industry such as wholesale and retail trade accounts for a substantial 8.3 percent of aggregate export value added, but exports for this industry account for only 3.4 percent of its total value added. Thus, the industries in which the greatest absolute export expansion can be expected to occur are not necessarily the industries in which these export expansions will be large relative to the industry's own total output (value added).

## 6.6 VAT-CIT SUBSTITUTION AND IMPORT-COMPETING OUTPUT: INTERINDUSTRY EFFECTS

The probable interindustry effects of any substitution of domestic import-competing output for imports can be similarly traced back, at least in a general way, using estimates by industry of imports relative to domestic value added (exclusive of imports). As with the export expansion, those industries for which imports constitute a large fraction of total output *and* in which tax-substitution-induced price reductions are greatest would appear likely to experience the greatest import-substitution-induced increases in activity. Imports loom particularly large relative to domestic value added in six industries: metal mining (80 percent), oil and gas (27 percent), footwear (25 percent), miscellaneous manufacturing (24 percent), transportation equipment (20 percent), and lumber and wood products (20 percent). However, relative price reductions in the first three of these are significantly less than average, only 3.8 percent in metal mining, 4.5 percent in oil and gas, and 4.9 percent in footwear, suggesting that these industries might not experience marked import-substitution expansions. Although prices would decline markedly in such industries as tobacco (9.2 percent), printing (7.6 percent), and fabricated metals (6.5 percent), imports of these products are so small (0.6, 1.0, and 2.3 percent, respectively) that any import substitution effect would be almost unnoticeable.

## 6.7 DEVALUATION AND VAT-CIT SUBSTITUTION

In the introductory pages of this chapter it was suggested that any net change in the balance of trade resulting from the VAT-CIT substitution could also be obtained by an appropriate overall adjustment in exchange rates. This point can now be easily demonstrated. The effect of a devaluation of the United States currency by $100\eta$ percent is to reduce the index of *foreign* prices of U.S. exports from its original value $P_x$ to $(1 - \eta)P_x$. Of course, the *domestic* price of exports does not change ($dP_x = 0$), at least initially. Thus, the devaluation is equivalent to an increase in world prices from $P_w$ to $P_w/(1 - \eta)$. Given the definition of the relative price elasticity of exports, equation (6-3), the effect of a change in world prices equivalent to a devaluation of the domestic currency is:[4]

$$d V_x = - P_x x \epsilon_x \frac{dP_w}{P_w}, \qquad (6\text{-}14)$$

---

4. Since $dP_x = 0$,

$$d(P_x/P_w) = \frac{1}{P_w} dP_x - \frac{P_x}{P_w^2} dP_w = - \frac{P_x}{P_w^2} dP_w,$$

so that

$$\epsilon_x = \frac{dx}{(-P_x/P_w)dP_x} \frac{(P_x/P_w)}{x} = - \frac{dx}{dP_w} \frac{P_w}{x}$$

or

$$dx = - \epsilon_x x \frac{dP_w}{P_w}.$$

The change in the domestic value of exports ($V_x = P_x x$) is then

$$\frac{dV_x}{dP_w} = P_x \frac{dx}{dP_w} = - P_x \left( \epsilon_x x \frac{dP_w}{P_w} \right) \frac{1}{dP_w}.$$

Equation (6-14) is obtained from this relationship.

which will be positive since $\epsilon_x$ is negative.

On the import side, the devaluation increases the domestic price of imports, $P_m$, by $1/(1 - \eta)$, but the prices of import-competing goods ($P_d$) remain unchanged. The change in the value of imports ($V_m = P_m m$) resulting from an increase in import prices is then:[5]

$$dV_m = m\, P_m\, (1 + \epsilon_m)\left(\frac{dP_m}{P_m}\right). \tag{6-15}$$

Because the devaluation increases domestic import prices by a known amount– from $P_m$ to $P_m/(1 - \eta)$–the effect on import value can be determined.

Finally, as in the case of the tax substitution, it is necessary to incorporate the interaction between increased exports and imports, i.e., the increase in imports induced by the export expansion resulting from the devaluation. The increase in imports, were import prices unchanged, would simply be the product of the total import coefficient of exports ($\gamma$) and the export expansion ($dx$), i.e.,

$$\gamma dx = -\gamma\epsilon_x x \frac{dP_w}{P_w}.$$

Then, from equation (6-15), the export-induced expansion in imports, after taking into account the import price increase, is

$$dV_{m'} = -\gamma\epsilon_x\, x\, \frac{dP_w}{P_w}\, P_m\left(1 + \frac{dP_m}{P_m} + \frac{dP_m}{P_m}\epsilon_m\right). \tag{6-16}$$

---

5. If $dP_d = 0$, then

$$d(P_m/P_d) = \frac{1}{P_d}\, dP_m - \frac{P_m}{P_d^2}\, dP_d = \frac{dP_m}{P_d}$$

and the relative price elasticity of imports, equation (6-8), can be expressed as:

$$\epsilon_m = \frac{dm}{d(P_m/P_d)}\, \frac{P_m/P_d}{m} = \frac{dm}{(dP_m/P_d)}\, \frac{P_m/P_d}{m}$$

$$= \frac{dm}{dP_m}\, \frac{P_m}{m},$$

or

$$dm = \epsilon_m\, m\, \frac{dP_m}{P_m}.$$

$dV_{m'}$ must be subtracted from the export expansion to obtain the increase in exports net of induced imports.

The net effect of the devaluation on the balance of trade is simply the sum of the import, and export, and export-induced import effects, i.e.,

$$dV = dV_x - dV_m - dV_{m'}.$$

Substituting from equations (6-14), (6-15), and (6-16), and noting that

$$P_x = P_m = 1, V_x = P_x x, V_m = P_m m,$$

and

$$\frac{d P_w}{P_w} = \frac{d P_m}{P_m} = \frac{1}{1 - \eta} - 1 = \frac{\eta}{1 - \eta},$$

the net change in the balance of trade, as a function of the degree of devaluation, is

$$dV = - V_x \epsilon_x \left( \frac{\eta}{1 - \eta} \right) - V_m (1 + \epsilon_m) \frac{\eta}{1 - \eta}$$

$$+ \gamma \epsilon_x V_x \left[ \left( \frac{\eta}{1 - \eta} \right) + \left( \frac{\eta}{1 - \eta} \right)^2 (1 + \epsilon_m) \right]. \qquad (6\text{-}17)$$

In the present instance, however, we are concerned not with the change in the balance of trade which would result from any specific

---

Thus

$$\frac{d V_m}{d P_m} = m + P_m \frac{dm}{dP_m},$$

or

$$dV_m = mdP_m + P_m dm$$

$$= mdP_m + \epsilon_m mdP_m$$

$$= P_m m \left( \frac{dP_m}{P_m} \right) + P_m m \, \epsilon_m \left( \frac{dP_m}{P_m} \right)$$

from which equation (6-15) is obtained.

degree of devaluation, but rather with the degree of devaluation necessary to generate a change in the balance of trade equivalent to the change which would result from the VAT-CIT substitution under specific assumptions concerning the degree of CIT reduction and shifting, i.e., equation (6-17) must be solved for $\eta$, given the change in the trade balance. Thus,

$$\eta = \frac{-[\gamma\epsilon_x V_x - V_m(1 + \epsilon_m) - V_x\epsilon_x] \pm \sqrt{A}}{2(\gamma\epsilon_x V_x)(1 + \epsilon_m) - [\gamma\epsilon_x V_x - V_m(1 + \epsilon_m) - V_x\epsilon_x] \pm \sqrt{A}}$$

(6-18)

where

$$A = [\gamma\epsilon_x V_x - V_m(1 + \epsilon_m) - V_x\epsilon_x]^2 + 4(\gamma\epsilon_x V_x)(1 + \epsilon_m)(dV).$$

Under the most favorable stipulations of repeal and full forward shifting of the CIT, the balance of trade improves by \$2.697 billion under the assumption of the Houthakker-Magee export and import price elasticities ($\epsilon_x = -1.24$, $\epsilon_m = -0.88$) and by \$4.696 billion if the higher elasticities ($\epsilon_x = -2$, and $\epsilon_m = -1$) are assumed. Setting $dV$ equal to these alternative values and employing observed 1969 values of exports (\$43.5 billion) and imports (\$44.2 billion), equation (6-18) can be used to identify the degree of dollar devaluation equivalent to each type of tax substitution.

The results of this exercise are displayed in Table 6-3, which contrasts the balance-of-trade effects flowing from the tax substitution with the consequences of an equivalent devaluation. To achieve the \$2.7 billion improvement resulting from the repeal of a fully shifted CIT, given the Houthakker-Magee elasticities, would require a devaluation of approximately 5.5 percent, implying a 5.8 percent reduction in export prices relative to world prices and an equal increase in import prices relative to domestic import-competing prices. Thus, the devaluation would produce changes in *real* export and import quantities very close in magnitude to the changes implied by the VAT-CIT substitution. However, the *apparent* (i.e., nominal) changes in exports and imports would be quite different. As a result of the tax substitution domestic export prices decline. Consequently, an increase in the real level of exports of almost \$2.9 billion would generate an increase in the dollar *value* of exports of only \$0.5 billion. With the devaluation, however, nominal export prices are unchanged, and the full increase in the real level of exports appears as an improvement in the export contribution to the

**Table 6-3.  Hypothetical Balance of Trade: Devaluation Versus CIT Repeal with Full Shifting, 1969**

| | Houthakker-Magee Elasticities $(\epsilon_x = -1.24; \epsilon_m = -0.88)$ | | Higher Elasticities $(\epsilon_x = -2.0; \epsilon_m = -1.0)$ | |
|---|---|---|---|---|
| | CIT Repeal | Devaluation | CIT Repeal | Devaluation |
| *Percentage Changes* | | | | |
| Degree of devaluation ($\eta$) | | 5.5% | | 5.4% |
| Change in relative export prices $[d(P_x/P_w)]$ | −5.4% | −5.8[a] | −5.4% | −5.7[a] |
| Change in relative import prices $[d(P_m/P_d)]$ | 5.8 | 5.8[a] | 5.8 | 5.7[a] |
| *Amounts in Billions at Pre-Policy-Change Prices* | | | | |
| Increase in export quantity ($dx$) | $2.888 | $3.150 | $4.654 | $4.916 |
| Reduction in import quantity ($-dm$) | 2.260 | 2.272 | 2.568 | 2.497 |
| Export-induced increase in import quantity ($dm'$) | 0.122 | 0.134 | 0.196 | 0.208 |
| *Amounts in Billions at Post-Policy-Change Prices* | | | | |
| Increase in export value ($dV_x$) | $0.559 | $3.150 | $2.327 | $4.916 |
| Reduction in import value ($-dV_m$) | 2.260 | −0.310[b] | 2.568 | 0 |
| Export-induced increase in import value ($dV_{m'}$) | 0.122 | 0.142 | 0.196 | 0.220 |
| Net change in balance of trade ($dV$) | 2.697 | 2.698 | 4.699 | 4.696 |

[a] $\left| d(P_x/P_w) \right| = \left| d(P_m/P_d) \right| = \eta/(1 - \eta)$.

[b] Import value increases by $0.310 billion.

balance of trade. Imports, however, exhibit identical changes in quantity and dollar values under the tax substitution, since the domestic price of imports is unchanged. But, with devaluation the reduction in the *quantity* of imports is insufficient to offset the effect of increases in domestic import prices, and the dollar value of imports actually *increases*. Thus, the real consequences of the devaluation and the tax substitution (assuming full CIT shifting) on the balance of trade are virtually identical, although as these changes would be revealed in the trade accounts the tax substitution appears to be most effective in reducing imports and the devaluation, in increasing exports.

The $4.7 billion improvement in the balance of trade induced by the tax substitution under the assumption of the higher export and import price elasticities would require a devaluation of approximately 5.4 percent. Again, in terms of real export and import flows the effect of the devaluation and the tax substitution would be virtually equivalent, with export expansions between $4.5 and $5 billion and import contractions of about $2.5 billion. But as before, the devaluation would *appear* to be most effective in inducing export expansion.

There are two additional, and crucial, differences between the anticipated consequences of the tax substitution and a corresponding devaluation. First, the devaluation-induced change in the balance of trade is *a function primarily of the export and import elasticities*, while the trade effects of the tax substitution are a function *both of export and import elasticities and of CIT shifting parameters*. The former are certainly open to error, but it can be safely suggested that the latter are unknown. It might, of course, be discovered that the effects of a devaluation can also be "shifted," in the sense that domestic export, import, and import-competing prices can be altered in response to an effective change in exchange rates. However, it may also be expected that the greater competitiveness of international markets would quickly undermine such individual attempts to counteract the effects of exchange rate adjustments. Thus, much greater confidence can probably be attached to the anticipated consequences of the devaluation than to the consequences of the tax substitution. If, consistent with classical price theory, the CIT is not shifted (in the short-run sense employed here), then *no* trade consequences would be observed. If the CIT is fully shifted, the change in the balance of trade would be approximately equivalent to that induced by a 5 percent devaluation, and the actual effect could fall anywhere between these extremes.

Secondly, the foregoing analysis of the potential consequences of a VAT-CIT substitution and of a United States devaluation for international trade has been restricted to a discussion of effects on the *balance of trade*. The tax-substitution-equivalent degree of devaluation has been defined quite narrowly in terms of identical net changes in the trade balance. Thus, while the VAT-CIT substitution and its corresponding devaluation might, under rather restrictive assumptions, be identical in terms of the balance of trade, they might be quite different in their consequences for long- or short-term capital flows or both and hence for the *balance of payments.*

Unfortunately, a serious assessment of the possible balance-of-payments effects of these alternative policies is beyond the confines of the present study. However, it can be suggested that although repeal of an unshifted CIT would have no effects on the *trade* accounts, it would increase after-tax corporate profits and rates of return, which could stimulate significant capital inflows and reduce capital outflows. The consequences for these capital flows in the short run would depend critically on the response of monetary authorities, but longer-term capital adjustments could be expected to be favorable regardless of compensatory monetary policies.

However, it must be pointed out that differential responses of international capital flows to the VAT-CIT substitution versus a devaluation would be qualitatively different from differential consequences for the balance of trade. The latter consequences stem from a fundamental change in the terms of trade and would persist beyond the initial period of reequilibration. That is, the improvement in the balance of trade would represent, ceteris paribus, a relatively permanent response to the tax substitution or change in the rate of exchange. Differential capital flow adjustments, however, would be expected to persist only through the phase of reequilibration, and would in fact represent the operating method of capital account reequilibration. Thus, the trade consequences of the devaluation, which are more certain than consequences of the tax substitution, could be expected to be more lasting than any capital account consequences of the tax substitution.

## 6.8 CONCLUSIONS

The foregoing analyses clearly demonstrate that if the VAT itself is shifted its effect on international trade is neutral. Any short-term consequences for the balance of trade flow from the substitution of a neutral destination-based tax (e.g., the VAT) for a nonneutral, i.e., shifted, origin-based tax (e.g., the CIT). If the replaced tax is not shifted (exported) then no trade effects result.

Furthermore, even if the tax to be replaced had been shifted and thus its effect in the short term had been significantly to depress exports and stimulate imports, in the longer term, there would be appropriate modifications in exchange rates to compensate for these effects. In the case of the CIT such compensatory adjustments in exchange rates are particularly likely to have occurred. The trade imbalance engendered by the introduction of the CIT would almost necessarily have been corrected in the course of the restructuring of exchange rates which has taken place at various times over the last thirty to forty years. Given the relatively small balance-of-trade consequences which can be anticipated to accompany full CIT repeal, the very second-order effects of the changes in CIT rates which have occurred from time to time certainly must have been minor compared to other trade-disequilibrating processes which have occurred simultaneously, e.g., differential rates of inflation.

In the extreme, freely floating exchange rates would automatically correct any trade imbalances which might result from any country's tax policies. Given sufficient time to adjust "fixed" exchange rates, and certainly the period since the introduction of the CIT should have been "sufficient" in this context, the required adjustments will have in fact been made. Thus, the arguments in favor of the VAT which emphasize the depressive trade effects of the CIT seem to be somewhat misplaced in time; they should have been made when the CIT was first introduced (although they would have been no more compelling then than now). Therefore, it seems difficult to ascribe trade deficits in the early 1970s to a CIT which has been in existence for almost a half century, over which period the balance of trade has usually been in surplus.

This returns us to the other major international-trade argument for the VAT-CIT substitution: that the adoption by other countries of the VAT has been discriminatory vis-a-vis United States export and import-competing industries. But the relevant considerations are again the same: if the substitution of a VAT for another tax has no own-country balance-of-trade effects then it will have no effects for other countries' trade balances.

Specifically, the European value-added taxes introduced over the last decade would, in and of themselves, have adversely affected the U.S. trade position *only if* they replaced other taxes which were both *origin based* and *forward shifted*. In fact, in virtually every case, the European VATs replaced some form of indirect tax which was creditable on exports and was applied as a border tax to imports, i.e., a destination-based tax. These were generally very cumbersome, distortive, and inefficient taxes on wholesaler or manufacturer turnover, with very crudely estimated rebates on exports and inexactly compensatory import taxes. Their replacement by a relatively neutral and internally consistent VAT might have resulted in changes in interindustry trade *patterns*, due to vagaries in the application and administration of the displaced taxes, but these tax substitutions would not be expected to have resulted in major changes in trade *balances*, except to the degree that the more precise rates of export rebates and import-compensatory taxes under the VAT differed systematically from the effective rates imposed under the old taxes, especially the cascade turnover type of sales tax.

Thus, while a VAT-CIT substitution does have potential trade consequences, depending on the shifting of the CIT, these consequences should not enter as arguments for or against such a tax change. Overall trade effects appear as consequences to be compensated for in comparative assessments of alternative taxes (particularly if a preexisting trade balance is assumed).[6] Implications for the composition of the trade balance, export stimulation versus import contraction, are simply a subset of the more general allocative effects of this tax substitution. Stimulation of the corporate sector relative to the noncorporate sector has the same allocative importance in the context of export and import-competing industries as it has in the case of industries producing only for domestic purchasers. That is, as discussed in the next chapter, these are *allocative, not trade,* arguments for a VAT as a replacement for the CIT.

---

6. Of course, U.S. advocates of a VAT-CIT substitution have cited the contemporary persistence of U.S. balance-of-payments deficits and more recently balance-of-trade deficits as an argument for this tax substitution. However, as indicated by John Bossons, in terms of the differential consequences of alternative taxes, trade effects appear as macroeconomic control problems from which differential incidence analysis should abstract.

✳ *Chapter 7*

# A Miscellany of
# Additional Topics

The preceding chapters, which have been focused on the effects of the VAT-CIT substitution on income distribution, investment, and international trade, certainly do not exhaust the specific issues relevant to the evaluation of this proposed change in tax structure. The issues were selected both because they represented important areas of substantive concern and because they were amenable to meaningful analysis within the confines of the techniques employed here to assess the short-run consequences of the tax substitution. All three have been of significant policy concern and have been primary foci for the various debates over the desirability of the value-added tax within the context of United States tax structure.

However, a number of other important issues arise in connection with a VAT-CIT substitution, to which the preceding analysis can make some contribution. This chapter contains brief examinations of several of these topics, including (a) intergovernmental fiscal effects of the substitution, (b) resultant differential interindustry changes in tax liabilities, (c) interindustry implications of possible wage-adjustments accompanying the substitution, (d) probable differential regional consequences, and (e) potential allocative effects of the tax substitution.

*157*

## 7.1 INTERGOVERNMENTAL FISCAL
## CONSEQUENCE OF THE
## TAX SUBSTITUTION

Although nominally involving only two tax instruments, according to the relative yield criterion which has been employed (equal change in government revenue and expenditure), the VAT-CIT substitution would have a number of direct and indirect fiscal consequences, as discussed in sections 2.2 and 2.5. First, the reduction or repeal of the CIT, if the benefits of this tax reduction were shifted, would reduce prices of government-purchased goods and services. Similarly, any failure to fully shift new VAT liabilities forward to purchasers in the form of higher prices—a possibility that has not been considered here—would *reduce* the net-of-VAT prices effectively paid by government. Secondly, through the alteration of prices, the tax substitution would cause changes in the revenue yields of other ad valorem taxes. Also, yields of direct taxes, e.g., the personal income tax, would be affected if the various tax changes were fully or partially shifted backward to factors of production. Finally, further-round price and income adjustments, representing responses to the disequilibrium created by the tax substitution, would imply further changes in revenue yields of various taxes and in government expenditures. Strictly speaking, the compensating yield criterion used here requires that all of the "first-round" manifestations of these effects be incorporated. Specifically, *rates* of other taxes should in principle be held constant, and changes in yields of these taxes induced by tax substitution should be compensated for by appropriate adjustments in the VAT rate. However, for tractability it has simply been assumed that the nominal revenue yields of these taxes are unaffected by the simultaneous changes in the VAT and the CIT.

But even with these constraints, an important set of effects of the tax substitution can be considered: resultant changes in the relative budgetary positions of federal and state-local governments. Recall that the yield criterion defining a compensating tax substitution was applied to the consolidated budgets of all governments (equal monetary surplus or deficit in national accounts terms). That is, the change in revenue of all governments was required to equal the change in expenditure of all governments; only the consolidated surplus or deficit was held constant. Thus, the yield criterion could be met but the fiscal condition of individual jurisdictions, or of jurisdictions at different levels, could yet be markedly altered.

Consider the case of complete removal of the corporate income tax. Denoting original CIT revenue by $T_c$, VAT revenue by $T_v$, and the change in government expenditure induced by CIT shifting by $\Delta G$, the equal surplus or deficit criterion requires that

$$T_v - T_c = \Delta G . \tag{7-1}$$

The change in the surplus (deficit) is simply

$$T_v - T_c - \Delta G = 0 . \tag{7-2}$$

However, this does not insure that the budgetary positions (deficits or surpluses) of federal or state-local governments separately will be maintained. The (positive or negative) change in fiscal surplus at the state-local ($s$) and federal ($f$) levels can be simply defined as

$$\Delta S_s = - T_{cs} - \Delta G_s \tag{7-3}$$

and

$$\Delta S_f = T_v - T_{cf} - \Delta G_f . \tag{7-4}$$

It is simply required that the sum of these changes in the surplus (deficit) by zero. Note that repeal of both the federal and state corporate income taxes is stipulated, and imposition of a solely federal VAT is assumed.

Thus, implicit in the yield criterion is some degree of revenue sharing, either from federal to state-local governments or in the reverse direction. The magnitude of this effective transfer will depend upon the administration of the VAT, the degree of CIT shifting, and the relative importance of federal and state corporate income taxes.

For government as a whole, it is irrelevant whether government purchases are exempt from the VAT or not. In the former case, governments face VAT-exclusive prices (the VAT is not invoiced on sales to government but sellers are given full credit for the VAT invoiced on their intermediate purchases). In the latter case, governments face VAT-inclusive prices, since the VAT will appear both as government revenue *and* expenditure, which thus cancel each other in terms of the consolidated surplus or deficit. However, for state-local government vis-á-vis the federal government, the alternatives do differ significantly. If government purchases are exempt, state-local expenditures will either by unchanged (if the CIT is not shifted) or will fall (if the CIT is shifted). If purchases are not exempt (VAT invoiced on government purchases) state-local expenditures will almost certainly rise, in relative terms, by up to the VAT rate, with the magnitude of the increase depending on the degree of CIT shifting.

Assuming CIT repeal, shifting of the CIT thus enters through its effect on government expenditures. If the CIT is not shifted at all, government (federal and state-local) expenditures at VAT-exclusive prices are unaffected by the tax substitution. However, if the CIT is shifted, then government expenditures at VAT-exclusive prices will be reduced.

Relative state reliance on the CIT has an obvious effect, since a federal tax (VAT) is being substituted for a federal-state tax (CIT). If states make relatively little use of the CIT, then their *revenue* positions will be only marginally affected by CIT repeal. But if state corporation taxes are large relative to the revenues of these governments, then the tax substitution will amount to a major shift from state to federal taxation.

Briefly recapitulating, if state-local government purchases are exempt from the VAT and if the CIT is shifted forward and if state CITs are of minor revenue importance, then state-local surpluses will be increased and the federal surplus reduced as a result of the VAT-CIT substitution. But if state-local governments do incur a VAT liability and if the CIT is not shifted and state use of the CIT is important then the opposite will occur.

In fact, as indicated by Table 7-1, the state-local (state) use of the CIT is sufficiently important ($3.69 billion or about 10 percent of the federal CIT revenue of $38.99 billion) that even with full forward CIT shifting and federal exemption or rebate of VAT on state-local purchases, state-local surpluses *in the aggregate* would decline by $1.65 billion. At the other extreme, with zero CIT shifting and no exemption of state-local purchases from the VAT, state-local surpluses are reduced by $6.9 billion. In each case, the federal surplus is necessarily *increased* by an equal amount.

Of course, it is virtually certain, politically, that state-local purchases would be exempt from the VAT, i.e., either the VAT would not be invoiced on government purchases or a full federal credit would be provided to state-local governments on their VAT-invoiced purchases. Thus, the range of the contraction in state-local surpluses would be only from $1.65 billion (full CIT shifting) to $3.69 billion (zero CIT shifting), assuming, of course, the simultaneous repeal of federal and state corporate income taxes.

In any event, the tax substitution itself would involve a form of implicit revenue sharing *from* state-local governments *to* the federal government. Or, equivalently, it would be an effective substitution

**Table 7-1. Federal and State-Local Budget Effects, Assuming Full CIT Repeal and Either Zero or Full CIT Shifting (billions of dollars)**

| | VAT Invoiced on Government Purchases (no credit or rebate) (YES/NO) | CIT Revenue Loss | VAT Revenue Gain | Expenditure Change (at VAT-exclusive prices) | VAT Liability on Expenditure | Net Change in Surplus |
|---|---|---|---|---|---|---|
| | | | *Zero CIT Shifting ($\alpha = 0$)* | | | |
| Federal | No | 38.99 | 42.68 | 0 | 0 | +3.69 |
| State | No | 3.69 | 0 | 0 | 0 | −3.69 |
| Federal | Yes | 38.99 | 49.62 | 0 | 3.73 | +6.90 |
| State | Yes | 3.69 | 0 | 0 | 3.21 | −6.90 |
| | | | *Full CIT Shifting ($\alpha = 1$)* | | | |
| Federal | No | 38.99 | 38.06 | −2.58 | 0 | +1.65 |
| State | No | 3.69 | 0 | −2.04 | 0 | −1.65 |
| Federal | Yes | 38.99 | 44.25 | −2.58 | 3.32 | +4.52 |
| State | Yes | 3.69 | 0 | −2.04 | 2.87 | −4.52 |

of federal for state-local taxes, a substitution which would almost necessarily have to be supplemented by a reverse, but explicit, sharing of federal VAT revenues with adversely affected state-local governments.

The point to be made in this context is that all state-local governments would not be equally affected by the tax substitution. Assuming effective exemption of state-local governments from the VAT, those lower-level governments not employing a CIT would be either unaffected (no CIT shifting) or benefited (reductions in expenditure through CIT shifting). Local governments as a group would be in this position, as would those states not currently imposing a corporate profits tax (most notably Ohio, Illinois, Michigan, and Texas). Those states deriving the greatest proportions of their revenues from the CIT would be most adversely affected (e.g., North Carolina, for which CIT revenue was 8.7 percent of own general revenue in 1967; South Carolina, 8.5 percent; and Connecticut, 8.1 percent). Thus, any federal formula intended to offset the adverse state-local fiscal effects of this set of tax changes would either have to distinguish between states according to the degree of their reliance on the CIT or would differentially benefit those states not utilizing the CIT.

There is, of course, the possibility that federal removal of the CIT would not encourage the states to follow suit, or might even result in *increases* in revenues from the CIT. Indeed, in those states that allow the federal income tax as a deduction in computing the base of the state tax, CIT reduction by the federal government would, in the case of incomplete shifting, result in an immediate increase in state CIT revenues.

In addition states may be induced to raise their rates to partly fill the void left by the repeal of the federal CIT. However, such a reaction is unlikely on any large scale or even on the average. First, state CIT rates are as high as they are, at least in part, because the state CIT liability can be deducted in computing the base of the federal CIT.[1] With nominal (and in most cases, effective marginal) federal CIT rates of 50 percent (in 1969), this amounts to an effective federal credit equal to 50 percent of the state CIT paid by any corporation, thus dramatically reducing the effective rates of state CITs. This federal treatment of state CITs has almost certainly stimulated state reliance on this type of tax. Second, as has been often argued, the CIT is not an "ideal" state tax. The fact that most

---

1. If the *federal* CIT is similarly deductible in computing the state CIT liability, the reduction in effective state CIT rates may be even greater.

corporations operate in many states necessarily requires that corporate profits be allocated among states by arbitrary rules, e.g., in relation to property, payroll, or sales, using for sales either a destination or origin principle. Most adversely, from an allocative point of view, such arbitrary formulas almost certainly insure that even under competitive assumptions the state CITs are shifted in specific, discriminatory directions (onto wages in the case of origin formulas, or onto sales, with destination formulas). Because of the implied excess burdens at the state level, major increases in state reliance on the CIT would seem both undesirable and unlikely. Third, the loss of administrative benefits flowing from the simultaneous use of the CIT by state and federal governments would vastly increase the cost of administering state corporate income taxes.

Thus, although the assumption of simultaneous reductions in both state and federal corporate income tax rates was imposed by data limitations, with complete federal repeal of the CIT it would appear that states would probably not *increase* their CIT rates. While in fact they might not reduce their CIT rates in step with federal rate reductions, it is not too unrealistic to assume, as we do here (for analytic convenience) that reductions in state CIT rates would be made, paralleling the federal reductions.

As indicated above, in addition to differential fiscal consequences for federal and state-local governments, intrastate differentials would also be implied, i.e., local governments would necessarily benefit from any price reductions resulting from the shifting of the CIT reduction, but would not *directly* suffer from the CIT revenue loss. Thus, the tax substitution exerts very different budgetary impacts on different levels and units of government.

## 7.2 INTERINDUSTRY REDISTRIBUTIONS OF TAX LIABILITIES

Varying degrees of sophistication can be exhibited in assessing the effects of a tax substitution. At its most simplistic, everything other than tax liabilities could provisionally be assumed to be unchanged. The analysis would then be restricted to examination of changes in tax liabilities of relevant economic units. At a more complex level, changes in outputs, prices, and factor incomes in response to the tax substitution would be incorporated. The distinguishing mark of these more complex formulations is that the system is permitted to respond to the disequilibrium created by the initial restructuring and redistribution of tax liabilities.

Limitations of knowledge and the constraints of the input-output formulation have restricted us to the more simplisitic, first-round end of this analytical spectrum, although prices and profit incomes (capital earnings) have been permitted to vary in response to the tax substitution. However, it is possible to use the first-round results to project, albeit qualitatively, the likely directions of further dynamic adjustments by the economy to the change in tax structure.

This projective application of the first-round responses has in fact been suggested in the discussion of price responses (Chapter 3). These relative price effects were interpreted as indices of disequilibrium created by the tax substitution, a disequilibrium which would induce further-round responses. The investment and international trade chapters represented attempts to quantify the initial responses in these dimensions to the first-round price effects of the tax substitution. However, these price effects are derived entirely from assumed interindustry redistributions of tax liabilities, as represented in rather simple stipulations concerning the role of taxes in price formation. Thus, a more direct approach to the assessment of tax-substitution-induced changes in outputs, prices, and factor incomes can be obtained by an examination of the tax-liability redistributions themselves. This in effect represents an analysis of what Musgrave has called the "money differential incidence" of the tax substitution.

To assess the money differential incidence of the VAT-CIT substitution, it is necessary to assume that prices charged by sellers, inclusive of all taxes, are initially unaffected by the tax substitution. Price adjustments then appear themselves as later-round responses to the change in tax structure. Thus, it must be assumed that neither the VAT nor the CIT is shifted initially.

In the case of the CIT, zero shifting is, as before, straightforward: prices do not respond to the reduction or repeal of the CIT. The VAT case, however, is more complex: under the assumption of full shifting of the VAT, VAT-inclusive prices increased by the VAT rate. With zero shifting, it is necessary that VAT-inclusive prices equal prices prevailing prior to introduction of the VAT.

The first implication of zero VAT shifting is that the CIT-compensating VAT rate is no longer equal to the ratio of CIT revenue loss to the net base (personal consumption expenditure) of a consumption-type VAT. Rather, the base, consumption expenditure *net of the VAT liability*, will decline by the amount of the VAT liability itself. Thus, if $C$ is consumption expenditure prior to the tax substitution and $Z$ is the compensatory VAT rate, consumption expenditure net of VAT, $C'$, will become

$$C' = C - ZC'$$

$$= \frac{C}{1 + Z}. \qquad (7\text{-}5)$$

Resultant VAT revenue, $T_v = ZC'$, must then equal CIT revenue forgone, $\Delta T_c$, i.e.,

$$Z\left(\frac{C}{1 + Z}\right) = \Delta T_c$$

and

$$Z = \frac{\Delta T_c}{(C - \Delta T_c)}. \qquad (7\text{-}6)$$

Assuming CIT repeal ($\Delta T_c = \$42.68$ billion), the resultant compensatory VAT rate is 8.3 percent.

The second important implication of zero VAT shifting is that effective *purchaser* prices associated with VAT-exempt transactions, i.e., transactions for which the purchaser gets a credit for VAT invoiced, will decline by the amount of the VAT. Thus, effective export, investment, and government prices can be viewed as declining, and these declines represent an effective burden of the VAT for the seller. In effect, the seller can be treated as viewing his gross VAT liability as the VAT rate applied to his total value added, regardless of rebates his purchasers may (or may not) receive.

The net burden of the VAT for any industry is then the VAT rate applied to total value added (net of VAT) less credits for the VAT invoiced on this industry's net investment goods purchases.[2] The sum over industries of this net apparent VAT liability (VAT burden) will exceed net VAT revenues of government by the effective VAT credits on export and government purchases.

The effective burden of an unshifted VAT, computed in the foregoing manner by industry, is given in the first column of Table 7-2. The benefits of CIT repeal are given in the second column of this table. The effective *increase* in the tax burden by industry (the

---

2. Note that the credit for replacement of depreciated capital has already been incorporated by removing depreciation and other intermediate purchases from total sales in determining value added net of depreciation.

**Table 7-2.  Interindustry Changes in Tax Burdens, Two-Digit Disaggregated Industries**

| | | Billions of Dollars | | | Ratios: | | |
|---|---|---|---|---|---|---|---|
| | | VAT Burden | CIT Burden | VAT Less CIT | VAT/CIT | CIT/VA | I/VA |
| 1 | Agriculture | 2070.4 | 128.6 | 1941.76 | 16.10 | 0.00 | 16.0 |
| 2 | Metal Mining | 114.6 | 36.8 | 77.84 | 3.12 | 0.03 | 57.9 |
| 3 | Coal,Stn.,Clay Mng. & Prod. | 863.9 | 730.9 | 132.98 | 1.18 | 0.06 | 16.1 |
| 4 | Oil & Gas | 957.6 | 643.7 | 313.93 | 1.47 | 0.04 | 40.3 |
| 5 | Construction | 4528.0 | 1352.4 | 3175.59 | 3.35 | 0.02 | 2.4 |
| 6 | Ordnance | 275.1 | 142.5 | 132.64 | 1.93 | 0.04 | 5.4 |
| 7 | Food | 2265.0 | 1169.0 | 1067.97 | 1.89 | 0.05 | 8.4 |
| 8 | Tobacco | 303.9 | 529.8 | -225.86 | 0.57 | 0.13 | 1.8 |
| 9 | Textiles & Apparel | 1434.7 | 964.1 | 470.59 | 1.49 | 0.06 | 5.1 |
| 10 | Lumber, Wood Products | 533.7 | 380.6 | 153.15 | 1.40 | 0.05 | 11.9 |
| 11 | Furniture & Fixtures | 290.8 | 256.9 | 33.91 | 1.13 | 0.07 | 7.2 |
| 12 | Paper & Products | 785.9 | 872.7 | -86.83 | 0.90 | 0.09 | 17.1 |
| 13 | Printing & Publishing | 923.4 | 1079.5 | -156.16 | 0.86 | 0.09 | 5.6 |
| 14 | Chem., Plast., Drugs, Pnt. | 1545.8 | 3181.7 | -1635.92 | 0.49 | 0.15 | 15.0 |
| 15 | Rubber & Leather | 623.7 | 468.9 | 154.82 | 1.33 | 0.06 | 11.2 |
| 16 | Footwear | 226.4 | 101.7 | 124.68 | 2.23 | 0.05 | 3.1 |
| 17 | Primary Metal | 1714.9 | 1074.7 | 640.20 | 1.60 | 0.05 | 15.1 |
| 18 | Fabricated Metal | 1203.6 | 1316.9 | -113.27 | 0.91 | 0.03 | 7.2 |
| 19 | Nonelect. Machinery | 2016.1 | 2446.4 | -430.30 | 0.82 | 0.09 | 11.3 |
| 20 | Electrical Equipment | 2025.9 | 2182.1 | -156.24 | 0.93 | 0.09 | 7.4 |
| 21 | Transp. Equipment | 2775.2 | 2600.4 | 174.83 | 1.07 | 0.08 | 6.5 |
| 22 | Instruments | 437.0 | 831.7 | -344.67 | 0.59 | 0.14 | 6.2 |
| 23 | Misc. Manufacturing | 381.6 | 229.4 | 152.21 | 1.65 | 0.06 | 10.1 |
| 24 | Transp. & Warehousing | 2531.0 | 755.4 | 1825.59 | 3.42 | 0.02 | 15.1 |
| 25 | Communications | 1020.6 | 2657.1 | -1636.46 | 0.38 | 0.13 | 37.4 |
| 26 | Utilities | 228.8 | 2278.0 | -2049.15 | 0.10 | 0.12 | 85.2 |
| 27 | Finance & Insurance | 2349.1 | 7131.8 | -4852.72 | 0.32 | 0.23 | 5.9 |
| 28 | Real Estate & Rental | 5778.9 | 781.8 | 5997.09 | 8.57 | 0.01 | 3.7 |
| 29 | Hotels & Services | 2728.0 | 719.1 | 2008.95 | 3.79 | 0.02 | 9.3 |
| 30 | Auto Repair & Services | 710.4 | 179.9 | 530.51 | 3.95 | 0.02 | 10.4 |
| 31 | Amusements | 341.7 | 32.5 | 309.15 | 10.51 | 0.01 | 26.9 |
| 32 | Med., Ed. Serv. & Nonprof. | 2243.3 | -45.8 | 2294.10 | | -0.00 | 20.6 |
| 33 | Wholesale & Retail | 1420.4 | 21.9 | 1398.47 | 64.86 | 0.00 | 0.6 |

VAT = aggregate incidence of unshifted VAT at 8.3 percent rate.
CIT = aggregate incidence of unshifted CIT.
I = gross investment by capital goods user industry.
VA = gross value added (inclusive of depreciation).

difference between the VAT and CIT burdens) is given in the third column; and the VAT as a ratio to the CIT, is the fourth.

Thus, under the foregoing assumptions the tax substitution would replace CIT liabilities with apparently greater VAT liabilities. The benefits of the CIT repeal would obviously be greatest in the most highly incorporated industries primarily in the manufacturing sector, for which the ratio of CIT to value added (fifth column of Table 7-2) is highest. Conversely, those industries exhibiting the lowest degrees of incorporation, those benefiting most from special treatments under the corporate tax, and those growing most slowly (i.e., exhibiting the lowest ratios of investment to value added, as indicated in the sixth column of Table 7-2, relating *gross* investment to value added inclusive of depreciation) would be disproportionately affected by imposition of the VAT.

The net effect of the tax substitution is then simply the difference between the newly imposed VAT burden and the rescinded CIT liability. A positive number indicates that the VAT burden for the industry exceeds the original CIT liability; a negative net change indicates the reverse. Alternatively, the ratio of the VAT to the CIT (fifth column) indicates an increase in the tax burden if greater than unity, a decrease if less than unity.

Most manufacturing industries would benefit from the replacement of the CIT by the VAT because they are highly incorporated and their capital intensities (ratios of profit to value added) and rates of capital accumulation are also relatively high. Conversely, those industries which are not highly incorporated and which have low profit margins and low rates of investment relative to value added would experience the greatest increases in tax liabilities. This is particularly true of the agriculture, textile, lumber, footwear, transportation, and service industries.

These changes in tax liabilities thus measure the varying degrees of pressure which would be exerted on different industries by the tax substitution. That is, they reflect the magnitudes of the responses of factor incomes, outputs, and prices which could be expected ultimately to result from the change in tax structure.

## 7.3 SHORT-RUN INTERINDUSTRY EFFECTS OF POTENTIAL WAGE RESPONSES

It has been explicitly assumed throughout that nominal factor incomes, other than corporate profits, are unaffected by the tax substitution. However, significant initial increases in consumer prices have been projected to result from the tax change, particularly if the CIT is assumed not to be shifted forward. Specifically, consumption price increases of from 1.7 percent (full CIT shifting) to 7.7 percent (zero CIT shifting) have been estimated to follow from repeal of the CIT and its replacement by the VAT. These price changes then imply corresponding reductions in real wages.

If it were assumed that in the short run the supply of labor were infinitely elastic at the prevailing real wage, it would be possible to project initial wage adjustments and changes in labor cost by industry. This would provide another direction from which the question of the longer-run, later-round responses to the tax substitution could be approached. Specifically, consider the case of full CIT removal and zero shifting: consumer prices rise by 7.68 percent. If it is assumed that initially wages rise, also by 7.68 percent, what pressure will this exert on prices?

The short-run interindustry effect of this wage increase would obviously reflect differences in the labor intensity of different industries. The ratio of employee compensation to value added, presented by industry in Table 7-3, provides a direct measure of this labor intensity. Labor-intensive industries, those in which employee compensation is a relatively large proportion of value added, will be initially most affected by the tax-substitution-induced wage change. Those industries include mining (75 percent), ordnance (85 percent), textiles (81 percent), furniture (82 percent), footwear (84 percent), and miscellaneous manufacturing (83 percent). On the other hand, employee compensation relative to value added is notably low in such industries as agriculture (14 percent), oil and gas (26 percent), tobacco (17 percent), utilities (28 percent), and real estate and rental (2 percent).

Under the assumption of zero CIT shifting, of course, net corporate profits have increased by the amount of initial CIT liabilities. It might be assumed that at least initially the increase in employee compensation is absorbed by profits rather than being passed on in price changes. The pressure for further-round adjustments in prices, profits, and wages would then be greater in those industries in which the increase in wages exceeded the increase in net profit, i.e., exceeded the original CIT liability. The CIT savings (as a proportion of value added), the hypothesized change in the wage bill, or employee compensation (also as a proportion of original value added), and the difference between the two are indicated by industry in Table 7-3. Further adjustments will be most severe in' those industries in which this difference is positive (change in employee compensation exceeds original CIT liability). Conversely, downward pressure on prices would be greatest in those industries in which net profit increases

Table 7-3. Short-Run Interindustry Effects of Potential Wage Increases, Two-Digit Disaggregated Industries

| | Employee Compensation | Ratio to Value Added | | |
|---|---|---|---|---|
| | | CIT Savings | Potential Labor Cost Increase[a] | Labor Cost Increase Less CIT Savings |
| 1 Agriculture | 0.14 | 0.00 | 0.01 | 0.01 |
| 2 Metal Mining | 0.75 | 0.03 | 0.06 | 0.03 |
| 3 Coal, Stn.,Clay Mng.& Prod. | 0.70 | 0.06 | 0.05 | -0.01 |
| 4 Oil & Gas | 0.26 | 0.04 | 0.02 | -0.02 |
| 5 Construction | 0.69 | 0.02 | 0.05 | 0.03 |
| 6 Ordnance | 0.85 | 0.04 | 0.07 | 0.02 |
| 7 Food | 0.61 | 0.05 | 0.05 | 0.00 |
| 8 Tobacco | 0.17 | 0.13 | 0.01 | -0.12 |
| 9 Textiles & Apparel | 0.81 | 0.06 | 0.06 | 0.00 |
| 10 Lumber, Wood Products | 0.52 | 0.06 | 0.05 | -0.01 |
| 11 Furniture & Fixtures | 0.82 | 0.07 | 0.06 | -0.02 |
| 12 Paper & Products | 0.67 | 0.09 | 0.06 | -0.03 |
| 13 Printing & Publishing | 0.75 | 0.09 | 0.06 | -0.03 |
| 14 Chem., Plast., Drugs, Pnt. | 0.58 | 0.15 | 0.04 | -0.10 |
| 15 Rubber & Leather | 0.71 | 0.06 | 0.05 | -0.00 |
| 16 Footwear | 0.84 | 0.05 | 0.06 | 0.01 |
| 17 Primary Metal | 0.74 | 0.05 | 0.06 | 0.01 |
| 18 Fabricated Metal | 0.76 | 0.08 | 0.06 | -0.02 |
| 19 Nonelect. Machinery | 0.74 | 0.09 | 0.06 | -0.04 |
| 20 Electrical Equipment | 0.77 | 0.09 | 0.06 | -0.03 |
| 21 Transp. Equipment | 0.71 | 0.09 | 0.05 | -0.03 |
| 22 Instruments | 0.64 | 0.14 | 0.05 | -0.09 |
| 23 Misc. Manufacturing | 0.83 | 0.06 | 0.06 | 0.01 |
| 24 Transp. & Warehousing | 0.68 | 0.02 | 0.05 | 0.03 |
| 25 Communications | 0.44 | 0.13 | 0.03 | -0.09 |
| 26 Utilities | 0.28 | 0.12 | 0.02 | -0.09 |
| 27 Finance & Insurance | 0.74 | 0.23 | 0.06 | -0.17 |
| 28 Real Estate & Rental | 0.02 | 0.01 | 0.00 | -0.01 |
| 29 Hotels & Services | 0.59 | 0.02 | 0.05 | 0.03 |
| 30 Auto Repair & Services | 0.47 | 0.02 | 0.04 | 0.02 |
| 31 Amusements | 0.60 | 0.01 | 0.05 | 0.04 |
| 32 Med., Ed. Serv. & Nonprof. | 0.66 | -0.00 | 0.05 | 0.05 |
| 33 Wholesale & Retail | 0.81 | 0.00 | 0.06 | 0.06 |

[a]Short-run labor cost increase = 0.0768 (employee compensation).

are still observed (a negative difference between the change in the wage bill and the CIT liability).

Because these short-run effects depend not only on labor intensity (the labor share of value added), but also on average CIT rates, and in particular on the degree of incorporation, the pressure will not necessarily be greatest in labor-intensive industries. Thus, agriculture, which is not at all labor intensive in terms of the labor share of value added, registers an increase in the wage bill in excess of CIT savings simply because of the very low original CIT liabilities. In general, however, in capital-intensive industries, e.g., communications and utilities, labor cost increases are considerably less than CIT savings, while in labor-intensive industries, e.g., textiles and apparel, the increases significantly exceed CIT savings.

It should be clearly understood that these consequences of a short-run increase in wage rates, of a magnitude necessary to hold real wages constant, do not represent an equilibrium adjustment of labor and output markets to the tax substitution. Specifically, only in the short run, before the system has fully adjusted to the change in tax structure, would differential interindustry effects related to the degree of labor intensity be observed. Ultimately, as wage increases are incorporated in prices of capital goods, increases in capital good prices induced by wage increases would lead to corresponding price increases in more capital-intensive industries, and this effect is independent of the effective CIT liability of the industry. That is, downward price pressure exerted by increases in net rates of return in industries incurring high CIT liabilities operates independently of the upward pressures exerted by longer-run, economy-wide wage adjustments. Nonetheless, the comparison of potential increases in labor cost and reductions in CIT liabilities does provide an index of differential short-run price pressures.

## 7.4 DIFFERENTIAL REGIONAL CONSEQUENCES OF THE TAX SUBSTITUTION[3]

In section 1.2, we noted that the predictive econometric models commonly utilized to assess the effects of potential changes in federal fiscal policy are inadequate for examing the *differential* effects of

---

3. These regional consequences were discussed more fully in a paper by Dresch [1972a].

alternative public policies. One of the most important of these in-adequacies relates to the level of disaggregation at which such models operate. In particular, regional disaggregation has received virtually no attention at all in this type of analysis. While the aggregative models have often been critized for their lack of detail in the house-hold and industrial dimensions, very little attention has been paid to the potential differential regional effects of alternative federal policies.

Correspondingly, the concern of regional policy analysts has been focused, with few exceptions, on the effects of explicitly regional policies for individual geographic areas. Government programs to promote private investment in depressed areas, for example, have been examined under quite confined assumptions concerning the relationship of these policies to broader federal fiscal policies. The possibility that general, ostensibly nonregional federal policies might have as great or even greater effects for the geographic dis-tribution of economic activity than ostensibly regional policies has been left almost entirely unexplored.

The obvious source of this void in policy analysis is the lack of a sufficiently refined conception of the determinants of the spatial distribution of activity. Unless regions are viewed individually, as closed, small-scale representations of national economies, no well-elaborated schema for the analysis of regional economic phenomena is provided by the corpus of economic theory.

While the development of an adequate conceptual representation of the relationship between national and regional economic processes is clearly beyond the scope of the present study, a rough approxi-mation of the first-round differential regional consequences of the VAT-CIT substitution can be attempted (the regions used for our analysis are described in Table 7-4). This discussion will focus on the potential regional impact of the initial changes in income dis-tribution, investment, and international trade which would be in-duced by the VAT-CIT substitution, and on the differential re-gional consequences of possible wage adjustments.

### 7.4.1 Income Distribution

Just as the VAT-CIT substitution has been shown (Chapter 4) to be regressive nationally, redistributing income from low- to high-income households, so it is also likely to be regressive region-ally, redistributing income from low- to high-income regions. This regional regressivity is in fact observed in this model, as indicated in Table 7-5, which contains net changes in regional tax liabilities

**Table 7-4. Regional Divisions of the United States**

New England (NE)
  Maine
  New Hampshire
  Vermont
  Massachusetts
  Rhode Island
  Connecticut

Middle Atlantic (MA)
  New York
  New Jersey
  Pennsylvania

East North Central (ENC)
  Ohio
  Indiana
  Illinois
  Michigan
  Wisconsin

West North Central (WNC)
  Minnesota
  Iowa
  Missouri
  North Dakota
  South Dakota
  Nebraska
  Kansas

South Atlantic (SA)
  Delaware
  Maryland
  District of Columbia
  Virginia
  West Virginia
  North Carolina
  South Carolina
  Georgia
  Florida

East South Central (ESC)
  Kentucky
  Tennessee
  Alabama
  Mississippi

West South Central (WSC)
  Arkansas
  Louisiana
  Oklahoma
  Texas

Mountain (MT)
  Montana
  Idaho
  Wyoming
  Colorado
  New Mexico
  Arizona
  Utah
  Nevada

Pacific (PAC)
  Washington
  Oregon
  California
  Alaska
  Hawaii

Note: In comparisons between the South and the rest of the country (non-South) the South comprises the South Atlantic, East South Central, and West South Central regions. The regions in this analysis correspond to U.S. Census Bureau "Divisions," as found in, e.g., U.S. Bureau of the Census, *County and City Data Book, 1967* (A Statistical Abstract Supplement), p. 2.

under the extreme assumptions of complete and zero CIT shifting, assuming in both cases complete CIT repeal.

To avoid the necessity of developing household income distributions by region, the regional distribution of retail sales was used to distribute any increase in nominal (VAT-inclusive) consumption expenditure over regions. Similarly, on the basis of the regional dis-

**Table 7-5. Change in Regional Tax Liabilities Resulting from VAT–CIT Substitution, Assuming Full CIT Repeal (1969)**

| Region^a | Distribution of Retail Sales | Distribution of Dividends Received | Zero CIT Shifting; Full VAT Shifting ΔC (billions) | ΔCIT (billions) | ΔC-ΔCIT (billions) | ΔC-ΔCIT / N | Full CIT and VAT Shifting ΔC (billions) | ΔI (billions) | ΔC-ΔI (billions) | ΔC-ΔI / N | ΔC-ΔCIT / Y | ΔC-ΔI / Y | Disposable Income per Capita |
|---|---|---|---|---|---|---|---|---|---|---|---|---|---|
| NE | 6.2% | 10.7% | $2.62 | $4.58 | -$1.95 | -$167 | $0.57 | $0.73 | -$0.16 | -$13 | -.049 | -.004 | $3,370 |
| MA | 18.7 | 28.2 | 7.97 | 12.04 | -4.07 | -110 | 1.74 | 1.92 | -0.18 | -5 | -.032 | -.001 | 3,490 |
| ENC | 20.6 | 18.8 | 8.78 | 8.04 | 0.75 | 19 | 1.92 | 1.28 | 0.64 | 16 | .006 | .005 | 3,330 |
| WNC | 8.4 | 5.8 | 3.59 | 2.45 | 1.14 | 70 | 0.79 | 0.39 | 0.39 | 24 | .023 | .008 | 3,020 |
| SA | 14.4 | 13.0 | 6.15 | 5.57 | 0.58 | 19 | 1.34 | 0.89 | 0.46 | 15 | .007 | .005 | 2,760 |
| ESC | 5.2 | 2.8 | 2.21 | 1.20 | 1.01 | 79 | 0.48 | 0.19 | 0.29 | 23 | .034 | .010 | 2,340 |
| WSC | 8.7 | 5.2 | 3.70 | 2.24 | 1.46 | 76 | 0.81 | 0.36 | 0.45 | 24 | .028 | .009 | 2,710 |
| MT | 4.0 | 2.8 | 1.69 | 1.19 | 0.50 | 62 | 0.37 | 0.19 | 0.18 | 22 | .022 | .008 | 2,830 |
| PAC | 14.0 | 12.6 | 5.96 | 5.39 | 0.57 | 22 | 1.30 | 0.86 | 0.44 | 17 | .006 | .005 | 3,400 |
| US | 100.0 | 100.0 | 42.68 | 42.68 | 0.00 | 0 | 9.34 | 6.82 | 2.52 | 13 | 0 | .004 | 3,120 |
| South | 28.3 | 21.0 | 12.06 | 9.01 | 3.05 | 49 | 2.63 | 1.44 | 1.20 | 19 | .021 | .007 | 2,660 |
| Non-S | 71.7 | 79.0 | 30.62 | 33.67 | -3.05 | -22 | 6.71 | 5.38 | 1.32 | 11 | -.007 | .003 | 3,320 |

Notes:

$\Delta C$ = increase in nominal consumption expenditures.

$\Delta CIT$ = CIT reduction.

$N$ = population.

$\Delta I$ = savings in investment expenditures.

$Y$ = disposable income.

Source: Figures for the United States are computed from 1969 U.S. input-output model. Data on 1969 retail sales are taken from U.S. Bureau of the Census, *Monthly Retail Trade*, January 1970. Data on dividends received are taken from Internal Revenue Service, *1968 Individual Income Tax Returns*. Data on population are taken from *1971 Statistical Abstract of the United States.*

^aThe list of states included in each region is contained in Table 7-4. NE = New England; MA = Middle Atlantic; ENC = East North Central; WNC = West North Central; SA = South Atlantic; ESC = East South Central; WSC = West South Central; MT = Mountain; PAC = Pacific; South includes South Atlantic, East South Central, and West South Central regions.

tribution of dividend income, as reported for federal income tax purposes, increases in net profits (zero CIT shifting) and reductions in investment cost (complete CIT shifting) were distributed.

It is readily apparent from the final three columns of Table 7-5 that the VAT-CIT substitution is regionally regressive, regardless of the value of the CIT shifting parameter. For example, with zero CIT shifting, the low-income Southern regions in the aggregate experience an $3.05 billion increase in tax liabilities and an increase in the tax burden in excess of 2 percent of disposable income in this area (see penultimate row of Table 7-5). For the rest of the country, tax liabilities are correspondingly reduced by almost 1 percent of disposable income. With full shifting of the CIT, on the other hand, the South's loss is reduced to $1.2 billion, or about 0.7 percent of disposable income, while the non-South experiences an absolutely greater increase in tax liability of $1.3 billion, but an increase relative to disposable income of only 0.3 percent.

In this context the relative significance of the regional effects of national policy changes can be vividly indicated. Great energy is expended modifying formulas for federal intergovernmental grant programs to achieve particular distributions and debating the relative desirability of alternative distributions. However, the *net* regional redistributions achieved through these programs are almost invariably less than those implied by the ostensibly "nonregional" substitution of a VAT for the CIT. For example, Dresch [1972a] has shown that the net increase in the South's tax liability due to the VAT-CIT substitution, between $1.2 billion and $3 billion depending on CIT shifting, *exceeds* the net benefit to the South of the $4 billion federal welfare grant program ($0.403 billion net Southern benefit), of the $11 billion federal nonwelfare categorical programs ($0.939 billion), or of any of three $5 billion income-tax-financed general revenue-sharing (GRS) programs under discussion in 1971 ($0.467 billion for the original House of Representatives' program, $0.78 billion under Congressman Wilbur Mills's GRS proposal and $0.419 billion under the Nixon Administration's original GRS program). Thus, while attention is focused on the regional implications of various intergovernmental grant-in-aid programs, their effects may be literally swamped by changes in national tax policy, the regional implications of which are rarely even explicitly considered.

### 7.4.2 Investment Effects

The analysis of the potential first-round investment effects of the tax substitution (Chapter 5) was restricted to national responses disaggregated only by industry. To project potential investment consequences by region it is necessary to distribute each industry's investment expansion spatially, not a simple problem. Information is available on the geographic distribution of gross plant and equipment expenditure by industry in 1969, but there is no reason to expect that the investment *expansion* will be distributed proportionately to base levels of investment. Specifically, any increase in investment is much more likely to be "new" investment, i.e., in new plants and in basic new equipment, than is preexpansion gross investment. The latter almost undoubtedly reflects heavily the maintenance of preexisting, spatially distributed industry capital stocks, while marginal investments reflect the *changing* geographic distributions of these stocks, which these marginal investments in fact bring about.

Although the capability for differentiating between total and marginal distributions of investment does not exist, even ad hoc assumptions employed to reach admittedly tentative conclusions provide some insight into potential regional implications. For present purposes, it is simply assumed that for each industry any region's share of the short-run investment expansion is equal to its share of base-year plant and equipment expenditures. However, the South's share of plant and equipment expenditures (29.8 percent), for example, is greater than its share of manufacturing value added (23.3 percent), probably reflecting its differential growth. Thus, simple proportionality will almost certainly result in an understatement of the South's share of the investment expansion.

If regional distributions of investment activities of all industries were identical, then under the proportionality assumption each region's share of the investment expansion would equal its share of base-year investment. However, as indicated in Table 7-6 (zero shifting) and Table 7-7 (unitary shifting), this regional uniformity does not exist. For the subset of manufacturing industries for which sufficient data are available, the tax substitution with zero CIT shifting results in an *aggregate* investment expansion of 10 percent. However, individual regions experience increases in investment ranging from 7.5 percent (West South Central) to 12.5 percent (New England), even on the assumption of intraindustry proportionality. Although the increase for the South is about equal to that for the nation, the South's industrial composition is quite different and its average expansion is explained by the counterbalancing of such regionally important industries as paper and allied products (27 percent investment increase, of which the South's share is 38 percent) at the high end, against tobacco (only 4.8 percent investment expansion with a Southern share of 67 percent) and

Table 7-6. Short-Run Regional[a] Investment Expansion Resulting from VAT-CIT Substitution, Assuming Zero CIT Shifting (millions of dollars)

| | NE | MA | ENC | WNC | SA | ESC | WSC | MT | PAC | US | South | Non-South |
|---|---|---|---|---|---|---|---|---|---|---|---|---|
| Food | 4.52 | 13.83 | 19.96 | 11.89 | 13.10 | 4.11 | 7.23 | 3.94 | 13.35 | 91.93 | 24.44 | 67.49 |
| Tobacco | — | 0.22 | 0.06 | — | 2.14 | 0.46 | — | — | — | 2.36 | 2.60 | 0.28 |
| Textile products | 6.68 | 9.72 | 2.02 | 0.31 | 55.87 | 9.26 | 1.12 | — | — | 84.98 | 66.25 | 18.73 |
| Apparel | 0.83 | 16.03 | 3.34 | 1.47 | 4.61 | 2.25 | 1.39 | 0.23 | 1.85 | 30.15 | 8.25 | 23.75 |
| Paper | 30.42 | 60.26 | 80.40 | 21.22 | 75.27 | 37.88 | 32.33 | 3.07 | 40.78 | 380.63 | 144.48 | 236.15 |
| Chemical | 3.76 | 25.43 | 26.59 | 5.06 | 30.06 | 12.76 | 48.29 | 1.66 | 5.61 | 159.22 | 91.11 | 68.11 |
| Petroleum and coal | 0.23 | 2.90 | 8.34 | 1.26 | 0.54 | 1.34 | 12.65 | 0.46 | 5.53 | 33.25 | 14.53 | 18.72 |
| Rubber and plastic | 8.63 | 13.52 | 35.11 | 5.22 | 9.42 | 14.14 | 5.57 | — | 8.63 | 100.24 | 29.13 | 71.11 |
| Stone, clay, and glass | 2.91 | 18.15 | 22.75 | 4.49 | 11.70 | 6.52 | 4.85 | 3.26 | 8.84 | 83.47 | 23.07 | 60.40 |
| Primary metal | 3.62 | 37.94 | 83.01 | 3.28 | 12.61 | 8.47 | 7.83 | 6.31 | 8.71 | 172.08 | 28.91 | 143.17 |
| Fabricated metal | 4.86 | 13.55 | 34.37 | 3.98 | 5.84 | 4.62 | 3.84 | 0.60 | 6.82 | 78.48 | 14.30 | 64.18 |
| Machinery | 33.92 | 91.76 | 165.14 | 30.40 | 25.85 | 12.63 | 20.25 | 4.84 | 36.36 | 421.15 | 58.73 | 362.42 |
| Electrical equipment | 14.27 | 32.14 | 38.47 | 6.14 | 13.51 | 7.18 | 10.31 | 2.77 | 16.33 | 141.12 | 31.00 | 110.12 |
| Total | 114.65 | 335.45 | 519.56 | 94.72 | 260.52 | 121.62 | 155.66 | 27.14 | 152.81 | 1781.43 | 536.80 | 1244.63 |
| Percentage change of total | 12.5 | 10.3 | 10.1 | 10.6 | 10.3 | 10.4 | 7.5 | 7.9 | 10.2 | 10.0 | 9.3 | 10.3 |

Note: Figures are obtained by applying percentage changes in gross investment by industry, estimated from the 1969 input-output tables, to 1969 capital expenditures by industry over regions, taken from the U.S. Bureau of the Census, *Annual Survey of Manufactures*, 1969.

[a]The list of states included in each region is contained in Table 7-4.

176

Table 7-7. Short-Run Regional[a] Investment Expansion Resulting from VAT-CIT Substitution, Assuming Full CIT Shifting (millions of dollars)

| | NE | MA | ENC | WNC | SA | ESC | WSC | MT | PAC | US | South | Non-South |
|---|---|---|---|---|---|---|---|---|---|---|---|---|
| Food | 1.22 | 3.75 | 5.41 | 3.22 | 3.55 | 1.11 | 1.96 | 1.07 | 3.62 | 24.91 | 6.62 | 18.29 |
| Tobacco | — | 0.06 | 0.02 | — | 0.58 | 0.12 | — | — | — | 0.78 | 0.70 | 0.08 |
| Textile products | 0.97 | 1.42 | 0.29 | 0.04 | 8.14 | 1.35 | 0.16 | — | — | 12.37 | 9.65 | 2.72 |
| Apparel | 0.12 | 2.33 | 0.49 | 0.21 | 0.67 | 0.33 | 0.20 | 0.03 | 0.27 | 4.65 | 1.20 | 3.45 |
| Paper | 5.32 | 10.53 | 14.05 | 3.71 | 13.15 | 6.62 | 5.65 | 0.54 | 7.13 | 66.70 | 25.42 | 41.28 |
| Chemical | 0.47 | 3.18 | 3.32 | 0.63 | 3.76 | 1.59 | 6.04 | 6.21 | 0.70 | 19.90 | 11.39 | 8.51 |
| Petroleum and coal | 0.11 | 1.40 | 4.04 | 0.61 | 0.26 | 0.65 | 6.12 | 0.22 | 2.68 | 16.09 | 7.03 | 9.06 |
| Rubber and plastic | 1.29 | 2.02 | 5.24 | 0.78 | 1.40 | 2.11 | 0.83 | — | 1.29 | 14.96 | 4.34 | 10.62 |
| Stone, clay, and glass | 0.60 | 3.75 | 4.70 | 0.93 | 2.42 | 1.35 | 1.00 | 0.67 | 1.83 | 17.25 | 4.77 | 12.48 |
| Primary metal | 1.25 | 13.06 | 28.58 | 1.13 | 4.34 | 2.92 | 2.70 | 2.17 | 3.00 | 59.15 | 9.96 | 49.19 |
| Fabricated metal | 1.67 | 4.66 | 11.83 | 1.37 | 2.01 | 1.59 | 1.32 | 0.21 | 2.35 | 27.01 | 4.92 | 22.09 |
| Machinery | 5.10 | 13.80 | 24.84 | 4.57 | 3.89 | 1.90 | 3.05 | 0.73 | 5.47 | 63.35 | 8.84 | 54.51 |
| Electrical equipment | 1.82 | 4.11 | 4.92 | 0.79 | 1.73 | 0.92 | 1.32 | 0.35 | 2.09 | 18.05 | 3.97 | 14.08 |
| Total | 19.94 | 64.07 | 107.73 | 17.99 | 45.90 | 22.56 | 30.35 | 6.20 | 30.43 | 345.17 | 98.81 | 246.36 |
| Percentage change of total | 2.2 | 2.0 | 2.1 | 2.0 | 1.8 | 1.9 | 1.5 | 1.8 | 2.0 | 1.9 | 1.7 | 2.0 |

[a]The list of states included in each region is contained in Table 7-4.

chemicals (investment expansion of 3.1 percent; Southern share, 44 percent) at the sluggish end of the spectrum. The average expansion of the textile industry, 10.3 percent, of which the South's share is 65 percent, also contributes to the South's average standing.

Under the assumption of full forward shifting of the CIT, the national investment expansion in these manufacturing industries is only 1.9 percent. And in this case the South's share is somewhat less than average, only 1.7 percent. The smallest expansion is observed in the West South Central region (1.5 percent), the largest again in New England (2.2 percent). Under both shifting assumptions the New England phenomenon is primarily explained by the rapid expansion of the nonelectrical machinery industry (22.6 percent with zero shifting, 3.4 percent with unitary shifting of the CIT).

Even granting that the South's share of the investment expansion may be understated by the assumption of intra-industry proportionality, it would still appear that the region would not benefit disproportionately from the investment response to the tax substitution, although further analysis might indicate otherwise.

In this discussion investment effects by the *purchaser* (investor) industry have been examined. While this focus is most important in longer-run terms, i.e., in terms of differential regional growth, the short-run consequences would be most sensitive to increases in the activity of investment goods *producer* industries. The latter would not necessarily have the same spatial distributions as investor industries. While beyond the scope of this examination, it is nevertheless desirable that differential regional (and national) consequences of the investment-induced expansion in industrial activity be treated endogenously and examined explicitly.

Our data for the geographic distribution of investment goods producer industries suggest that the regional distribution of these increases in industrial activity would not be uniform. In Table 7-8 the regional distribution of all industries is presented. The data in Table 7-9 indicate the proportion of value added of investment goods contributed by each producer industry. On this basis the regional impact of the increase in capital goods output can be roughly projected. Ignoring construction, which would probably closely approximate the regional distribution of investment purchases and which accounts for 43 percent of investment value added, the largest contribution is by the nonelectrical machinery industry (25 percent). On the basis of the spatial distribution of this industry's activity in 1969, 9.0 percent of its expansion would be concentrated in New England, certainly a disproportionate share.

**Table 7-8. Regional[a] Distribution of Value Added in Selected Industries, 1969 (percent)**

| | NE | MA | ENC | WNC | SA | ESC | WSC | MT | PAC | SUM |
|---|---|---|---|---|---|---|---|---|---|---|
| Ordnance | 6.36 | 4.62 | 11.92 | 12.74 | 7.73 | 3.01 | 5.42 | 5.16 | 42.18 | 99.14 |
| Food | 3.64 | 17.34 | 24.26 | 11.78 | 11.32 | 5.61 | 7.84 | 2.99 | 14.60 | 99.38 |
| Tobacco | 0.20 | 5.39 | 1.24 | — | 67.54 | b | — | — | — | 74.37 |
| Textiles | 9.13 | 16.73 | 3.45 | 0.47 | 58.23 | 8.10 | 1.38 | 0.70 | — | 97.49 |
| Apparel | 5.39 | 43.61 | 8.92 | 3.74 | 16.03 | 9.31 | 5.22 | 5.99 | 6.49 | 99.41 |
| Lumber and wood | 4.27 | 6.07 | 10.86 | 3.53 | 13.38 | 9.49 | 8.30 | 0.87 | 37.42 | 99.36 |
| Furniture | 5.04 | 16.82 | 24.05 | 4.39 | 23.55 | 8.13 | 5.28 | 0.94 | 11.36 | 99.49 |
| Paper | 10.13 | 18.34 | 23.33 | 5.38 | 15.98 | 7.70 | 7.08 | 2.04 | 11.22 | 100.10 |
| Printing | 6.50 | 33.35 | 24.76 | 7.97 | 8.86 | 3.34 | 4.53 | 1.07 | 9.74 | 101.07 |
| Plastics and chemicals | 4.00 | 24.67 | 20.79 | 5.21 | 16.08 | 9.15 | 12.93 | 2.68 | 6.10 | 101.00 |
| Petroleum | 0.76 | 11.39 | 17.66 | 6.30 | 3.01 | 2.50 | 40.60 | — | 14.73 | 99.63 |
| Rubber | 10.44 | 16.82 | 37.76 | 6.46 | 8.31 | 6.93 | 4.51 | — | b | 91.23 |
| Leather | 26.60 | 23.13 | 15.39 | b | 6.52 | b | b | — | b | 71.64 |
| Stone, clay, and glass | 4.62 | 21.44 | 26.18 | 7.22 | 13.77 | 5.39 | 7.28 | 2.60 | 10.77 | 99.27 |
| Primary metal | 4.38 | 25.23 | 40.22 | 2.54 | 6.53 | 5.95 | 4.31 | 3.90 | 7.01 | 100.07 |
| Fabricated metal | 7.31 | 19.01 | 41.08 | 5.49 | 6.33 | 4.33 | 5.20 | 1.02 | 9.76 | 99.53 |
| Machinery | 8.74 | 18.48 | 42.12 | 8.97 | 4.39 | 3.51 | 4.41 | 1.63 | 7.83 | 100.08 |
| Electrical equipment | 9.34 | 24.34 | 30.81 | 4.93 | 7.71 | 5.10 | 3.31 | 1.72 | 12.74 | 100.00 |
| Transportation | 5.50 | 11.85 | 39.53 | 6.99 | 6.55 | 2.46 | 6.17 | 6.36 | 17.42 | 102.83 |
| Instruments | 14.80 | 45.19 | 17.61 | 4.61 | 3.75 | 1.46 | 2.72 | 1.77 | 7.31 | 99.22 |
| Miscellaneous mfr. | 17.93 | 32.46 | 19.85 | 5.39 | 6.28 | 3.98 | 3.12 | 0.90 | 9.80 | 99.71 |

[a]The list of states included in each region is contained in Table 7-4.

bWithheld to avoid disclosing identity of individual firms.

179

**Table 7-9. Industry Share of Investment and Export Value Added and Imports as Proportion of Domestic Value Added**

| | Share of Plant and Equipment Value Added | Share of Export Value Added | Imports as Percentage of Value Added |
|---|---|---|---|
| 1.  Agriculture | | 9.11 | 6.81 |
| 2.  Metal mining | | 0.23 | 79.75 |
| 3.  Coal, stn., clay mng. & prod. | | 1.98 | 6.15 |
| 4.  Oil and gas | | 0.52 | 26.73 |
| 5.  Construction | 42.99 | | |
| 6.  Ordnance | | 3.07 | 11.75 |
| 7.  Food | | 2.74 | 14.15 |
| 8.  Tobacco | | 0.40 | 0.63 |
| 9.  Textiles and apparel | 0.07 | 0.98 | 15.96 |
| 10.  Lumber, wood products | 0.02 | 1.06 | 19.68 |
| 11.  Furniture and fixtures | | 0.09 | 5.22 |
| 12.  Paper and products | | 1.43 | 15.99 |
| 13.  Printing and publishing | | 0.66 | 1.04 |
| 14.  Chem., plast., drugs, pnt. | | 7.82 | 5.32 |
| 15.  Rubber and leather | 0.18 | 0.90 | 7.68 |
| 16.  Footwear | 0.02 | 0.04 | 24.83 |
| 17.  Primary metal | | 3.36 | 14.12 |
| 18.  Fabricated metal | 1.75 | 2.51 | 2.34 |
| 19.  Nonelect. machinery | 24.87 | 11.36 | 6.86 |
| 20.  Electrical equipment | 6.84 | 5.99 | 8.21 |
| 21.  Transp. equipment | 12.67 | 12.29 | 19.72 |
| 22.  Instruments | 3.49 | 2.22 | 8.22 |
| 23.  Misc. manufacturing | 0.82 | 0.69 | 23.57 |
| 24.  Transp. and warehousing | 1.51 | 13.31 | 7.75 |
| 25.  Communications | 1.79 | 0.41 | |
| 26.  Utilities | | 0.02 | 0.29 |
| 27.  Finance and insurance | | | 1.40 |
| 28.  Real estate and rental | | 4.47 | |
| 29.  Hotels and services | | 11.10 | |
| 30.  Auto repair and services | | | |
| 31.  Amusements | | 0.08 | |
| 32.  Med., ed. serv., and nonprof. | | | |
| 33.  Wholesale and retail | | 1.12 | |

Source: Input-output tables, 1969, from Cybermatics, Inc.

Again, there is no more justification for the proportionality assumption in allocating producer than user expansion. Certainly, the geographic distribution of users (investors) will affect the distribution of producers, and even if this were not true, it would be unlikely that marginal expansions of output would be distributed spatially in proportion to total output. Different ages of capital stocks and different technologies will serve to alter the geographic distribution of industrial activity in an expansion. Until such processes and factors are considered it will be impossible adequately to predict the full regional consequences of federal policy.

### 7.4.3 International Trade Effects

As in the case of expansion in industries producing investment goods, it is virtually impossible adequately to project the regional consequences of an expansion of exports or of import substitutes that results from the VAT-CIT substitution. As discussion of the aggregate trade effects (Chapter 6) indicated, the consequences for the balance of trade were estimated on the basis of aggregate export and import elasticities and indices of price change. While involving serious inconsistencies at the national level, this procedure breaks down completely at the regional level.

However, at least a qualitative feel for the consequences of changes in trade flows at the regional level can be obtained from an examination of Tables 7-8 and 7-9. As was indicated in Table 6-3, the tax substitution, assuming repeal and full shifting of the CIT, would lead to an increase in the physical volume of exports of between $3 billion and $5 billion, depending on the relative price elasticity of export demand, and a real contraction of imports of between $2 billion and $3 billion. Real consequences of an equivalent balance-of-trade devaluation (of about 5 percent) would be quantitatively similar. Tables 7-8 and 7-9 clearly indicate that many of the most important import-competing industries are heavily concentrated in the South. Thus, for example, any import-substitution expansion in the textile and paper products industries would have pronounced stimulative effects in this region. Conversely, the only quantitatively important export industry in the South is chemicals, but the region lacks any significant concentration of such major export industries as nonelectrical machinery and transportation equipment.

### 7.4.4 Potential Wage Adjustments

As indicated in section 7.3, full replacement of the CIT by a consumption-type VAT has been estimated to increase consumption prices by 7.7 percent if the CIT reduction is not shifted forward in the form of lower prices and by 1.7 percent if full shifting occurs. In either case, these price increases imply corresponding reductions in real wages. If the supply of labor is initially assumed to be infinitely elastic at the prevailing real wage, it is possible to project the first-round wage adjustment to the tax substitution.

Such wage increases would obviously exert upward pressure on prices. Interindustry variations on this pressure would depend on differences in labor intensity, measured by employee compensation as a proportion of value added (Table 7-3). Those industries in which this ratio is highest would be most affected by this wage adjustment.

Included in this class would be such important Southern industries as textiles (employee compensation 81 percent of value added) and furniture (82 percent). On the other hand, the employee compensation ratio is relatively low in oil and gas (26 percent) and tobacco (17 percent), also important industries in the South.

Under the assumption of zero CIT shifting, of course, net profits increase by the amount of initial CIT liabilities. It could be assumed that, at least in the first instance, the increase in employee compensation is absorbed by profits. The pressure for further-round price changes would then be greater in those industries in which the increase in employee compensation exceeded the original increase in net profit (CIT liability). Original CIT liabilities (= CIT savings), the hypothesized labor cost changes, and the difference between the two, all as proportions of value added, are also indicated in Table 7-3. Further adjustments would be most severe in industries in which the increase in labor cost exceeds the CIT reduction. In no important Southern industry would the net excess of labor cost increase over CIT savings be greater than 2 percent; but in such major regional industries as tobacco, chemicals, and paper significant net profit increases would be observed even if the wage increases were fully absorbed by profits.

In the case of manufacturing industries it is possible to estimate the aggregate regional effects of CIT removal and wage increases, as shown in Table 7-10. For manufacturing for the United States as a whole, the original CIT liability (= CIT reduction) greatly exceeds the hypothetical labor cost adjustment. Nationally, the net increase in profit (CIT liability minus increase in wage bill) in manufacturing is 20 percent of original (pre-tax-substitution) net capital earnings (Table 7-10, last column). This is explained by the predominance of the corporate form in manufacturing, as compared to other sectors. However, regional variations in this net increase are very great, ranging from only 1.5 percent in New England to 35.3 percent in the West South Central. Significantly, the highest increase in capital earnings adjusted for wage increases, 30.2 percent, is found in the combined Southern regions. The consequences of this adjusted profit increase would be an above-average stimulus to investment in the South.

As with the discussion of other effects of the tax substitution, these hypothetical regional consequences do not represent equilibrium adjustments to the tax substitution. Rather they characterize the initial disequilibrium created by this change in tax structure. Again, it is possible only to identify these first-round consequences as indices of disequilibrium. However, that they exist is an indication

Table 7-10. Regional Labor Cost-CIT Differentials for Manufacturing, Assuming Full CIT Reduction, Zero CIT Shifting, and Full VAT Shifting (billions of dollars)

| Regions[a] | Net Value Added (1) | Employee Compensation (2) | Net Capital Income (col. 1 less col. 2) (3) | CIT Reduction (4) | Increase in Employee Compensation (5) | Increase in Profit (col. 4 less col. 5) (6) | Profit Increase Relative to Net Capital Income (col. 6/col. 3) (7) |
|---|---|---|---|---|---|---|---|
| United States | 221.3 | 179.9 | 41.4 | 21.9 | 13.8 | 8.1 | 19.6 |
| New England | 15.3 | 13.3 | 2.0 | 1.05 | 1.02 | 0.03 | 1.5 |
| Middle Atlantic | 47.2 | 39.8 | 7.4 | 3.93 | 3.05 | 0.88 | 11.9 |
| East N. Central | 63.3 | 52.6 | 10.7 | 5.67 | 4.03 | 1.64 | 15.3 |
| West N. Central | 14.3 | 11.0 | 3.3 | 1.77 | 0.84 | 0.93 | 27.8 |
| South Atlantic | 25.1 | 19.8 | 5.3 | 2.79 | 1.52 | 1.27 | 24.1 |
| East S. Central | 12.1 | 8.7 | 3.4 | 1.80 | 0.67 | 1.13 | 33.2 |
| West S. Central | 14.4 | 10.0 | 4.3 | 2.30 | 0.77 | 1.53 | 35.3 |
| Mountain | 4.1 | 3.1 | 1.0 | 0.52 | 0.24 | 0.28 | 28.3 |
| Pacific | 25.6 | 21.8 | 3.9 | 2.05 | 1.67 | 0.38 | 9.8 |

Note:

Col. 1: Based on value-added data from U.S. Bureau of the Census, *Annual Survey of Manufactures*, 1969.

Col. 2: Based on data on 1969 personal income by region and income and employment by industry, from *Survey of Current Business*, July 1970.

Col. 4: Allocated on the basis of the distribution of net capital income (column 3).

Col. 5: Assumed to increase by the VAT rate, 7.68 percent.

[a]The list of states included in each region is contained in Table 7-4.

of the degree of regional nonneutrality inherent in the assumed plan of changes in federal policy.

The primary purpose of this section was to indicate the importance of assessing the differential regional consequences of federal policies that are not often discussed in regional terms or recognized to have significant regional impacts. The identification of these differential regional effects is important for three reasons. First, to the degree to which a particular area is severely affected by a federal policy change, compensating adjustments in other federal programs are indicated. Secondly, in general there exists more than one federal action which will achieve a nationally desired end, and the choice between these should be made on the basis of differential consequences in other dimensions, of which the regional dimension would be one of the more important. And finally, the very effectiveness of a program may itself be affected by its differential regional impacts. For example, a selective tax reduction designed to stimulate demand and employment may be primarily inflationary if, due to the characteristics of those benefited, the expansion is concentrated in industries and areas already relatively fully employed. Only by explicitly assessing the differential effects of alternative policies in disaggregated, including regional, terms is it possible to make rational and effective policy choices.

## 7.5 ALLOCATIVE EFFECTS OF THE TAX SUBSTITUTION

The most substantive economic argument in favor of the VAT vis-á-vis the CIT emphasizes its allocative efficiency characteristics. Regardless of the assumptions made about *short-run* CIT shifting, to the degree to which the CIT is a tax on capital earnings (as opposed to, e.g., monopoly surpluses) it will necessarily result in (a) the inefficient allocation of capital between the corporate and noncorporate sectors, (b) output price ratios which do not reflect relative opportunity costs of converting one product into another, and (c) suboptimal rates of capital accumulation.

Improper allocations of capital between incorporated and unincorporated sectors result from differences in the tax treatment of capital earnings in each sector. If, prior to the introduction of the CIT, rates of return to capital are equal in the two sectors, imposition of a CIT will result in a net flow of capital from the incorporated sector. The immediate effect is to reduce the net rate of return in the sector subject to the tax. This results in a flow of capital out of the taxed sector, the consequence of which is an increase in the gross-of-tax rate of return in the taxed sector, which now has less capital, and a decline in the rate of return in the untaxed sector, which now has relatively more capital. This process continues until the net-of-tax rates of return are equal in the two sectors.[4]

Even if the CIT were fully shifted forward, with no initial reductions in net rates of return in the taxed sector, capital would flow from the taxed to the nontaxed sector as a result of demand responses to the relative increase in prices in the taxed sector. Demand would increase in the unincorporated sector and decline in the incorporated sector, resulting in changes in rates of return which would serve to shift capital (and labor) into the untaxed sector.

Thus, the CIT implies a deadweight welfare loss regardless of whether or not it is shifted in the short-run. This is true regardless of the scope for capital-labor substitution. Even with fixed capital-labor coefficients, the imposition of the CIT will result in artificially high relative prices for capital-intensive commodities, with consequent reductions in their consumption.

Furthermore, by reducing the net rate of return to capital, the CIT will result in reductions in the rate of capital accumulation unless the supply of savings is completely interest-inelastic. The initial response of investment demand to the tax substitution, examined in Chapter 5 under the assumption of an unchanged rate of interest, would necessarily result in an increase in the rate of interest and possibly an increase in the savings rate.

By comparison, the VAT, with one exception, is proportionate to price and hence does not serve to alter *relative* prices. If relative prices prior to the introduction of the VAT reflect opportunity costs, post-VAT relative prices will be unchanged and will also reflect opportunity costs. The one significant exception is the VAT treatment of leisure. By not taxing leisure, the VAT would serve to induce the substitution of leisure for market-purchased goods in consumption, with resultant overconsumption of leisure and undersupply of labor. This result, of course, assumes that work-leisure choices would be affected by a decline in the relative price of leisure.

Similarly, the VAT applied to total value added does not result in distortions of relative factor prices. Thus, the attempted substitution of labor for capital resulting from a CIT would not occur with the

---

4. In this discussion, it is assumed that *at the margin* debt-equity ratios are limited, and increases in investment must be accompanied by increases in equity capital.

VAT; net *and* gross (of tax) relative factor prices would be identical in all sectors, with no resultant allocative distortions. The potentially depressive effects of the CIT on the rate of capital accumulation would then not derive from the VAT.

In brief, the deadweight loss or excess burden associated with the CIT is virtually completely avoided under the VAT. It is on this basis that the VAT is argued to be the allocatively more desirable tax.

*Appendix A* <sup></sup>*

# Methods Used to Compute
# the Value-Added Tax

## A.1 GENERAL DESCRIPTION

The analysis of the possible effects of a single-level value-added tax (VAT) and of a two-level VAT have been computed by the Econoscope Group of Cybermatics, Inc., and are based on the methods used in the quarterly economic analysis service of Econoscope.

Although based on input/output tables previously published by the Department of Commerce, the Econoscope table used to analyze the VAT has been revised to represent the year 1969 with sufficient accuracy for the purposes of the study. For each quarter-year of its normal operation, Econoscope routinely updates the I/0 table with newly available data. For the VAT study, four quarterly tables have been consolidated into a single table for 1969. Some further specifications of this table are as follows:

1. The number of sectors is 106.
2. The Standard Industrial Classification (SIC) coverage of 95 of these sectors is shown in Appendix B.
3. The I/0 table is in 1969 prices.
4. Domestic final demand data are drawn from a variety of sources.
   a. Personal consumption expenditure (PCE) from the Bureau of Economic Analysis (BEA), formerly the Office of Business Economics.
   b. Constructure from the Bureau of the Census.

*Appendices A and B were prepared by Milton L. Godfrey, Cybermatics, Inc.

    c. Producers durable equipment (PDE) from the BEA-Securities and Exchange Commission survey of capital investment expenditures. Estimating procedures are used to remove the construction portion of capital investment, leaving the PDE investment of corporations. Other government data sources are used to enable Econoscope to estimate noncorporate and agricultural investment in PDE. The consolidated figures from these processes reconcile with the national income accounts as published in the *Survey of Current Business.*

    d. Since foreign trade is critically important in considering a VAT, processing of the export and import data is covered in detail in section A.2.

    e. Federal government expenditures are based on published Budget figures modified by later reports on actual expenditures.

    f. State and local government expenditures are based on the most recent Census of Governments and other summaries by federal agencies, by the Conference Board, and others.

5. The value added for each sector in 1969 has been reestimated for this VAT study. The major procedures followed are described in section A.3.

## A.2 FOREIGN TRADE

*Exports* of domestic merchandise as reported by the Census in Schedule B classifications are grouped by Econoscope into seven major end-use categories according to the Census definitions. Each group is then classified by SIC and assigned to the appropriate I/0 sector.

The category, "other exports," excluding reexports, is then augmented by adding nonmerchandise exports classified to match the I/0 sector definitions.

Military grant shipments and monetary transactions of government are excluded. Hence, Econoscope estimates of exports differ from the balance-of-payments reports to the extent of these government transactions.

Export values at port of embarkation are converted to producers' prices for each I/0 sector by subtracting transportation, trade, and insurance costs. The sums of the deductions are entered as purchases from the transportation, trade, and insurance sectors for each of the seven end-use groups.

The basic reference for classification is U.S. Foreign Trade Statistics Classifications and Cross-Classifications with revisions to January 1, 1970. The end-use categories are: food, feeds, and beverages; industrial supplies and materials; capital goods, except automobiles;

automobiles, vehicles, parts, and engines; consumer goods, nonfood, except passenger cars, special category; and exports, n.e.c.

For the conversion from Schedule B classifications to SIC classifications we follow the correlation table in U.S. Foreign Trade Statistics Classifications. However, we deviate from this table to conform to the standard BEA practice in I/0 tables. The basis for this deviation is the I/0 requirement that each product be assigned primarily to only one industry. For example, the Census classifies petroleum coke as primary to the petroleum industry and classifies coke from coal as primary to either the chemical or steel industry, depending on where it was made. Since coke from any industry is chemically the same, for I/0 purposes we define coke as primary to the chemical industry only, and classify it as secondary to or by-product of the other industries.

The nonmerchandise export trade included in the category exports, n.e.c., is as follows: gold exports, electric energy exports, freight valuation adjustment, transportation of foreigners on U.S. carriers, other travel expenses of foreigners in the United States, fees and royalties paid to American industry, other services sold in export by private industry and government, and income on U.S. investments abroad. In general, these items conform to the definitions used in the quarterly reports on the U.S. balance of payments issued by the Department of Commerce.

*Imports* of merchandise for consumption are taken from Census reports and converted to SIC classifications to match the input/ output definitions. They are further classified as competitive or non-competitive imports. By estimation, Econoscope adds insurance and freight costs to the published foreign port values to get a c.i.f. value of imports.

Nonmerchandise import data is collected from several sources. However, information from the balance-of-payments report in the *Survey of Current Business* is used as a control on the process so that our estimates can be successfully reconciled with the national income accounts.

Noncompetitive imports are all shown in the body of the I/0 table as a purchase by the actual buying industry from the import sector.

Competitive imports are all shown in the body of the I/0 table as a purchase by the industry that makes the competitive product. We assume that further distribution of these imports follows normal trade channels. This is identical to one of the methods used by the BEA in the official I/0 tables for 1958 and 1963. However, since this is a "dummy" transaction, the value added of the competitive domestic industry is not affected by the imports and reflects only the actual sales of the domestic industry.

## A.3 ESTIMATION OF VALUE ADDED

For the base year of an I/O table, the value added is an accurate report of what happened. However, when an I/O table is applied to
other years with changed prices, making the assumption that value
added is a fixed portion of sector expense can lead to major errors
in estimating profitability or other details.

The value-added sector covers three major items, labor, depreciation, and profit as well as some minor items.[1] Although more than
half of gross income of some industries goes to value added, the
I/O tables show no breakdown into labor, depreciation, etc. Instead,
value added is treated as a lump sum, in contrast to the fine detail
shown for purchases of goods and services. However, as indicated
earlier, it is desirable to break value added into components of
labor, depreciation, etc. Information on these components is available from a variety of government files but none of these is an exact
match to the I/O tables. The major differences are of three general
types: (a) a different definition of value added (in the Census files),
(b) different definitions of industry than those used in I/O tables
(gross product originating files), and (c) data on enterprises which
contain establishments in two or more industries (SEC and Internal
Revenue Service data). Only the data file for gross product in current
and constant dollars, by industry is establishment-based and is con-
structed using the same definition of value added as the I/O table.
A summary is published annually in the July issue of the *Survey of
Current Business* (Tables 1.21 and 1.22) and the file in full detail
is available on magnetic tape. This file will be referred to as gross
product originating or GPO. Sixteen industries in the GPO file can
be matched almost exactly to the I/O sectors.

For Econoscope, we developed a method for estimating the
details of value added to match our updated I/O table for each
quarterly period, and we used the same procedure for this study. The
base for estimating 1969 is BEA data on the reconciliation between
gross product originating and the I/O table for 1963. This shows the
changes in allocations of value added due to the different sector
definition in GPO.

For 1969 we have assumed a continuity of the patterns of 1963
and have reallocated accordingly. While almost all sectors are affected to some extent, the major impact of shifted value added falls on:
new construction, repair and maintenance construction, crude
petroleum and natural gas, petroleum refining and related industries,
wholesale and retail trade, business services, and auto repair.

---

1. The minor items include interest payments, net rental income, transfer
payments, inventory valuation adustment, subsidies from government. For
government enterprises it includes a net surplus item.

The causes of reallocation can be separated into seven major classes, described in the following paragraphs:

a. *Force account.* This covers new and maintenance construction work performed by the employees of other industries; for example, the construction and maintenance of distribution systems by electric power companies.

b. *Industry reclassification.* This covers situations where the GPO industries and the I/0 secotrs are differently defined: for example SIC 138 (oil and gas field services) is considered part of the crude petroleum and natural gas industry in the GPO file, while in the I/0 table it is considered part of the new and maintenance construction sectors.

c. *Installation work.* This covers the installation labor supplied by manufacturers of elevators, escalators, heating and air-conditioning equipment, and other items where the installation labor should be applied to the construction sectors.

d. *Manufacturer's sales offices.* Where these offices are separate from the plants or mines and perform only a marketing function apart from retailing, the associated costs are transferred to the trade sector of the I/0 table.

e. *Trade activity.* This covers direct wholesale and retail sales of nontrade sectors, for example, the sale of drugs by hospital dispensaries, which is reallocated to the trade sector of the I/0 table.

f. *Manufacturing activity.* This covers manufacturing processes performed in stores or warehouses. It is reallocated to the appropriate manufacturing sector. Examples are food processing in retail stores, or custom-made clothing fabricated in retail stores.

g. *Service activity.* Some wholesale and related establishments sell services that are normally provided by sectors such as transportation, warehousing, equipment rental, auto repair, and others. In each case the associated costs are reallocated to the proper service sector.

The impact of these reallocations of value added is small in many sectors. The accompanying table shows the net effects of shifting on selected sectors where the change is substantial.

## A.4 DEPRECIATION AND CAPITAL INVESTMENT

In this study, gross capital investment is not subject to the VAT. Since a large part of the funds for investment are generated by depreciation charges (normally part of value added), we estimated the straight-line depreciation flows using IRS Bulletin F [U.S. Treasury

Table A-1. GPO-I/O Value Added Reconciliation

| | GPO File | Value Added, 1969 (millions of dollars) | Increase |
|---|---|---|---|
| | | I/O Table | |
| All construction | 43,685 | 60,403 | +38.3% |
| Crude petroleum and natural gas | 10,861 | 7,218 | -33.5 |
| Petroleum refining and related industries | 7,235 | 7,868 | +8.7 |
| Wholesale and retail | 155,421 | 142,474 | -8.3 |
| Business services | 20,470 | 24.172 | +18.1 |
| Auto repairs | 4,704 | 10,320 | +119.4 |

Department] modified to conform to the actual service lives of fixed capital assets (see *Survey of Current Business*, December 1966).

The composition of capital investment purchases of each industry was estimated on the basis of 1969 data on total purchases by type, 1969 data on total expenditures by each industry, and earlier data on purchase patterns of each industry.

Since dependable data on capital stocks by industry are not available at the necessary level of detail, the rate of growth of real product of each industry was used to determine the portion of capital investment for expansion and the portion for replacement of retired capital stocks. Hence, the replacement and expansion investments of each industry were estimated. The replacement part was deducted from value added and from final demand, and added to the proper cell in the body of the I/O table. To determine the reasonableness of this procedure, total estimated depreciation was compared with total depreciation in the GPO files with the following results:

Estimated 1969 depreciation: $59,594 millions
GPO 1969 depreciation: $76,715 millions

The IRS data used for the gross product originating file reflects the accelerated depreciation schedules of recent years. Hence, the difference above is in the expected direction.

## A.5 CORPORATE PROFIT TAXES

Corporate profit taxes are reported only on an enterprise base. The GPO file shows profits, but not taxes, on an establishment base. Hence, while our tax estimates for each I/O sector are reasonable approximations, there is no benchmark that can be used for validation. The Census report titled *Enterprise Statistics 1963* provides the most recent data on the structure and industrial coverage of enterprises, bridging the enterprise-establishment gap to some extent. It was necessary to assume that tax liability ratios (tax to profit) based on enterprise data could be applied to establishments. However, it was necessary to deviate from this practice for the petroleum industry (sectors 8 and 45, and for medical, educational services, and nonprofit organizations (sector 95).

A very large part of oil field operations of the petroleum industry are run by integrated corporations. The GPO files show on an establishment base that oil field operations are profitable while refinery operations show a net loss. The GPO operations figures for 1969 (in millions of dollars) are:

|  | *Oil and Gas Fields* | *Refineries* |
|---|---|---|
| Corporate profits | 4,102 | -265 |
| Noncorporate profits | 285 | 5 |
| Total | 4,387 | -260 |

After adjustment to I/0 definitions by reallocation of value added, the 1969 corporate profit and tax figures (in millions of dollars) are:

|  | *Oil and Gas Fields* | *Refineries* |
|---|---|---|
| Corporate profits | 3,321 | -228 |
| Corporate tax liability | 698 | -54 |

The negative income tax liability of the petroleum refining industry must be viewed as a tax credit for the crude petroleum and natural gas industry. In a similar fashion the net loss indicated by the medical, educational services, and nonprofit organization sector must be viewed as a tax credit primarily for the wholesale and retail trade sector.

*Appendix B*

# Industry Numbering
# for the Econoscope
# Input/Output Table

| Indus-trial Sector # | Industry Titles | Related SIC Codes |
|---|---|---|
| 1 | Livestock and Livestock Products | 013, pt. 014, 0193, pt. 02, pt. 0729 |
| 2 | Other Agricultural Products | 011, 012, pt. 014, 1092, 0199, p. 02 |
| 3 | Forestry and Fishery Products | 074, 081, 082, 084, 086, 091 |
| 4 | Agricultural, Forestry and Fishery Services | 071, 0723, pt. 0729, 085, 098 |
| 5 | Iron and Ferroalloy Ores Mining | 1011, 106 |
| 6 | Nonferrous Metal Ores Mining | 012, 103, 104, 105, 108, 109 |
| 7 | Coal Mining | 11, 12 |
| 8 | Crude Petroleum and Natural Gas | 1311, 1321 |
| 9 | Stone and Clay Mining and Quarrying | 141, 142, 144, 145, 148, 149 |
| 10 | Chemical and Fertilizer Mineral Mining | 147 |
| 11 | Residential Buildings | pt. 1511 |
| 12 | Private Industrial Buildings | pt. 1511 |
| 13 | Other Private Nonresidential Buildings | pt. 1511 |
| 14 | Other Private Construction | pt. 1511 |
| 15 | Public Nonresidential Buildings | pt. 1511 |
| 16 | Highways | pt. 1511 |
| 17 | All Other Public Construction | 1611 |
| 18 | Maintenance and Repair Construction | pt. 15, pt. 16, pt. 17 |
| 19 | Ordnance and Accessories | 19 |
| 20 | Meat Products | 201 |
| 21 | Dairy Products | 202 |
| 22 | Canning, Preserving Fruits, Vegetables, and Sea Foods | 203 |
| 23 | Grain Mill Products | 204 |
| 24 | Bakery Products | 205 |
| 25 | Sugar | 206 |
| 26 | Confectionery and Related Products | 207 |
| 27 | Beverage Industries | 208 |

195

| Industrial Sector # | Industry Titles | Related SIC Codes |
|---|---|---|
| 28 | Miscellaneous Food and Kindred Products | 209 |
| 29 | Tobacco Manufactures | 21 |
| 30 | Broad and Narrow Fabrics, Yarn and Thread Mills | 221, 222, 223, 224, 226, 228 |
| 31 | Misc. Textile Goods and Floor Coverings | 227, 229 |
| 32 | Apparel | 225, 23 (Ex. 239), 3992 |
| 33 | Misc. Fabricated Textile Products | 239 |
| 34 | Lumber and Wood Products, Exc. Containers | 24 (Ex. 244) |
| 35 | Wooden Containers | 244 |
| 36 | Household Furniture | 251 |
| 37 | Other Furniture and Fixtures | 25 (ex. 251) |
| 38 | Paper and Allied Products Exc. Containers | 26 (Ex. 265) |
| 39 | Paperboard Containers and Boxes | 265 |
| 40 | Printing and Publishing | 27 |
| 41 | Chemicals and Selected Chemical Products | 281 (Ex. Alumins pt. of 2819), 286, 287, 289 |
| 42 | Plastics and Synthetic Materials | 282 |
| 43 | Drugs, Cleaning, and Toilet Preparations | 283, 284 |
| 44 | Paints and Allied Products | 285 |
| 45 | Petroleum Refining and Related Industries | 29 |
| 46 | Rubber and Miscellaneous Plastic Products | 30 |
| 47 | Leather Tanning and Industrial Leather Products | 311, 312 |
| 48 | Footwear and Other Leather Products | 31 (Ex. 311, 312) |
| 49 | Glass and Glass Products | 321, 322, 323 |
| 50 | Stone and Clay Products | 324, 325, 326, 327, 328, 329 |
| 51 | Primary Iron and Steel Manufacturing | 331, 332, 3391, 3399 |
| 52 | Copper Manufacturing | 3331, 3351, 3362 |
| 53 | Aluminum Manufacturing | pt. 2819, 3334, 3352, 3361 |
| 54 | Other Nonferrous Metals Manufacturing | 3332, 3333, 3339, 3341, 3356 3357, 3369, 3392 |
| 55 | Metal Containers | 3411, 3491 |
| 56 | Heating, Plumbing and Structural Metal Products | 343, 344 |
| 57 | Stampings, Screw Machine Products and Bolts | 345, 346 |
| 58 | Other Fabricated Metal Products | 342, 347, 348, 349 (Ex. 3491) |
| 59 | Engines and Turbines | 351 |
| 60 | Farm Machinery and Equipment | 352 |
| 61 | Construction, Mining, and Oil Field Machinery | 3531, 3532, 3533 |
| 62 | Materials Handling Machinery and Equipment | 3534, 3535, 3536, 3537 |
| 63 | Metalworking Machinery and Equipment | 354 |
| 64 | Special Industry Machinery and Equipment | 355 |

| Indus-<br>trial<br>Sector<br># | Industry Titles | Related SIC Codes |
|---|---|---|
| 65 | General Industrial Machinery and Equipment | 356 |
| 66 | Machine Shop Products | 359 |
| 67 | Office Computing and Accounting Machines | 357 |
| 68 | Service Industry Machines | 358 |
| 69 | Electric Industrial Equipment and Apparatus | 361, 362 |
| 70 | Household Appliances | 363 |
| 71 | Electric Lighting and Wiring Equipment | 364 |
| 72 | Radio, TV and Communication Equipment | 365, 366 |
| 73 | Electric Components and Accessories | 367 |
| 74 | Misc. Electrical Machinery, Equipment and Supplies | 369 |
| 75 | Motor Vehicles and Equipment | 371 |
| 76 | Aircraft and Parts | 372 |
| 77 | Other Transportation Equipment | 373, 374, 375, 379 |
| 78 | Scientific and Controlling Instruments | 381, 382, 384, 387 |
| 79 | Optical, Ophthalmic and Photographic Equipment | 383, 385, 386 |
| 80 | Miscellaneous Manufacturing | 39 (Ex. 3992) |
| 81 | Transportation and Warehousing | 40, 42, 42, 44, 45, 46, 47 |
| 82 | Communications, Exc. Radio and TV Broadcasting | 481, 482, 489 |
| 83 | Radio and TV Broadcasting | 483 |
| 84 | Electric Utilities | 4911 |
| 85 | Gas Utilities | 492 |
| 86 | Water and Sanitary Services | 494–497 |
| 87 | Wholesale and Retail Trade | 50 (Ex. Manufact. Sales Offices), 52, 53, 54, 55, 56, 57 58, 59, pt. 739 |
| 88 | Finance and Insurance | 60, 61, 62, 63, 64, 66, 67 |
| 89 | Real Estate and Rental | 65 (Ex. 6541 and pt. 6561) |
| 90 | Hotels, Personal and Repair Services Exc. Auto | 70, 72, 76, (Ex. 7694 & 7699) |
| 91 | Business Services | 6541, 73 (Ex. 7361, 7391, pt. 7399), 7694, 7699, 81, 89 (Ex. 8921) |
| 92 | Research and Development | No SIC Code |
| 93 | Automobile Repair and Services | 75 |
| 94 | Amusements | 78, 79 |
| 95 | Medical, Educational Services, and Nonprofit Org. | 0722, 7361, 80, 82, 84, 86, 8921 |

Note: Sectors not shown here do not have any directly selected SIC Codes.

❋

# References

Aaron, H. "The Differential Price Effects of a Value-Added Tax," *National Tax Journal*, June 1968.

Bossons, J. "Economic and Redistribution Effects of a Value Added Tax," *Proceedings*, National Tax Association 64th Annual Conference on Taxation, Kansas City, September 1971 (forthcoming).

Bossons, J. and C.S. Shoup "Analyzing the Effects of Large-Scale Changes in Fiscal Structure: A Proposed Systems Approach," in *New Challenges for Economic Research*, 49th Annual Report of the National Bureau of Economic Research, New York, 1969.

Brittain, J.A. *Corporate Dividend Policy*, The Brookings Institution, Washington, D.C., 1966.

Committee for Economic Development, *A Better Balance in Federal Taxes on Business*, New York, April 1966.

Dobrovolsky, Sergei *Corporate Income Retention, 1915–43*, National Bureau of Economic Research, New York, 1951.

Dresch, Stephen P. [1972a] "Assessing the Differential Regional Consequences of Federal Tax-Transfer Policy," *Proceedings*, Regional Economic Development Research Conference, U.S. Department of Commerce, Economic Development Administration (April 19, 1972).

Dresch, Stephen P. [1972b] "Disarmament: Economic Consequences and Developmental Potential," A Report Prepared for the United Nations Department of Economic and Social Affairs, December 1972.

Dresch, Stephen P. and Robert D. Goldberg "IDIOM: An Inter-Industry, National-Regional Policy Evaluation Model," *Annals of Economic and Social Measurement*, July 1973.

Due, John F. "The Case for the Use of the Retail Form of Sales Tax in Preference to the Value Added Tax," Committee for Economic Development, August 1972 (unpublished).

Gordon, R.J. "The Incidence of the Corporation Income Tax in U.S. Manufacturing 1925–62," *American Economic Review*, Sept. 1967.

Hall, R.E. and Jorgenson, D.W. "Tax Policy and Investment Behavior," *American Economic Review*, June 1967.

Houthakker, H.S. and Magee, S.P. "Income and Price Elasticities in World Trade," *Review of Economics and Statistics,* May 1969.

Jorgenson, D.W. and Siebert, C.D. "A Comparison of Alternative Theories of Corporate Investment," *American Economic Review,* September 1968.

Kaldor, N. *An Expenditure Tax,* George Allen and Unwin, London, 1955.

Katona, G. *et al. 1969 Survey of Consumer Finances,* Survey Research Center, The University of Michigan, Ann Arbor, 1970.

Krzyzaniak, M. and Musgrave, R.A. *The Shifting of the Corporation Income Tax,* John Hopkins, Baltimore, 1963.

Lindholm, R.W. "The Value Added Tax; Rejoinder to a Critique," *Journal of Economic Literature,* December 1971.

Lindholm, R. W. "The Value Added Tax: A Short Review of the Literature," *Journal of Economic Literature,* December 1970.

Lintner, John. "Distribution of Incomes of Corporations Among Dividends, Retained Earnings and Taxes," *American Economic Review,* May 1956.

Meyer, J.R. and Glauber, R.R. *Investment Decisions, Economic Forecasting, and Public Policy,* Harvard University, Boston, 1964.

Meyer, John R. and Edwin Kuh *The Investment Decision,* Harvard University Press, Cambridge, Mass., 1959.

Musgrave, R.A. *The Theory of Public Finance,* McGraw-Hill Co., New York, 1959.

National Economic Development Office, *Value Added Tax,* 2nd Edition, Her Majesty's Stationery Office, London, 1971.

Shoup, C.S. "Factors Bearing on an Assumed Choice between a Federal Retail Sales Tax and a Federal Value Added Tax," Committee for Economic Development, August 1972 (unpublished).

Shoup, C.S. "Incidence of the Corporation Income Tax: Capital Structure and Turnover Rates," in *Readings in the Economics of Taxation,* Richard D. Irwin, Inc., Homewood, Illinois, 1959.

Shoup, C.S. *Public Finance,* Aldine Publishing Co., Chicago, 1970.

Smith, D.T. "Value Added Taxation in Relation to Income, Excise and Sales Taxation," in *Excise Tax Compendium* (Part I), Committee on Ways and Means, U.S. Congress House of Representatives, 1964.

Stout, D.K. "Value Added Taxation, Exporting and Growth," *British Tax Review,* September/October 1963.

U.S. Bureau of Labor Statistics, *Consumer Expenditures and Income: Total United States, Urban and Rural, 1960-61,* BLS Report No. 237-93.

U.S. Treasury Department, Bureau of Internal Revenue, *Income Tax Depreciation and Obsolescence: Estimated Useful Lives and Depreciation Rates,* Bull. F, Rev. January 1942.

Vickrey, William S. "The Problem of Progression," *University of Florida Law Review,* 1968.

# Index

# About the Authors

**Stephen P. Dresch** is president of the Institute for Demographic and Economic Studies and a research associate of the National Bureau of Economic Research and of Yale University's Institution for Social and Policy Studies. He received his baccalaureate degree from Miami University (Ohio) in 1963 and his Ph.D. in economics from Yale University in 1970. Mr. Dresch has undertaken studies for and/or served as advisor to the Ford Foundation, the Alfred P. Sloan Foundation, the United Nations Department of Economic and Social Affairs, the U.S. Departments of Health Education and Welfare, of Commerce, and of the Interior, the U.S. Office of Education, the Comptroller General of the United States, the National Institute of Education, and other agencies on such subjects as disarmament, tax policy and higher education. A frequent participant in conferences and symposia devoted to issues in education, public finance and related fields, Mr. Dresch is the author of many publications and papers dealing with these topics.

**An-loh Lin** is an economist with the Federal Reserve Bank of New York. He is a graduate of the University of Rochester, Ph.D., 1972. A former Research Associate with the National Bureau of Economic Research, he participated in numerous research projects and publications for NBER and is the author of several publications on economic research.

**David K. Stout** is a graduate of Sydney University and Magdalen College, Oxford. He was an Official Fellow in Economics at University

College, Oxford, from 1959 to 1976 when he was appointed the Economic Director of the Office of the United Kingdom National Economic Development Council (the tri-partite planning and discussion body set up in 1962). Mr. Stout is the author of numerous publications, many of them on the subject of the Value-Added Tax, and a frequent consultant to governmental commissions on taxation policy.